To my father, Richard Gosney, for inspiring my dreams.
To my mother, Marilyn Gosney, for helping me so much
in achieving them. I love you both very much.

ASP

Programming

for the absolute beginner

THE FUN WAY TO LEARN PROGRAMMING

WITHDRAWN

An accompanying
CD is enclosed
inside this book

Premier

Press JOHN GOSNEY

Premier Press and For the Absolute Beginner are registered trademarks of Premier Press, Inc.

Microsoft, Windows 95, Windows 98, Windows 2000, Windows NT, Internet Explorer, FrontPage, and VBScript are trademarks or registered trademarks of Microsoft Corporation.

Important: Premier Press cannot provide software support. Please contact the appropriate software manufacturer's technical support line or Web site for assistance.

Premier Press and the author have attempted throughout this book to distinguish proprietary trademarks from descriptive terms by following the capitalization style used by the manufacturer.

Information contained in this book has been obtained by Premier Press from sources believed to be reliable. However, because of the possibility of human or mechanical error by our sources, Premier Press, or others, the Publisher does not guarantee the accuracy, adequacy, or completeness of any information and is not responsible for any errors or omissions or the results obtained from use of such information. Readers should be particularly aware of the fact that the Internet is an ever-changing entity. Some facts may have changed since this book went to press.

ISBN: 1-931841-01-2

Library of Congress Catalog Card Number: 2001091383

Printed in the United States of America

01 02 03 04 05 BH 10 9 8 7 6 5 4 3 2 1

Publisher:
Stacy L. Hiquet

Marketing Manager:
Heather Buzzingham

Managing Editor:
Sandy Doell

Acquisitions Editor:
Melody Layne

Project Editor:
Heather Talbot

Technical Reviewer:
Chad Beckner

Copy Editor:
Kate Talbot

Interior Layout:
Danielle Foster

Cover Design:
Mike Tanamachi

Indexer:
Katherine Stimson

Proofreader:
Jenny Davidson

Acknowledgments

I have written several books, and I am always struck by the same thought as the writing process for each one comes to an end: that is, over the course of a few short months, life can take a fantastic array of twists and turns. Working on a project like this one provides neat bookends to a beginning and an end, and always—without fail—forces me to pause and review the previous months of my life.

Sometimes, these periods are filled with joy, as occurred with my last project and my son being born as the book neared completion. Yet other times, life takes unexpected and traumatic turns. As I write this, my mind continues to dwell on the tragedy of September 11, 2001, and the thousands of people who have lost their lives. It has been difficult to accept the events of that day. Moreover, it has marked the ending of this particular project as indeed one of the darker bookends in my, and the world's, lifetime.

But as with all things, healing does begin, and the pain (if not the memory) of such a tragedy is gradually lessened. As befits a computer book, the real promise of technology (that is, of making the world a better place) reminds me, as I write this, that there is still great promise in the world, and that human ingenuity, creativity, perseverance, and kindness can (and will) prevail. Technology and all the benefits it brings can help deliver this promise, and it is this thought (among many) that has gotten me through these sad and mournful days.

That said, there are many people who have worked on this book who, through their efforts, have kept this promise of technology alive and well, and have in turn helped to make this book far better than it ever could have possibly been. Once again, Emi Smith has come through with her fantastic organizational details, always willing to lend a sympathetic and understanding ear to the trials and tribulations of her authors. Thanks as well to Heather Talbot who picked up this book after many internal changes, keeping it on track and thus guiding it to the light of day. Also, thanks to Chad Beckner for ensuring the technical accuracy of the book, and for continuing to answer—always with good humor—my silly technology questions. And to all the other folks at Premier Press who, while perhaps going specifically unmentioned, have my enduring gratitude for making sure a project is done right, and done well.

Finally, and as always, all my love and thanks to Melissa, Genna, Jackson, and George who make everything possible and inspire me to always do my best.

About the Author

John W. Gosney is currently Director of Technology Services for the Indiana University School of Dentistry, Indianapolis. He has also served as a technical writer and Web development consultant for a major pharmaceutical corporation. John has worked extensively with Microsoft applications and Web development tools for several years, and has experience with ColdFusion and other Web development technologies. He is the author of several books, ranging from test preparation guides to e-business titles. John is also an adjunct instructor for the Community College of Indiana.

John received his B.A. in Technical Writing and Psychobiology in 1992 from Purdue University. In 1996, he was awarded an M.A. in English from Butler University. When not working (which is rare these days!), John enjoys spending as much time as he can with his family, cheering for his favorite teams (Pacers, Colts, and Boilermakers) and furthering his reputation as an expert in all things popular culture.

Contents at a Glance

Contents

Working with ASP Objects   43

Working with ASP Components   71

Essential Programming Logic, Part I   143

Essential Programming Logic, Part II   161

Formatting Processed Output   189

ASP and HTML Scripting with FrontPage 2000   215

Looking Back and Looking Forward 261

VBScript Variable Reference 267

APPENDIX B SQL Reference 277

APPENDIX C Access Essentials 285

Index 301

Introduction

Welcome to *ASP Programming for the Absolute Beginner*. By developing an interest in Active Server Pages (ASP), you stand at the threshold of a very exciting programming adventure. When first introduced, ASP offered the promise of an easy, powerful method of breaking through the functional shackles of the Common Gateway Interface (CGI)—it has delivered on that promise. Now, several years into its history, ASP technology has become a central component of the Microsoft development strategy. Moreover, it has become the scripting language of choice for literally thousands of programmers, so you are in good company in wanting to learn more.

Although ASP is relatively easy to learn, it does require some degree of general programming knowledge to best utilize its power. Additionally, ASP allows for easy integration of data sources (Access, SQL Server, and so on), so an understanding of basic database development comes into play. Finally, because ASP is, at its core, a Web scripting language, you should have some basic knowledge of HTML to better understand how ASP can be used to bring a previously unleashed power and functionality to your Web pages.

This book *does* assume that you have some working knowledge of HTML. You've probably created a few Web pages, perhaps using a development tool such as Microsoft FrontPage or Macromedia HomeSite. Maybe you've also added some advanced functionality to said Web pages, perhaps by adding tables, Cascading Style Sheets (CSS), and forms. Maybe you're familiar with another type of scripting language, such as JavaScript.

If you have done this level of Web development, you can build on this experience while learning to work with ASP. Even if you haven't done much Web development (again, aside from having a general understanding of HTML), you can still learn to work with ASP—and have fun in the process. Don't be intimidated by the programming aspect of ASP. Yes, you do have to learn some programming to most effectively work with ASP. However, I'm assuming from your purchase of this book that you are willing and ready to dive into the exciting and rewarding world of ASP development. This book shows you how to do just that.

Why Learn ASP, and What Can You Do with It?

If you've purchased this book or are thinking about purchasing it, you probably have some interest in advanced Web development. As already mentioned, you don't need any prior programming experience to read and learn from this book. However, I am going to assume that although you might not know much about programming (yet), you do have a keen interest in understanding how to utilize ASP in your work and thus, by default, become a programmer.

Aside from your general interest, why else would you want to learn to work with ASP? Consider the following compelling reasons:

- Of all the Web scripting languages, ASP is probably the easiest to learn. I talk more about this issue throughout the book, but the programming language at the heart of ASP is called *Visual Basic Script*, or *VBScript* for short. An extension of the Visual Basic programming language, VBScript is the programming language used by ASP to add all the power and functionality to your Web pages.

TRICK

If you already have a little programming experience, you might recognize the term *BASIC*. One of the original, easy-to-learn programming languages, BASIC (*Beginner's All-Purpose Symbolic Instruction Code*) has been developed and improved over the years, gaining power without losing its inherent simplicity. VBScript benefits from both this power and simplicity, and you will learn how to program with it to best utilize ASP.

- ASP code is processed on the server (more about this server-side processing later in the book), so this brings a tremendous amount of freedom to your development because you don't have to be as concerned with how your ASP-enabled Web pages will appear and function in different browsers. Your code is processed on the server, and only the results of that processing are sent to the Web browser, in the form of regular HTML.

TRAP

Because ASP is a technology developed by Microsoft, it should come as no surprise that you can gain additional functionality with ASP via the use of the Microsoft Web browser, Internet Explorer. Although I talk about this extra functionality in various sections of the book, the primary focus of your learning will be on getting ASP to work across browsers, regardless of whether they are Microsoft-based. The important thing here is that, when developing Web pages, you always keep in mind the requirement of cross-functionality between different kinds of browsers to ensure that you don't alienate potential visitors to your site.

- If you have information stored in a data source, for example, a Microsoft Access database, you can use ASP to read and manipulate that information inside your Web pages. You might want to use ASP to build an inventory search form for your small business so that your customers can quickly and easily browse through your products while on-line. If your inventory data is stored in a database, you can connect to it via ASP so that customers can search information. This integration of database information with Web pages is easily made possible via ASP.

- Aside from integration with a database, you can use ASP to facilitate more advanced Web page functionality. For example, you can use ASP to process Web forms so that you can gather and manipulate information entered into your Web pages and to send information to a Microsoft Word or Excel document, or any text file, for that matter. I show you how to perform all these advanced functions as you move through the book.

- As with other information technology skills, knowing how to develop with ASP can be a real boost to your professional career. As I've mentioned, ASP is an incredibly popular technology, with literally thousands of developers working on ASP-enabled applications in a variety of industries. Consider your work through this book beneficial to not only your interest in computer programming but also, potentially, your career.

What Do You Need to Know First?

Fortunately, you don't need much prior knowledge to begin working with ASP. In fact, given the nature of this book, you don't need any programming background. After all, the purpose of this book is to show you how to program. However, I am going to assume that you know or have access to a few things:

- **A general understanding of the Hypertext Markup Language (HTML).** You don't need to be an expert Web developer, but you should have some knowledge of the various codes that make up HTML. Moreover, if you've previously created Web pages, even basic ones, you will benefit greatly from this experience as you learn to program with ASP.
- **A computer.** Preferably, you should have at least a 266MHz/Pentium II grade (the faster the better, of course). Your computer should also have at least 32MB of RAM. Like processor speed, the more memory you have, the better off you are.
- **An operating system (OS).** Windows 98, Windows NT 4.0, or Windows 2000.
- **A personal Web server.** The type depends on which OS you choose. You will, in essence, turn your machine into a complete Web development environment. Don't worry about this Web server issue for now. I discuss what you need to load onto your machine in Chapter 1, "Preparing to Work with ASP." Regardless of which OS you use, this Web server component is free. You can download it from the Web or install it from the CD-ROM that came with your computer and contains your OS.
- **A Web browser application.** Preferably Netscape Navigator or Microsoft Internet Explorer.

That's it for the absolute requirements. Unlike many programming languages, ASP is not compiled, so you don't need an advanced interface to work with the programs you develop.

Even though the following items are not required, you will find them useful as you learn how to program with ASP:

- **A direct connection to the Web.** This is useful in further testing the Web pages you develop with ASP.
- **A copy of Microsoft Access 2000.** One of the major benefits of ASP (which are explored extensively throughout this book) is the power it brings to you in integrating your Web pages with a data source, such as an Access database or some other database engine. Several chapters of this book, including your final game project, utilize this database-connectivity functionality of ASP. If you have a copy of Access 2000 or are in the position to purchase a copy, you will greatly benefit.
- **A copy of Microsoft FrontPage 2000.** FrontPage is an HTML editor that aids in the otherwise rudimentary tasks of Web development. It also comes complete with

built-in support for ASP. However, when you are learning any programming language, ASP included, it is best to do things by hand, without the aid of an editor like FrontPage, so that you can be sure to fully understand the central concepts at the core of the language. After you have a solid grasp of the fundamentals, in Chapter 10, "ASP and HTML Scripting with FrontPage 2000," you will take a look at how using an editor like FrontPage can speed up your ASP development. Other HTML editors support ASP (one such example is Macromedia HomeSite), so if you have access to one of these applications, you will benefit from that, too. Here, at least in Chapter 10, you will be focusing on how to use FrontPage to enhance your ASP development work.

How to Use This Book

Learning how to program in any language is best done in a step-by-step approach. Moreover, like many advanced topics, you don't just jump right in the middle of a difficult concept without first understanding the fundamentals.

It is best to read this book in the order the material is presented. That is, start with Chapter 1, and work your way through the chapters in numerical order. You might be tempted to skip ahead—especially if you browse through the book and in later chapters see the exciting things that are possible with ASP. Try to contain your enthusiasm (at least in this regard!) and work through the information in the order it is presented. This will ensure that you don't miss anything and that you indeed understand all the basics before moving on to more advanced material.

At the end of each chapter, you will also find a short listing of learning exercises. Use these exercises to expand your understanding of the material and to challenge (and inspire!) your own programming creativity. Generally speaking, there are no "right or wrong" answers to these exercises: rather, they are designed to get you thinking as a programmer and to give you an opportunity to experiment with what you learn. So, take advantage of these exercises, using them as a fun way to challenge your understanding of the text.

Conventions Used in This Book

The following are all conventions used in this book:

Look to the Trick elements for inside advice and hints to help you better understand a subject or otherwise gain insight into a more effective way of working with the subject.

The Hint elements provide information that is not commonly known or otherwise documented in the general reference material for the subject or the Help files that accompany the software.

IN THE REAL WORLD

These special elements provide you with real-world insight into not only ASP but also other issues that surround the programmer, including career development, project management, customer relationship management, and various factors of being an outstanding ASP developer.

Traps help you avoid common pitfalls that new programmers often experience. Be sure to watch out for these special elements because they can save you lots of time (not to mention headaches) by steering you clear of everyday problems that crop up as you program with ASP.

CHAPTER 1

Preparing to Work with ASP

In this chapter, you will

- Learn what ASP is and how it interacts with both Web servers and Web browser software.

- Learn which type of server to configure with ASP, depending on the type of operating system you are using, and install the server, learning its administrative features.

- Learn the various development environments you can use to program with ASP, such as Microsoft FrontPage, Macromedia HomeSite, and even simple text editors such as Windows Notepad.

You've made a wise choice in deciding to learn more about Active Server Pages (henceforth referred to as *ASP*). Deceptively simple on the surface, ASP is a powerful element in any high-powered Web site, enabling you to create dynamic content and provide a high degree of interactivity to your Web pages.

Before you begin your programming adventure, you need a clear understanding of how to configure your server to work with ASP. Undoubtedly, you have noticed the word *server* in *Active Server Pages*. Understanding how ASP interacts with—you guessed it—a server (a Web server, in this case) is critical to your development of Web pages that utilize ASP.

In this first chapter, you will be doing just that—configuring your Web server to work with ASP.

Understanding ASP and the Web Server

One great benefit of working with ASP is that the programs you create are processed on the server, instead of your asking the individual Web browser clients to do any of the work. When an ASP Web page is loaded into a browser, only the processed HTML is sent to the browser—all the hard work is performed on the server.

Are you still with me? Although the method by which ASP functions might sound complicated, it's quite easy to understand. You will take a closer look at what this server-side processing means and how it differs from other Web scripting languages, such as JavaScript.

Imagine that you are interested in purchasing a new music CD. Because your favorite record store has a Web site, you go on-line to purchase the disc. You are quickly becoming a savvy Web developer, so you notice that the home page of the record store Web site has an .asp extension (short for *Active Server Pages*).

 HINT

You are probably familiar with the typical .html extension on Web pages (for example, `http://www.somewebsite.com/homepage.html`**). As you know,** *html* **is short for** *Hypertext Markup Language.* **With ASP-enabled pages, the usual .html extension is replaced with .asp. You will learn more about the differences between regular .html and .asp pages in Chapter 2, "Programming ASP Web Pages with VBScript."**

Because in ASP all the code processing is performed on the Web server, only the results are sent to the Web browser. Even though you'd like to see how the record store home page has been programmed, you realize that the ASP code has already been processed on the server.

The Advantages of Server-Side Processing

You might be asking yourself: What are the advantages of this server-side processing? There are several answers.

One of the biggest reasons for server-side processing is that it allows a wide variety of Web browsers to display the information because they are being sent only the processed

HTML. When you utilize ASP, you don't have to worry about how different Web browsers, such as Internet Explorer and Netscape Communicator, will display the information. If the browser is capable of displaying regular HTML (it wouldn't be a Web browser if it couldn't handle that task), it can handle the results of an ASP-processed Web page.

HINT Compare ASP to a scripting language, such as JavaScript. In JavaScript, the code processing is done within the Web browser. As you might guess, various Web browsers interpret, and thus process, JavaScript code differently, which leads to your Web pages being displayed inconsistently. Worse, your JavaScript can work in one type of browser but fail in another.

This is not meant to belittle the power of a well-programmed JavaScript Web page, but you should realize that ASP provides you with a certain freedom from the potential differences in how Web browsers process code.

TRAP Even though ASP code is processed on the server, you should still be aware that some elements of your Web page—such as table layout, cascading style sheets, and other DHTML elements—can and do appear differently, depending on the type of Web browser used to view your pages. As with any Web development, be sure to take the time to load your pages into a variety of browsers to ensure the greatest level of cross-compatibility.

Another advantage of server-side processing is security. Because only the results of your code processing are sent to the Web browser, you can keep confidential information—passwords, credit card numbers, and even your own code—on the server.

Finally, having code processed on the server can increase how fast your Web pages perform. This is somewhat dependent on the power of the Web server, the amount of processing being performed, and your connection speed. Still, you can usually expect ASP pages to perform more quickly than JavaScript-enabled pages because the code processing is not performed on the client's machine.

VBScript, the Heart of ASP

ASP is not a scripting language in and of itself but rather a mechanism for integrating a scripting language into your Web pages. This scripting language is *VBScript*, short for *Visual Basic Script*.

Developed by Microsoft, VBScript is closely related to its big brother programming language, Visual Basic. Like JavaScript, VBScript can be executed directly within the Web browser, but only if that browser is Microsoft Internet Explorer.

HINT Processing VBScript directly within the Web browser (in this case, Internet Explorer) can produce some stunningly powerful Web pages. However, to focus your attention exclusively on ASP and how it is processed on a Web server, I do not discuss client-side VBScript in this book.

The focus of this book is to show how VBScript is processed on the Web server, in other words, ASP.

You will really be learning how to program with VBScript in this book. However, because the processing of that VBScript is performed on a Web server, you can more accurately say that you are learning how to program with ASP.

Configuring Your Web Server for ASP

At this point, you should have a good idea of what ASP is and how it functions in conjunction with a Web server. It's time to configure your Web server to work with ASP.

Depending on the type of Windows operating system you are using (98, NT, 2000), you already have a Web server available for your use, but it might not be loaded or configured on your machine. The following sections show you how to determine which type of Web server to use and how to configure it for use with ASP.

ASP functionality is available with Web servers other than those manufactured by Microsoft, for example, Apache. For the sake of simplicity and to ensure that you are getting as well rounded an overview of ASP as possible, I focus on the Microsoft Web servers that can be used with Windows 98, NT, and 2000.

If the phrase *configure your Web server* sounds complicated, let me reassure you. It is an easy task to get your computer ready to work with ASP. As mentioned, you might already have a Web server installed on your computer without your realizing it. Regardless, the following sections take you through the steps of locating (if necessary), installing, and configuring a Web server that you can use on your own machine to work with ASP.

At this point, you might be asking, "I know that my Internet service provider allows me to develop Web pages utilizing ASP, so why can't I just use its servers rather than worry about configuring one on my own computer?"

That's a great question, and for all intents and purposes, you can use your ISP to develop your ASP-enabled Web pages. To see immediate results of your work and learn more about how ASP functions, however, it is essential that you make your own computer a development machine, complete with its own Web server, which you can use to build and test your ASP Web pages quickly.

It is easy and in your best interests to have a Web server running on your own computer.

Configuring Internet Information Server with Windows 2000

Windows 2000 provides a major advance in the Windows operating system. For the first time, you have access to a full-featured, robust Web server (the Microsoft Internet Information Server, or *IIS* for short) via the typical Windows client. Utilizing IIS on your own Windows 2000 machine, you can see the power and experience the fun of working with ASP.

Better still, IIS is incredibly easy to install and configure with Windows 2000. This section takes you through the steps of installing and configuring IIS and shows you how to administer the Web server via an easy-to-use interface.

Installing Internet Information Server

Before you configure and work with IIS, you need to install it. Here's how you do it.

To load IIS on your computer, you must use the professional client edition of Windows 2000. Earlier versions of Windows (for example, Windows NT 4.0) do not support IIS on the client machine. Instead, you have to have access to the Windows NT server to work with IIS.

Be sure to note the difference between client and server in this context. By loading IIS onto your Windows 2000 client machine, you eliminate the need to connect to an external computer (server) because you have everything necessary on your own machine. Again, this is a major benefit to having a Web server on your own computer, as opposed to using an external source, such as your ISP.

To install IIS, follow these steps:

1. From the Start menu, select Settings, Control Panel. In the Control Panel dialog box, select the icon Add/Remove Programs (see Figure 1.1).
2. Within the Add/Remove Programs dialog box, click the icon Add/Remove Windows Components (see Figure 1.2).

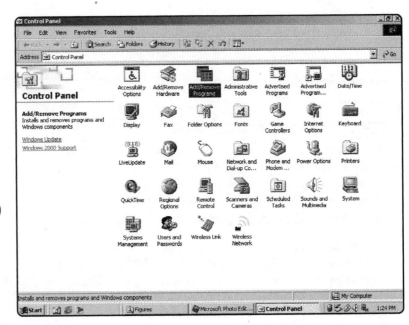

FIGURE 1.1

Select Add/Remove Programs as a first step in installing IIS on your Windows 2000 client computer.

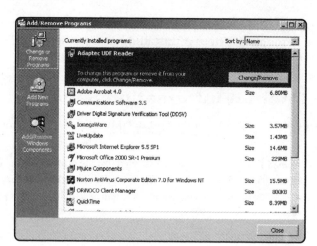

FIGURE 1.2

Click Add/Remove
Windows
Components to gain
access to the IIS
installation features.

3. The Windows Components Wizard dialog box opens. Select the Internet Information Server (IIS) option (see Figure 1.3).

4. Click the Details button to get a better idea of what you will be installing along
with IIS (see Figure 1.4).

5. Leave all the options checked for installation. This ensures that you have complete IIS functionality.

TRAP

When installing IIS, be sure to disable the FTP Server option. Leaving it on can pose
some very serious security breaches.

6. Click Install. Note that you might be asked to provide your Windows 2000
CD-ROM to complete the installation process.

FIGURE 1.3

Note the
Description
information shown
when you click the
IIS option. Along
with general details
about the
component option,
total disk space
required for the
installation is
displayed.

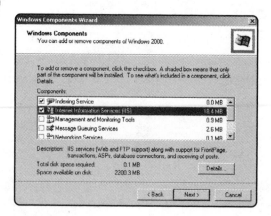

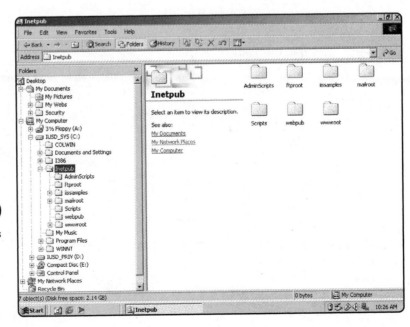

FIGURE 1.4

Various components
are installed with
IIS, including ways
for administering
IIS, FrontPage 2000
Server Extensions,
and other tools.

Confirming Your IIS Installation

Although I'll talk much more about working with your Web server when I begin the
discussion of manipulating Web page files (in the next chapter), there are a few things
you can look at now to get a better idea of how IIS functions on your machine:

1. Open the Windows 2000 Explorer, and navigate to your C: drive. Find the folder
   Inetpub and select it (see Figure 1.5).
2. Note that below the Inetpub folder are several subfolders (AdminScripts, ftproot,
   iissamples, and so on). These folders correspond to additional IIS components
   placed on your computer during the installation process described in the preceding section.

FIGURE 1.5

The Inetpub folder is
the central storage
location for all the
Web pages you
create and
administer with IIS.

Think of the Inetpub folder as your central location for storing, manipulating, and displaying your Web pages via IIS (Web pages of all kinds, not just ASP-enabled Web pages). As you begin to develop Web pages, you will become quite familiar with the Inetpub folder, as well as its subfolders.

3. Aside from the creation of the Inetpub folder, take a look at the tools used to administer IIS on your computer. Again, from the Start menu, select Settings, Control Panel. Then, click the icon Administrative Tools (see Figure 1.6).

4. In the Administrative Tools screen, you notice a few icons that deal specifically with IIS (see Figure 1.7).

5. Double-click the Internet Services Manager icon to gain access to the Internet Information Services control panel. Throughout this book, I'll be talking more about administering the Web pages you create via the aid of your Web server of choice. For now, just note the availability and location of these administration services. Close the Internet Information Services control panel.

6. Now, in the Administrative Tools screen (refer to Figure 1.7), double-click the Personal Web Manager icon. The Personal Web Manager control panel appears (see Figure 1.8).

7. Note the information immediately available to you on this Main screen. You can gain quick access to your home page and home directory (note the location of your home directory within the Inetpub folder). You can also view statistics about your Web site, such as the number of active connections and the number of visitors.

HINT

Take a look at the address of your home page (refer to Figure 1.8). This address will differ, depending on the configuration of your machine. If your home address doesn't look like the one shown here (and, indeed, it shouldn't!), that is completely normal.

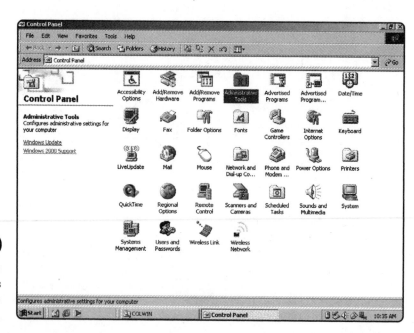

FIGURE 1.6

Click Administrative Tools to gain access to IIS administrative features.

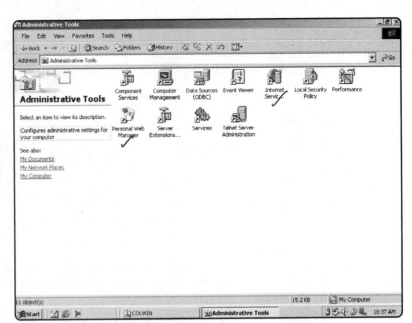

FIGURE 1.7

Several icons under Administrative Tools deal specifically with IIS, or configuring data sources, which I'll discuss specifically in Chapter 5, "Database Access with ADO."

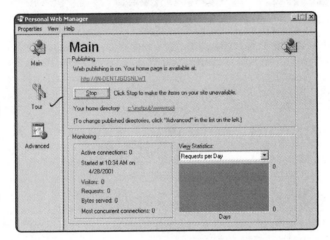

FIGURE 1.8

The Personal Web Manager control panel provides a quick overview of the general features of your computer's Web server.

8. For more general information on IIS, click the Tour icon in the Personal Web Manager control panel. You are then given a guided tour through the features of IIS (see Figure 1.9).

TRICK

Take a closer look at Figure 1.9. Note the text *Or, use IIS as a development staging platform before uploading your site to an Internet provider.* As discussed earlier, you can use your ISP's servers to develop your Web site (assuming that it offers support for ASP). However, by utilizing the power of IIS, you have a convenient staging platform for developing your Web pages before you deploy them for public consumption (thus ensuring that they appear and function as you intend). This holds true whether you are planning on making your Web pages available on the World Wide Web or within the confines of a corporate intranet.

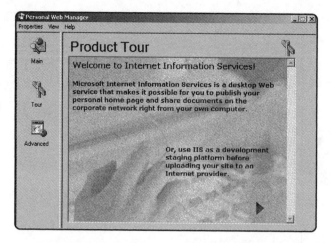

The Tour option presents a general overview of the features and benefits of working with IIS on your own computer.

Again, I talk more about the administration of your Web pages via IIS in later chapters. For now, just familiarize yourself with the location of these administrative tools.

Configuring Personal Web Server with Windows 98

Although Windows 2000 offers a full-featured Web server in the IIS, you can load a functional Web server on your computer if you are using Windows 98. This Web server is the Personal Web Server (PWS) and is just as easy to install and configure as IIS is with Windows 2000. Also, it offers full support for ASP.

TRICK

If you have upgraded from Windows 98 to Windows 2000, the IIS described in the preceding section should already be installed on your computer.

Installing Personal Web Server

To begin the discussion of the PWS, you will first install it on your computer:

1. Place your Windows 98 CD-ROM into your computer.
2. Click the Windows Start button, and choose Run. In the Run dialog box, type **d:\add-ons\pws\setup.exe** (substituting the letter of your computer's CD-ROM drive for the letter *d*, if necessary). Then click OK.
3. The PWS installation procedure begins. You are first greeted with the Microsoft Personal Web Server setup greeting (see Figure 1.10). Click Next.
4. On the next screen, click the option Add/Remove (see Figure 1.11).
5. The next screen asks you which components you want to install. Be sure that the following items are checked for installation (see Figure 1.12):
   - Common Program Files
   - FrontPage 98 Server Extensions
   - Microsoft Data Access Components 1.5
   - Personal Web Server

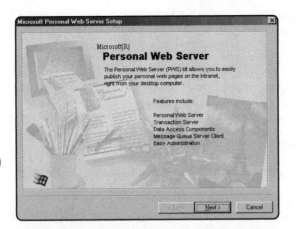

FIGURE 1.10

The Personal Web
Server installation
welcome screen.

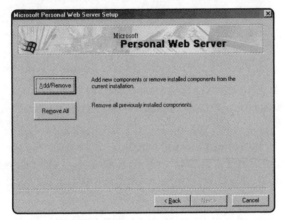

FIGURE 1.11

Regardless of
whether you have
installed PWS in the
past, click Add/
Remove.

TRICK

You don't have to install all the options presented in Figure 1.12. You don't need them
to use the PWS effectively. Also, they take up precious space on your computer.

6. Click Next. When the installation process is complete, a message appears, asking
   you to restart your computer. Go ahead and restart your machine at this time.

HINT

Given that you are a savvy computer user, what I'm about to say will come as no
surprise, but I'm going to say it anyway: the Windows operating system (any flavor
of it) can be a fickle, frustrating piece of software to work with. That said, you may
notice—from time to time—that after you install the PWS in Windows 98, you may
experience slow startups, or startup may hang. If the latter occurs, press
Ctrl+Alt+Delete and see if any files are not responding. If they are, go ahead and
stop them and then see if Windows finishes the startup process (it probably will).
Chances are good that you won't have this problem (especially if you are running on
a Pentium III machine or higher, with at least 64MB of memory). If you continue to
have problems, consult http://www.microsoft.com/support, for the latest product/
troubleshooting updates.

FIGURE 1.12

Be sure to select
only the necessary
components for
installation of
the PWS.

Confirming Your PWS Installation

After your computer restarts, the PWS icon appears in your Windows taskbar (in the status area of your screen).

When you click the PWS icon, you are presented with the Personal Web Manager control panel, shown in Figure 1.13.

Take a quick look at some of the Personal Web Manager features so that you have an idea of how to work with the PWS. In later chapters, as you start developing your ASP pages, you will learn in detail how to work with these features.

HINT

Notice the address of your home page (refer to Figure 1.13). This address will differ, depending on the configuration of your machine. If your home address doesn't match the one shown here (and it shouldn't), that is completely normal.

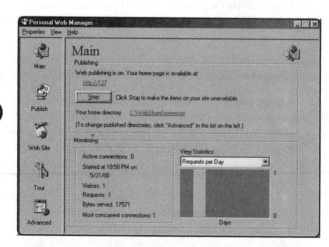

FIGURE 1.13

The Personal Web
Manager offers
convenient, easy
access to a variety
of PWS
administrative
features.

- **Publish.** This button calls up the Publishing Wizard, which is one way to Web-enable your pages (ASP or otherwise). Although it is easy to use, I don't discuss this feature in this book.

- **Web Site.** This button brings forth the Home Page Wizard, which guides you through the creation of a simple home page for display in conjunction with PWS. Again, our focus here is the creation of far more robust Web pages, utilizing the power of ASP.

- **Tour.** This option provides a general overview of the PWS features (see Figure 1.14). This is an excellent source of basic information about what a Web server is and how you can use PWS in conjunction with your Web design efforts.

TRICK

Take a closer look at Figure 1.14. Note the text *Or, use PWS as a development staging platform before uploading your site to an Internet provider*. As discussed earlier, you can use your ISP's servers to develop your Web site (assuming that it offers support for ASP). However, by utilizing the power of PWS, you have a convenient staging platform for developing your Web pages before you deploy them for public consumption (thus ensuring that they appear and function as you intend). This holds true whether you are planning on making your Web pages available on the World Wide Web or within the confines of a corporate intranet.

- **Advanced.** This option allows you to customize and edit specific directories within your home directory (refer to Figure 1.13).

Confirming Your Web Server's ASP Functionality

Regardless of which Web server you are running on your Windows computer (IIS or PWS), you can do a quick check to make sure that the server supports ASP functionality.

FIGURE 1.14

Be sure to note how to use the PWS as a development staging platform to test your Web pages before you deploy them for public consumption.

To do this, you will quickly create a very simple ASP Web page and use the Windows Notepad as your editor.

HINT

I am using a Windows 2000 client machine, with the IIS installed. Unless specifically noted, you should have no problem using a Windows 98 or NT machine running PWS. You might notice some (very slight) differences in screen appearance (that is, how the figures in this book compare to the ones on your computer) if you are not using Windows 2000, but this should give you no reason for concern—the functionality described remain the same.

1. From the Start menu, select Programs, Accessories, Notepad.
2. Enter the following ASP code exactly as it appears here (see Figure 1.15):

```
<html>
<body>
<p>
<b>This is my first ASP Web page!</b>
</p>
Today's date is <%=Date()%>
</body>
</html>
```

TRICK

The line of code shown here:

```
Today's date is <%=Date()%>
```

will display the current date within your ASP page. You'll be learning much more about VBScript and functions like the `Date()` function later in the book.

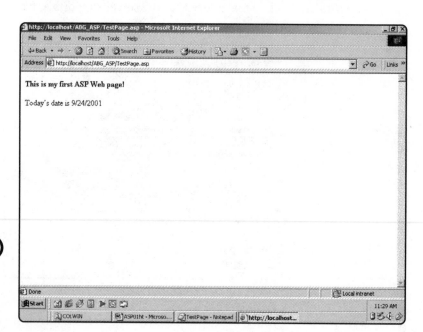

FIGURE 1.15

Testing your Web server's ASP functionality with some simple code.

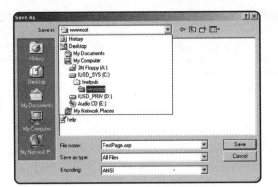

FIGURE 1.16

Saving your first
ASP Web page in
your Web server's
home directory.

3. From the File menu within Notepad, select the Save As option.

4. In the Save In field, navigate to the wwwroot folder, below the Inetpub folder (see Figure 1.16). For a more detailed discussion of the Inetpub folder, see the earlier discussions of your specific Web server, IIS or PWS.

5. As shown in Figure 1.16, give this page the name **TestPage.asp**. Be sure to name the page with the .asp extension. If you don't save your ASP pages with the .asp extension, any VBScript contained within those pages will not function.

Now that you've created your first ASP page, it's time to test it on your Web server:

1. Open your Web browser of choice.

2. If you are using Windows 2000, type the following URL into your browser's location field: **http://localhost/TestPage.asp**.

   If you are using Windows 98, type the following URL into your browser's location field: **http://127.0.0.1/TestPage.asp**.

Assuming that you saved your TestPage.asp Web page into the wwwroot subfolder of your Inetpub folder, your screen should now look like Figure 1.17.

Admittedly, this isn't an exciting page—especially compared to the things you will be doing throughout this book—but this is an important first step in ensuring that you've accomplished the following critical tasks:

• On your own machine, you've successfully installed a Web server that you can use to develop and test your ASP Web pages.

• You understand how to save your ASP Web pages with the appropriate .asp extension (versus .html or some other extension) to ensure that the ASP programming you build into these pages functions as you intend.

• You've created your first ASP Web page. Although this is perhaps not a very interesting page, it does confirm your ability to embark on this exciting path of Web development!

Displaying Your Web Server's Default Home Page

You probably noticed in the preceding section the address of your TestPage.asp Web page. Again, whether you are using IIS or PWS, the complete URL to access this page

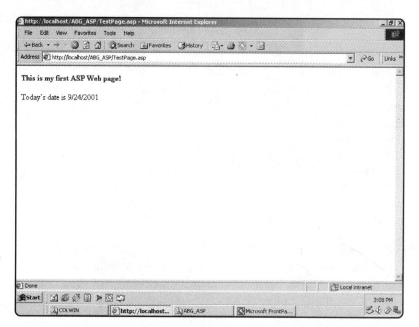

FIGURE 1.17

Your first ASP
Web page.
Congratulations!

consists of a few parts. To confirm that you understand how these URLs are constructed (thus confirming that you understand how to access the Web pages you create in this book), take a moment to review the elements of the URL you entered to display your TestPage.asp page (`http://localhost/TestPage.asp` or `http://127.0.0.1/TestPage.asp`):

- The `http://` is the typical association with the hypertext transfer protocol—no surprises here.
- The next part of the URL is the name of your server running on your computer. If you are using Windows 2000 with IIS, this is the `localhost` section of the URL. If you are using Windows 98 and the PWS, the name of your server is the default `127.0.0.1`.

TRICK

Although it's probably easy to remember `127.0.0.1` or `localhost`, **you might want to bookmark this home page address of your server within your browser application so that you don't have to retype it each time you want to access it.**

- Finally, `/TestPage.asp` is the name of the Web page you want to view.

Note that, as you develop different Web sites and organize your pages within the Inetpub folder, you can create subfolders underneath the wwwroot folder. For example, say that you create a Web site describing your family history. The home page of this particular Web site is History_Home.asp. The full URL for accessing this page could be `http://localhost/Family_History/History_Home.asp`.

`Family_History` is the name of the subfolder you created to store all Web pages associated with this particular site, and `History_Home.asp` is one of perhaps many Web pages related to this family history Web site (see Figure 1.18).

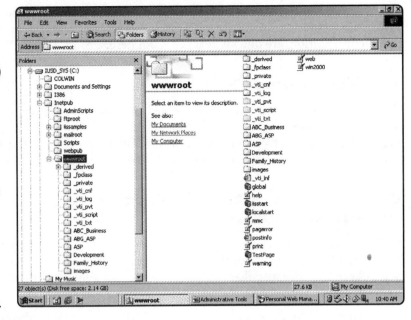

FIGURE 1.18

A typical folder
hierarchy, showing
different Web
folders underneath
the Inetpub and
wwwroot folders.
Under the wwwroot
folder, the folders
Family_History and
ABC_Business are
specific Web sites
and contain the
Web pages that
make up those sites.

Displaying the Default IIS Home Page

If you are using IIS, you access the default home page of the server by opening your
Web browser and entering the following URL: http://localhost/. The default home page
will load, as shown in Figure 1.19.

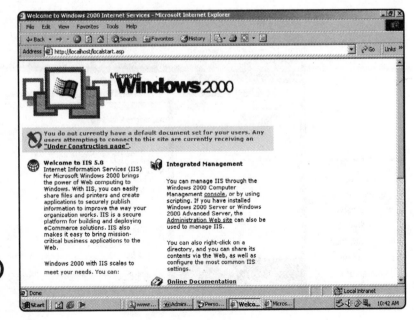

FIGURE 1.19

The default home
page for IIS.

As you see in Figure 1.20, you can access additional information about IIS from this page. Links to the administrative tools discussed earlier, as well as more extensive on-line documentation, are quickly reached from here.

Displaying the Default PWS Home Page

If you are using PWS, you can access the default server home page, including on-line documentation, just like the information available via IIS. To access the default home page of PWS, open your Web browser and enter the following URL: http://127.0.0.1/. The default home page will load, as shown in Figure 1.21.

Choosing an ASP Application Development Tool

You're nearly set to begin your ASP programming adventure, now that you have your developmental Web server installed and configured. However, there is one major question I haven't yet discussed: With what tool are you going to enter all your ASP program code?

This is an excellent question, and one I'll address in a variety of ways as you move through this book. For now, though, you should keep the following in mind:

• When learning a new programming language, it is best to do things "by hand" first, rather than rely on an application development package, Through the use of wizards, on-line help, or other "crutch" features, you circumvent gaining a real understanding of the fundamental concepts. Although useful, these crutches don't expose you to how things work.

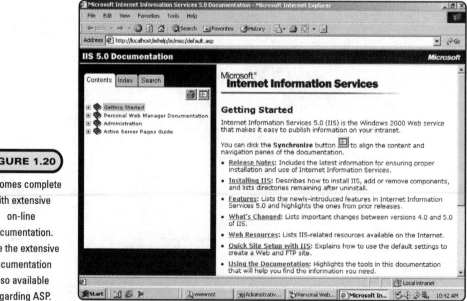

FIGURE 1.20

IIS comes complete with extensive on-line documentation. Note the extensive documentation also available regarding ASP.

FIGURE 1.21

On-line
documentation is
also available via
the PWS default
home page.

- Application development packages oftentimes insert their own special code on top of or in addition to the code you enter. Again, although potentially useful (and taking a lot of the grunt work out of programming), this extra code can be confusing as you attempt to learn the fundamentals of the language.

- After you get a solid understanding of the fundamental concepts of the language, you can move to an application development package to enhance the skills you already have learned. Thus, you gain the benefit of working with the development package.

What does all this mean? Put simply, as you begin programming with ASP, you're going to stick with a straight text editor (Notepad should suffice). Because you will hand-code all your programming, you will gain a much stronger understanding of ASP fundamentals.

If you take a quick look at the table of contents, you will see that I also provide detailed information on how to work with Microsoft FrontPage 2000 in conjunction with your ASP development (see Figure 1.22). FrontPage is a wonderful tool and makes

IN THE REAL WORLD

Even though ASP is a Microsoft technology, its popularity and power have caused other companies to integrate support for ASP into their products. FrontPage remains (in my humble opinion) the tool of choice for quick and easy ASP Web development, but other products are available. For example, HomeSite, manufactured by Macromedia, is another very solid Web application development tool that natively supports ASP development (see Figure 1.23). By *natively supports*, I mean that ASP functionality is built in.

Your choice of application development tool (if you choose to use one) is ultimately your decision. Eventually, you will want to use one because these types of applications make your development work much easier and faster.

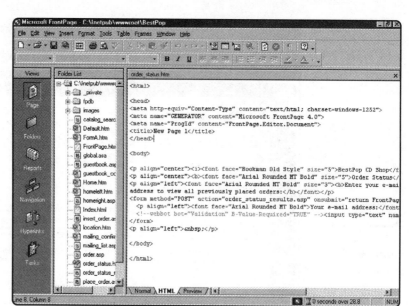

FIGURE 1.22

Working with
Microsoft FrontPage
2000 as your ASP
development tool.

the development of your Web sites much easier, more productive, and more fun. Before you get to FrontPage, you will do everything by hand to ensure that you understand how all this ASP programming works. You might have to enter a few extra keystrokes (there are no Web development wizards in Notepad), but your effort will be well worth it!

Summary

In this first chapter, you learned what ASP is and how it interacts with Web servers and Web browser software. You also took a look at the Web servers you should load on your

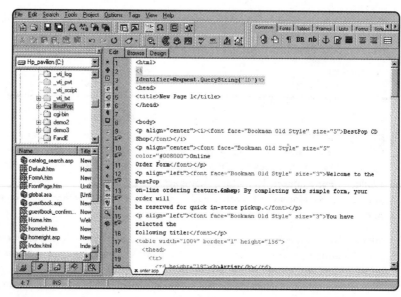

FIGURE 1.23

Utilizing
Macromedia
HomeSite to
develop with ASP.

computer to work most effectively with ASP in general and with the information provided in this book. Finally, I quickly talked about the use of FrontPage 2000 and other application development tools. I stressed that it is in your best interest to hold off on using these tools until you gain a solid understanding of ASP fundamentals.

EXERCISES

To ensure you have a good understanding of the Web server configuration issues presented in this chapter, take a look at the following exercises:

1. Open Notepad, Word, and so on, and describe the advantages of working with ASP.

2. Continuing with the above, write another paragraph that describes the differences between ASP and a regular HTML Web page.

3. Create at least two new ASP Web pages so that you are comfortable with where to save them (i.e., in the Inetpub directory) and how to save them (that is, with the .asp extension).

4. Take a few moments to search the Web for more information on both Microsoft FrontPage (http://www.microsoft.com) and Macromedia HomeSite (http://www.macromedia.com). Although you may not have experience with either program, take a moment to review their features to see how they both support ASP development. Also, see if you can find information on other Web development tools that support ASP.

5. Finally, review the enclosed CD-ROM to see the goodies that have been included and to fire your imagination and interest as to the exciting things that await you in this book!

CHAPTER 2

Programming ASP Web Pages with VBScript

I n this chapter, you will

- Learn how Visual Basic Script (or *VBScript*) is at the center of all your ASP development and how you can integrate VBScript into all your ASP programming.

- Learn the core concept of variables and why (and how) they are an essential programming component.

- Learn fundamental programming statements that bring your VBScript code to life.

- Build your first ASP game, Hello, World!, which will utilize all the concepts you learn in this chapter.

Before you begin developing the whiz-bang ASP pages I know you've been dreaming about since you first purchased this book(!), there are some fundamental concepts of programming with which you need to become familiar. I can hear the groans now, and I know what you're probably thinking: "Fundamental concepts! That sounds like a synonym for *boring*!" Although it's true that the material you will learn in this chapter might not be as interesting as the games you will soon be developing, keep in mind the operative phrase here: *soon be developing*. In other words, I'll try my hardest to get you through this perfunctory yet critical material as quickly as possible, and we'll try to have a little fun along the way, too.

This chapter was written to give you a general overview of VBScript, to get your programmer's feet wet, and, I hope, get you excited about the wonderful things you can learn and do by reading the rest of this book. As you read sections that particularly interest you, be sure to note the additional reference chapters, which go into far more detail, including lots of coding examples, on the subject being discussed.

All the code examples in this chapter can be found on the enclosed CD-ROM. If you want to follow along and test the examples, you can open them with Notepad or any other text editor at your disposal and save them in the Inetpub folder on your hard drive. If you don't know what the Inetpub folder is, take another look at Chapter 1, "Preparing to Work with ASP." You might create a separate folder in the Inetpub folder and call it *ABG_ASP*. In this folder, you can place all the code examples you work through in this book, which will help you keep everything organized.

Integrating VBScript with ASP

This discussion of VBScript begins with a quick demonstration. Figure 2.1 shows a simple Web page with a typical .html extension.

Take a closer look at this page:

- Notice the name of the page: *ABC.html*. As you know, *HTML* is short for *Hypertext Markup Language*, the primary method of posting information on the Web.

- Note the following text: *Upon receipt of your letter of inquiry, you should receive information about the company in 4-6 weeks.* The ABC Company is fictitious, of course, but four-to-six weeks, in my opinion, is a long time to wait for information, especially if you have to go to the trouble of mailing an inquiry.

- Take a look at the HTML code that constructed this page:

Listing 2.1 ABC.html

```
<html>

<head>
<title>Welcome to the ABC Company</title>
```

```
</head>

<body>

<p align="center"><b>Welcome to the ABC Company </b></p>
<p align="center"><b>Today is Friday, June 15 2001</b></p>
<hr>

<p align="left">If you would like more information about our company, please
write to:</p>
<p align="left">ABC Company</p>
<p align="left">1234 Jackson Street</p>
<p align="left">North Vernon, Indiana 47265</p>
<p align="left"><i>Thanks for your interest in the ABC Company!  Upon
receipt of your letter of inquiry, you should receive information about the
company in 4-6 weeks.</i></p>

</body>
</html>
```

Notice that the date (in this case, June 15, 2001) is *hard-coded* into the HTML. This means that for the page to remain accurate, the HTML has to be manually *updated* (that is, changed) each day to reflect the change in the date.

Now, consider the same page as an ASP page, illustrated in Figure 2.2. Note the .asp extension in place of the usual .html.

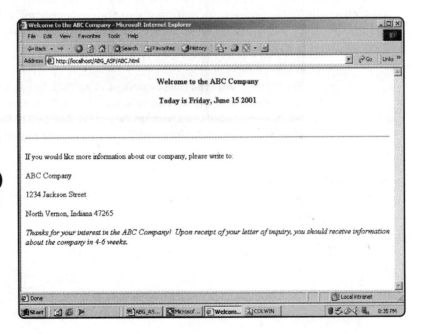

FIGURE 2.1

A simple Web page describing the fictitious ABC Company. Note the .html extension in the name of this Web page, *ABC.html*.

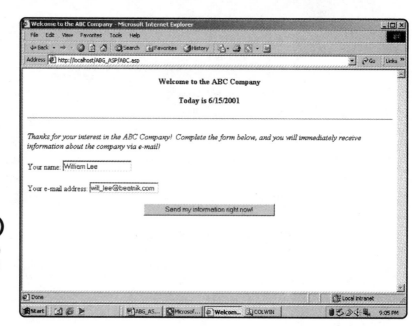

FIGURE 2.2

A simple ASP page
but with enhanced
functionality,
compared to the
.html version.

Aside from the obvious differences in appearance, there are some critical differences between ABC.html and ABC.asp:

- Note the name of the page in Figure 2.2 and how it has an .asp extension. This indicates that the page is an ASP page.

- Note how, compared to ABC.html (refer to Figure 2.1), the ABC.asp page offers the visitor the ability to receive information about the company immediately via e-mail rather than wait four to six weeks for delivery through regular "snail mail."

- Take a look at the code behind ABC.asp:

TRICK

The use of <%= and <% and other opening/closing VBScript commands and functions will be discussed in more detail throughout this book. For now, just be sure to recognize these special characters and the fact that they must be included within your code (as shown) in order for your ASP pages to function properly.

Listing 2.2 ABC.asp

```
<html>

<head>
<title>Welcome to the ABC Company</title>
</head>

<body>

<p align="center"><b>Welcome to the ABC Company </b></p>
```

```
<p align="center"><b>Today is <%=DATE%></b></p>
<hr>

<p align="left"><i>Thanks for your interest in the ABC Company!  Complete
the form below, and you will immediately receive information about the company
via e-mail!</i></p>
<form method="POST" action="ABCInfo.asp">
    <p align="left">Your name: <input type="text" name="T1" size="20"></p>
    <p align="left">Your e-mail address: <input type="text" name="T2" size="20"></p>
    <p align="center"><input type="submit" value="Send my information right now!"
    name="B1"></p>
</form>
<p align="left"> </p>

</body>
</html>
```

- Notice how, compared to ABC.html, the ABC.asp page uses the VBScript function DATE to display the current date on the Web page dynamically. Also, the page uses a form to capture information from the user on the spot so that the user can receive information immediately via e-mail.

By utilizing the DATE function, the ABC.asp page is self-sufficient in that the date displayed is always current and doesn't need to be manually updated. Remember, in ABC.html, the date is hard-coded, so the HTML used to display the data has to be changed each day to display the correct date.

Although a simple demonstration, this is a prime example of the power and functionality ASP brings to your Web development.

Client-Side versus Server-Side Processing

In the preceding section, you caught a glimpse of how ASP can take your Web pages to an entirely new level, but how does ASP work?

A critical element of ASP is that it executes on the server rather than the client, that is, the Web browser itself. What does this mean? Let me use an analogy to explain.

Imagine that your television goes on the blink. Rather than have it repaired at the shop, you ask the repairman to come out to your house. Although you give good directions to your home, and the repairman doesn't have a hard time finding you, the story changes considerably after he arrives. He quickly discovers that, because of the specific make and model of your television, he can't repair it in your home, even with his full set of tools and general skill.

Now, imagine another scenario. In this case, you take your television to the shop to have it repaired. Because the repairman doesn't need to anticipate any special requirements of your TV or guess which tools he'll need for the job, he can utilize his full complement of resources, both tools and skill, in repairing your TV. Moreover, because the repair work is being done in his shop, he has full control over how the repair proceeds. Not only does he have easy access to all his tools, but he can also use sophisticated testing equipment on your set. Ultimately, the TV is returned to you, repaired correctly and—in this case—more quickly because you didn't experience the delay of the repairman's first coming out to your house and discovering that he didn't have everything he needed.

What does this have to do with ASP? Think of client-side versus server-side processing in the same fashion. When you utilize a language that is processed in the client, for example, JavaScript, you risk the possibility of the repairman—in this analogy, the visitors to your site and their specific Web browser—not being configured to display or manipulate (or incapable of displaying or manipulating) the code you have placed within your Web page. In other words, if the code within your Web page executes in a browser that can't handle it, for whatever reason, the code malfunctions or, worse, doesn't display at all. You are then left with a broken TV, to carry out the analogy. However, if you use server-side processing, all the repair work can be taken care of on the server, with the browser client's only involvement being the receipt of the processed code. This processed code is straight HTML, so the vast majority of browsers can

SHOULD YOU ALWAYS USE SERVER-SIDE PROCESSING?

From the TV repair analogy I've presented here, you might think that the only way to make Web pages that utilize a programming language work properly is to use server-side processing. Although it's true that server-side processing has many advantages, it's not accurate to say that client-side processing is a bad thing. The real issue in this client-side/server-side processing debate is whether you can safely assume, or control, the type of Web browser that will be used to display your VBScript-enabled Web pages (in this case). For example, VBScript is a Microsoft innovation. It is designed to work, for the most part, exclusively in the Microsoft Web browser Internet Explorer. Now, that statement is true if you use VBScript in the manner of client-side processing or if the VBScript is executed in the Web browser itself. Usually, if you try to execute VBScript directly in other types of browsers, it will not function. If you have the VBScript executed on the Web server, though, the only thing sent to the Web browser client is the results of this execution. These are mostly straight HTML, which is capable of being displayed in any Web browser.

Some programming languages are designed from the onset to work in the client. JavaScript is a fine example of this. However, you need to keep in mind that with even the most universal client-side languages, there can be differences. For example, both Microsoft and Netscape have slightly different methods of interpreting JavaScript. A Web page you create with JavaScript will typically function the same in Internet Explorer and Netscape Navigator, but differences—some big and some small—will creep up when you try to execute JavaScript-enabled pages in the various browsers. Does this mean that you should avoid using them? Not necessarily. However, you should be cognizant of the fact that, like our friendly TV repairman, when you bring the repair into the client's house (that is, the client-side processing in the browser) versus doing the work at the shop (server-side processing), you introduce a level of unpredictability because you don't know what kind of environment you will be working in and which tools you will need to get the job done right.

display it. In a nutshell, server-side processing takes all the guesswork and variability out of utilizing a programming language such as VBScript within your Web pages because the code processing is done on the server, not in the browser.

Understanding VBScript Variables

Variables are perhaps the most essential programming elements because they allow you to assign values to specific markers in your code. With this assignment comes the power to further manipulate the values. A variable value can be nearly anything: a telephone number, an e-mail address, an order date, a customer's name–the list goes on.

Consider the following example:

Listing 2.3 VariableA.html

```
Email_Address="rsmith@zeppelin.com"
Age=31
UserName="Robert Smith"
```

You see three variables (Email_Address, Age, and UserName) being assigned specific values (rsmith@zeppelin.com, 31, and Robert Smith, respectively). After variables are assigned, they can be manipulated or otherwise referenced in your code, as in the following sample page, Variable.asp:

Listing 2.4 VariableB.asp

```
<html>

<head>
<title>Working with Variables</title>
</head>

<body>
<%
Email_Address="rsmith@zeppelin.com"
Age=31
Name="Robert Smith"
%>
<b>This is an example of working with variables within ASP</b><hr>
The e-mail address is: <%=Email_Address%><p>
The age is: <%=Age%><p>
The name is: <%=Name%>
</body>
</html>
```

When this code is executed, it appears as shown in Figure 2.3.

Also, as discussed in the preceding section, because Variable.asp has its code processed on the server, only the results are sent to the browser. When the source code for this page is viewed in the browser, only the processed HTML is visible. In other words, the

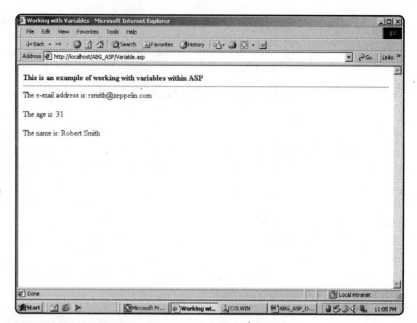

Working with Variables - Microsoft Internet Explorer

File Edit View Favorites Tools Help

Back · · Search Favorites History

Address http://localhost/ABG_ASP/Variable.asp   Go Links

This is an example of working with variables within ASP

The e-mail address is: rsmith@zeppelin.com

The age is: 31

The name is: Robert Smith

Done   Local intranet

Start   Microsoft Fr... Working wi... COLWIN ABG_ASP_O... 11:05 PM

FIGURE 2.3

The VBScript in this page allows variables to be assigned values and then allows those values to be displayed.

```
<html>

<head>
<title>Working with Variables</title>
</head>

<body>

<b>This is an example of working with variables within ASP</b><hr>
The e-mail address is: rsmith@zeppelin.com<p>
The age is: 31<p>
The name is: Robert Smith
</body>
</html>
```

FIGURE 2.4

Because the VBScript in Variable.asp is processed on the server, only the resulting HTML is sent to the browser.

assignment of the variables (the actual VBScript) is processed on the server and therefore not visible to users when they check the source code in their Web browser (see Figure 2.4).

HINT

Because only the resulting HTML is sent to the Web browser, server-side processing is more secure, in general, because a user can't see potentially sensitive program code when viewing the source code.

In VBScript, there are several subtypes of variables, but I'm going to focus on the following four:

- **Integer.** This subtype can have an assigned value anywhere in the range of -32768 to 32768. Think of an integer subtype as the number variable, where you can assign specific numeric values to the variable names you set. Examples of an integer variable are age=31 or weight=190.

- **Date.** This subtype stores (you guessed it) date values. The value range for the date subtype can range from January 1, 100, to December 31, 9999.

- **Currency.** Useful for storing monetary values. There are some specific formatting concerns with this subtype, as there are with the date subtype. By calling specific VBScript *functions* (special commands used to execute stored procedures), you can display currency and date values in different ways. You can see a variety of these formatting features illustrated in Appendix A, "VBScript Variable Reference."

- **String.** This is perhaps the most common subtype. In general, you use string variables to store textual values, such as FirstName="William Burroughs" or CityName="Indianapolis".

 Note in the examples that with string variables you use quotation marks around the value assigned to the variable, but with integer subtypes you do not use quotes. I'll talk more about this difference in the next section.

Declaring Constants in VBScript

Remember your senior prom or your wedding? Before you walked into the reception hall with your date or spouse, you were announced to the crowd so that everyone would know who you are. This is analogous to declaring constants in VBScript.

What does *declaring* mean, and why do you have to be concerned with it? When you assign a value to a variable, you declare a constant. That is, you assign a permanent value—until you declare it with a different value. The following are examples of declaring constants in VBScript:

- LastName="Johnson"

- DOB="4/12/70"

- Years_Employed=15

As you will see in coding examples throughout this book, variables can have their values changed as your code is executed, depending on how your code functions. This can be useful when you want to use a variable as a temporary holding container for a transient value. For example, you write a program that displays 10 random numbers to the screen. In the program, you use the variable Display_Number in which to assign the random number. However, because you are displaying 10 different numbers, you want Display_Number to be able to have its value changed.

In another section of this program, you want to refer back to the user's name at several points in the code, via the variable UserName. Because the user's name doesn't change, you want to declare a specific value for this UserName variable so that it will not change, unless you change it by assigning a new value to the variable.

The simple way to view this is that you are always declaring variables the moment you assign a value to them. However, when you assign a value to a variable that you don't want to change, you are declaring a constant for that variable.

TRICK

For more specific information on VBScript variable subtypes, including how to manipulate them, be sure to refer to Appendix A, "VBScript Variable Reference."

Learning to Program with VBScript

By all definitions, the following simple example is a VBScript program, which comes alive when placed within an ASP Web page:

Listing 2.5 Simple_Program.asp

```
<html>
<body>
<%
FirstName="John"
LastName="Gosney"
%>
Welcome to VBScript <%=FirstName%> <%=LastName%>!
I know you are really going to love it!
</body>
</html>
```

When this code is executed on the Web server, it appears in a Web browser, as shown in Figure 2.5.

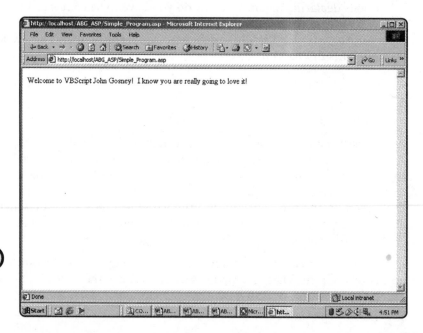

FIGURE 2.5

Simple as it is, this is an example of a VBScript program.

This is a fine program, a good place to start, but I'm sure that you're thinking right now that you want your ASP pages to do more than just display simple text.

I have good news for you. You can unleash all kinds of power and functionality and make your code run much more efficiently by utilizing some core VBScript statements. I want to give you a preview of two:

- `IF...THEN`
- `FOR...NEXT`

Many more statements are essential to your effective use of VBScript, but I will focus on these two statements in this introductory chapter.

The IF...THEN Statement

As I write this chapter, it is a very hot, humid summer afternoon. I live in Indiana, where we have the saying, "If you don't like the weather in Indiana, wait five minutes and it will change!" Although this can make things interesting sometimes—for example, a beautiful summer morning can give rise to very dark clouds and the threat of a tornado—this also makes it difficult to plan for outdoor activity.

Imagine that you live in Indiana or someplace where the weather is very unpredictable. You are on a much needed vacation, and tomorrow you want to take your kids to the park for a day of outdoor fun. You want to plan for any contingency, so you decide that if it rains, you will take the gang to the movies instead. To express this as an `IF...THEN` statement, you could write it as *IF it rains tomorrow, THEN I will take the kids to the movie.*

Basically, when you use an `IF...THEN` statement, you want your code to test for a particular condition. If that condition is *true* (equal to some value or condition you've set), a certain set of actions will take place. In the vacation example, you can see that `IF` the weather is bad, `THEN` you will go to the movies. Going to the movies is the action that takes place if the condition you are evaluating, the weather, is true, in other words, if it rains.

The following code illustrates this analogy as a VBScript program:

Listing 2.6 Weather_Fun.asp

```
<html>

<body>

<%
Good_Weather="We are going to the park!"
Bad_Weather="We are going to the movies!"

WeatherCheck=2

IF WeatherCheck=2 THEN
%>
The weather is bad --   <%=Bad_Weather%>
<%
END IF
```

```
%>
</body>
```

```
</html>
```

When this code is executed, it appears in the Web browser as shown in Figure 2.6.

Go through this code to be sure that you understand everything that is happening:

1. After inserting the usual `<body>` and `<html>` tags, a `<%` is placed to indicate that everything that follows (up to the closing `%>` tag) should be evaluated as VBScript.

2. Two variables are set, `Good_Weather` and `Bad_Weather`. Recall from the earlier discussion that you are declaring constants by assigning permanent values to these two variables.

3. A third variable, `WeatherCheck` (a variable of the integer subtype, by the way) is set to `2`. You will find that as you program, you assign various test variables so that depending on the value they are assigned, a specific condition will be true or false. In this example (and as you will see in a moment), a value of `2` for this variable indicates bad weather. A value of `1` could indicate good weather.

4. The `IF...THEN` statement comes into play. In this example, `IF` the `WeatherCheck` variable has been set to `2`, `THEN` the value assigned to the `Bad_Weather` variable is displayed, via the `<%=Bad_Weather%>` statement.

5. Finally (as with many statements in VBScript), you need to indicate the end of the statement so that your program knows that it can move on to the next section of your code. This ending, for the `IF...THEN` statement, is indicated by the line `END IF`.

TRAP

Be careful that you don't forget to place the closing statements (the `END IF` statement in the example). This is a very common oversight that results in program errors.

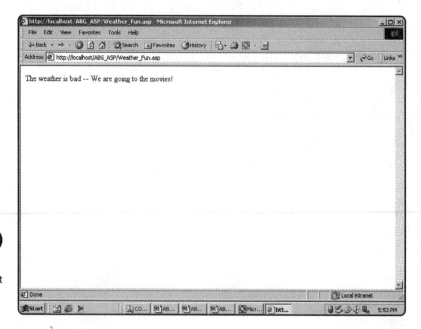

FIGURE 2.6

In this example, the IF...THEN statement results in some stormy weather.

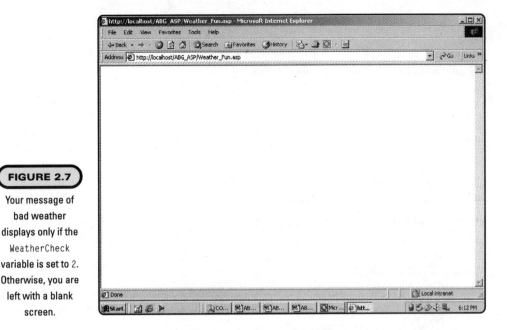

FIGURE 2.7

Your message of bad weather displays only if the `WeatherCheck` variable is set to 2. Otherwise, you are left with a blank screen.

You might be wondering at this point what would happen if you set the `WeatherCheck` variable to something other than 2. Go ahead and try it. Set the `WeatherCheck` variable to 49 or any numeric value other than 2. Be sure to save your changes, and then load the program again into your Web browser. Your screen should look like Figure 2.7.

Having a blank screen display when a certain condition is not true is generally not good. Imagine if you were visiting this Web page and suddenly you were confronted with a blank screen. You would probably, and rightly, wonder whether something is wrong with the code, even though the code is working perfectly.

The code is working too perfectly, in fact. What you need at this point is a way to designate another action to occur if the `WeatherCheck` variable is set to something other than 2.

You do this with the `IF...THEN...ELSE` statement. Take a look at the following code listing:

Listing 2.7 More_Weather_Fun.asp

```
<html>

<body>

<%
Good_Weather="We are going to the park!"
Bad_Weather="We are going to the movies!"

WeatherCheck=2

IF WeatherCheck=3 THEN
%>
The weather is bad --  <%=Bad_Weather%>
```

```
<%
ELSE
%>
The weather is good -- <%=Good_Weather%>
<%
END IF
%>
</body>

</html>
```

When this code is executed, your screen should look like Figure 2.8.

Can you see what's happening here? By adding the ELSE statement to the usual IF...THEN, you allow your code to evaluate more than one condition. In simple English, you can read it as IF the weather is bad, THEN we'll go to the movies. ELSE we will go to the park. Note that you still need the closing END IF statement.

TRICK   This type of program logic is illustrated in far greater detail in Chapter 7, "Essential Programming Logic."

I explain more about this concept in examples throughout the book, but let me mention now that it is possible to nest IF...THEN statements so that you evaluate a variety of conditions, based on the programming rules you set. Examine the following code:

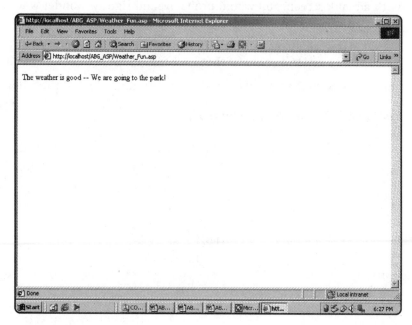

FIGURE 2.8

If the WeatherCheck variable is set to something other than 2, the condition for bad weather, this message is displayed.

Listing 2.8 Nested.asp

```
<html>
<body>
<%
Test_Variable_A=1
RecordName_A="Pretzel Logic"
RecordName_B="Aja"
Test_Variable_B=2
IF Test_Variable_A=1 THEN
        IF Test_Variable_B=2 THEN
%>
My favorite record has the title of <%=RecordName_A%>
<%
ELSE
%>
My favorite record has the title of <%=RecordName_B%>
<%
END IF
END IF
%>
</body>
</html>
```

Now see what's happening in this code:

1. As with the preceding example, four variables are set with specific values. These variables are `Test_Variable_A`, `RecordName_A`, `Test_Variable_B`, and `RecordName_B`.

2. The first `IF...THEN` statement is called. If `Test_Variable_A` is equal to 1, the second `IF...THEN` statement is executed, `IF Test_Variable_B=2 THEN`. If this second `IF...THEN` statement evaluates as `true` (the `Test_Variable_B` is equal to 2), the following statement is executed: `My favorite record has the title of <%=RecordName_A%>`. If the `Test_Variable_B` variable does not equal 2, the following statement is executed: `My favorite record has the title of <%=RecordName_B%>`.

3. Finally, note that two `END IF` statements are placed in the code. For every `IF...THEN` or `IF...THEN...ELSE` statement you use, there must be a corresponding `END IF` statement.

Be sure to note in this code that if the first `IF...THEN` statement does not evaluate to `true` (`Test_Variable_A` does not equal 1), the second `IF...THEN` statement does not execute. It can't because it falls within, or is *nested* within, the first `IF...THEN` statement. This results in a blank screen being displayed, which should be avoided.

The FOR...NEXT Statement

As will be the case with many, many programs you write, the need to have a specific action repeated, or *looped*, will occur. This is useful when you want to evaluate a variety of values against the same condition. For example, imagine that you have 10 names of visitors to your Web site, but you want to give the fifth name a prize for being the fifth person to visit your site. You have the list of names in random order, so you want to loop through them, and when you hit the fifth name, you want a special message to be displayed.

Take a look at the following code, and see how this is illustrated:

Listing 2.9 Loop.asp

```
<html>
<body>
<%
FOR i=1 to 10
IF i=5 THEN
%>
<b> Congratulations!  You are the fifth visitor to the site!</b> <p>
<%
ELSE
%>
Sorry, you are not the fifth visitor! <p>
<%
END IF
NEXT
%>
</body>
</html>
```

In this example, you are utilizing the FOR...NEXT statement to loop through a count of 10 numbers. This count is identified in the statement FOR i=1 to 10. i is a variable (you can name it anything—I just picked i for this example) that is temporarily assigned the count value (1 through 10).

Next, an IF...THEN statement is placed. If the loop count is equal to 5 (indicated here by the statement IF i=5 THEN), the message Congratulations! You are the fifth visitor to the site! is displayed. Otherwise, when the loop count is anything other than 5, the message Sorry, you are not the fifth visitor! is displayed.

Figure 2.9 shows this code displayed in a Web browser.

This is a simple example of the FOR...NEXT loop, but it gives you an idea of the power of this statement and the ways you can utilize it in your code. Throughout the book, you will see many, many examples of the FOR...NEXT statement.

 HINT

As with the IF...THEN statements, you need to close your FOR...NEXT statements. However, with FOR...NEXT statements, you don't close them with an END FOR but rather the simple statement NEXT. By placing this statement in your code, it completes the loop cycle you put into motion with the FOR i=1 to 10 statement in the example.

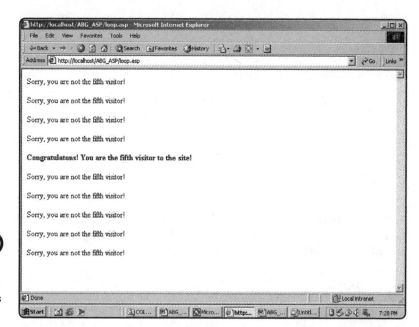

FIGURE 2.9

When the loop count gets to 5, the winning message is displayed.

Commenting Your VBScript Code

Although the code examples in this chapter are simple and not in need of much internal commentary, the more advanced programs you develop (including those in this book) require that you comment your code. By commenting your code, you place notes to yourself and, critically, to others who might view your code later, explaining the rationale behind the way you coded the program and reminding you how things work. You'd be surprised how quickly you forget your own programming, even after a short while.

Commenting your code in VBScript is very simple. You place a single quotation mark, also known as a tick mark, (') before the line, to indicate that it is a commented line. In looking at the preceding code example, you can see how it would appear if it were commented:

Listing 2.10 Loop.asp

```
<html>
<body>
<%
' The loop begins here.  In this loop, the count will run from 1-10
FOR i=1 to 10
' When the loop gets to five, I want a special message to be displayed
IF i=5 THEN
%>
<b> Congratulations!  You are the fifth visitor to the site!</b> <p>
```

```
<%
ELSE
%>
Sorry, you are not the fifth visitor! <p>
<%
END IF
' Don't forget the NEXT statement, which completes the loop
NEXT
%>
</body>
</html>
```

As you can see here, providing even basic commentary makes your code easier to review. Take advantage of this essential element of successful programming. You won't regret it, and neither will the programmers who need to review your code at a later date.

TRICK

Any line that begins with the ' character is considered a comment and is not executed. You can use this feature to disable a line of code temporarily, which is often helpful in troubleshooting your programs as you search for possible errors.

The Hello, World! Game

It is a tradition that when you learn a new programming language, your first program should be the Hello, World! program, which displays this very text to your computer screen.

Despite the groans of some of you who have learned a programming language before, I won't veer from tradition. The Hello, World! game is the first game you will program in this book. It is very similar to the sample code you saw in the section describing the FOR...NEXT statement earlier.

The code for the game is shown here:

Listing 2.11 HelloWorld.asp

```
<html>
<body>
<b>Welcome to the Hello, World! Game!</b><p>
<i>Admittedly, not much of a game, but hey...you gotta start somewhere,
right?</i>
<p>
<%
'Be sure to assign the value of the NAME variable to your own name!
NAME="John Gosney"
FOR i=1 to 15
IF i=5 THEN
'Again, you'll need to assign your own name here!
        IF NAME="John Gosney" THEN _
%>
```

```
<hr>
<center><b>Hello, World!</b><p>
Welcome, <%=NAME%>, to VBScript Programming and ASP!
</center><hr>
<%
'Don't forget you need two END IF statements, one for each IF...THEN
END IF
END IF
'And don't forget to include the NEXT statement so that your loop functions
NEXT
%>
</body>
</html>
```

You can see the game code in action in Figure 2.10.

Summary

In this chapter, you were introduced to essential concepts of working with VBScript as your programming tool of choice when developing ASP Web pages. You learned the difference between client-side and server-side scripting languages and the pros and cons of each. You learned about VBScript variables, including what they are and how to use them. You also examined some essential program statements, including the IF...THEN and FOR...NEXT statements, both of which you will use throughout this book. Also, you learned the importance of commenting your code, so you will take the time to provide this type of internal documentation in your code. Finally, you programmed your first ASP game and worked up a healthy programming appetite for the fun that lies ahead.

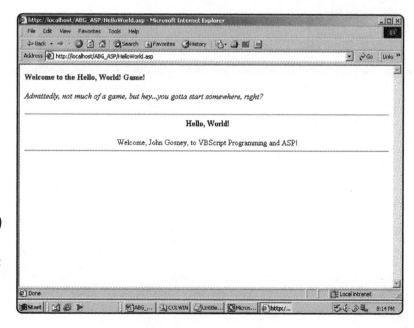

FIGURE 2.10

Your first game! As the screen says, not too exciting, but things will get more interesting soon.

EXERCISES

Work through the following exercises to help you gain a further understanding of the essential concepts you learned in this chapter:

1. Without referring to the text, take out a piece of scratch paper. To keep more in line with the flavor of this book, open a blank document in Word or your favorite text editor. Briefly describe in a short paragraph the difference between client-side and server-side code processing.

2. Go back to the code examples in this book, and in at least two of them, assign a variable with the value of your name. Have it displayed on screen when the code executes.

3. Write a program that utilizes the FOR...NEXT loop statement to count from 1 to 50, displaying each number on the screen. When this count hits 50, have the program display a special completion message.

4. Write a program that has at least three nested FOR...NEXT loops. Like the examples in this chapter, be sure that as the code executes, a blank screen is never displayed when the conditions you set are evaluated.

5. In the programs you develop in steps 3 and 4, add comments so that you clearly understand how your code is functioning.

CHAPTER 3

Working with ASP Objects

I n this chapter, you will

- **Learn to work with the** Response **and** Request **objects and use them to (among other things) process form results and display them on a Web page.**

- **Understand the difference between passing information between Web pages with the QueryString and form collections.**

- **Learn to manipulate the** File **object so that your ASP Web pages interact with common text files.**

- **Program the ASP MadLibs game, using the** Request, Response, **and** File **objects.**

In the first two chapters of the book, I introduce you to fundamental groundwork for working with ASP. In Chapter 1, "Preparing to Work with ASP," you configured a Web server of your choice for a solid development platform from which to build your ASP pages. In Chapter 2, "Programming ASP Web Pages with VBScript," you learned how VBScript brings your ASP pages to life. Although all this information is critical, you are probably ready to begin developing real ASP Web pages (and a game here and there, too).

You are in luck. With this chapter, you begin your journey into the exciting world of ASP by learning how to manipulate objects. Think of objects as the building blocks of your ASP pages, powerful tools to help you bring all that functionality you've been dreaming about to your own personal Web design toolbox. Without further delay, jump right in!

Introducing the Request and Response Objects

Of all the objects in ASP, you use the Request and Response objects the most frequently. As is my custom in this book, the discussion of these two powerful ASP objects begins with an example, in Listing 3.1.

Listing 3.1 Response.asp

```
<html>

<head>
<title>Example of the Response Object</title>
</head>

<body>
This is an example of the ASP Response Object! <hr>

<%
Name="Robert Smith"
Response.Write Name & ", welcome to ASP!"
%>
</body>

</html>
```

This code is straightforward. You know from Chapter 2 that you can define variables and declare constants. In this example, the variable Name is assigned the value Robert Smith. Then, by using the Response object, the variable is output to the Web page, along with the comment "welcome to ASP!". In essence, the Response object is an easy, effective way of presenting the values of your variables and any results of your code manipulation to the Web page.

TRICK

The use of the <%= can also be viewed as equal to Response.Write. You can think of <%= as a method of telling your VBScript to "write" to the screen what comes next. For example, <%=SomeVariable%> would write the contents of SomeVariable **variable to the screen.**

What are the Response and Request objects? The best way to understand these two objects is to think of a telephone call. When you place a call, you are requesting that someone on the other end of the line pick up the phone. When that person answers the phone, he or she issues a response to your request (the ringing phone). Depending on what the person says (your resulting conversation), you process the results of your request by taking specific actions, depending on whom you are talking to and for what purpose. Without much extrapolation, this is the way the Response and Request objects work with ASP.

The Request Object

Before any further explanation, take a look at the Request object in Listing 3.2. You can view the Request object as the "call to action" that the Response object, in turn, answers.

Listing 3.2 RequestForm.asp

```
<html>

<head>
<title>Example of the Request Object</title>
</head>

<body>

<p><b>This is an example of the Request Object!</b></p>
<form method="POST" action="RequestForm_Results.asp">
  <p>This is a typical HTML form.  In the space provided, enter your name
  and then click on the Submit button.</p>
  <p><input type="text" name="Name" size="20"><input type="submit"
  value="Submit" name="B1"></p>
</form>
<p> </p>

</body>

</html>
```

Although you will be learning all about working with forms in ASP in Chapter 6, "Using Forms," here you can see how easy it is via the power of the Request object. Take a look at Listing 3.3.

Listing 3.3 RequestForm_Results.asp

```
<html>

<head>
<title>Example of Form Processing with the Request Object</title>
</head>

<body>
```

```
Welcome <%=Request.Form("Name")%> to the world of ASP!
</body>


</html>
```

As you can see in Figures 3.1 and 3.2, the value you enter in the box on the RequestForm.asp page is displayed within the RequestForm_Results.asp page after

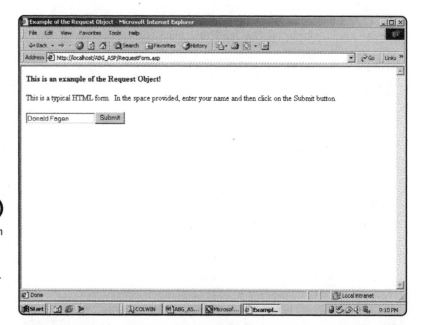

FIGURE 3.1

A typical HTML form you've probably seen (and used) many times on your journeys around the Web.

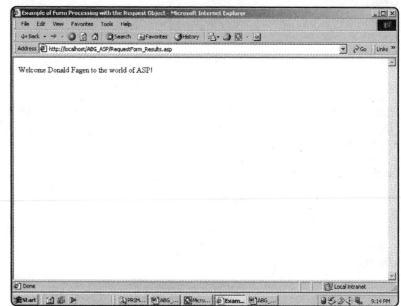

FIGURE 3.2

You can easily process and display form results in ASP, using the Request object.

you click the Submit button. This is done through the functionality and power of the Request object, as shown in the following line from Listing 3.3:

```
Welcome <%=Request.Form("Name")%> to the world of ASP!
```

What's happening in this line of code? I'm guessing that by looking at Listings 3.2 and 3.3, you can figure this out. To reiterate, though, here is a breakdown of the preceding line of code from both an ASP and a basic HTML perspective:

1. Notice in Listing 3.2 how you designate the page to point to when processing the form results. Take note of the following line:

```
<form method="POST" action="RequestForm_Results.asp">
```

Notice the section action="RequestForm_Results.asp". By using the action attribute of a form (which is straight HTML—nothing to do with ASP), you tell the form where to go after the user clicks the Submit button and puts the form into action. You are asking this form to point to the RequestForm_Results.asp page. On this page, the information entered into the form (the name entered in the text box shown in Figure 3.1) is processed and ultimately displayed on screen.

2. When the information gets to the RequestForm_Results.asp page, it can be processed. Remember the analogy of the telephone call? That is exactly what's happening here. The Web browser in which the user enters his or her name on the form makes a *request* that an action be taken by the Web server. In Listing 3.3, the following line accomplishes this:

```
Welcome <%=Request.Form("Name")%> to the world of ASP!
```

By using the form collection of the Request object (more about collections in the following section), you garner a *response* from the Web server—in this case, asking it to pass the information entered into the form field (which I named *Name*) to the RequestForm_Results.asp page.

3. Finally, after all the requesting and responding is completed, the Web browser displays the results, shown in Figure 3.2.

As you might guess, there is much more to both these objects, and you will see them in action throughout this book. In the next section, you will begin your exploration of Object collections, which will make the Request and Response objects more clear. You'll also see how they work in conjunction with other objects to really give ASP all of its power.

Understanding Object Collections

Think of *collections* as special subsets of objects that expose unique information about an object for extended manipulation. In a large company, you can have a manufacturing component, a sales component, a human resources component, and so on. In making an analogy to ASP object collections, think of these company components as exposing specific attributes of the company.

So it is with the ASP object collections. Depending on the object, the number of collections varies, and each collection makes available specific information about the object.

For the Request object, the following collections are available for your manipulation:

- **ClientCertificate.** On some pages, a user certificate is required for access to the page. This certificate contains a variety of information, from encrypted data to basic user profile information. The ClientCertificate collection makes available this information, as requested of the Web server.

- **Cookies.** If the Web page requesting information of the server contains cookies, those cookies (and the data they contain) are sent to the server for examination.

- **Form.** By far the most common collection of the Request object, the form collection takes all the values, as passed by an HTML form section, that are submitted as part of the request. In Listing 3.2, the text box form element (named *Name*) would be included in the form collection of the Request object. As shown in Listing 3.3, the line Request.Form("Name") illustrates the form collection in action.

- **QueryString.** Similar to the form collection, the QueryString collection makes available to the Web server all values contained in the URL of the user's request. I discuss the QueryString in more detail later in this chapter.

- **ServerVariables.** This collection makes available all the HTTP header values, as sent by the user with his or her request.

TRICK

Each object also has a set of unique properties that allow for even greater control of the data being submitted by the user. You will learn about specific object properties in the various code listings throughout this book.

The Request Object Form Collection

You already have an example of the form collection of the Response object in Listings 3.2 and 3.3. As you saw, it is very easy—via the form collection—to access and manipulate information submitted on a typical HTML form.

Even though that example is very simple, it shows you everything you need to know about reading form information from a Web page. However, here is a slightly more complex example, where you can see the true power of the form collection. Listing 3.4 is a regular HTML form, albeit with several form elements.

Listing 3.4 FormExample.asp

```
<html>

<head>
<title>A complete Request object form collection example</title>
</head>

<body>

<p><b>A complete Request object form collection example</b>
<hr>

<form method="POST" action="FormExample_Process.asp">
  <p>Enter your name here: <input type="text" name="Name" size="20"></p>
```

```
<p>What is your gender: <input type="radio" value="M"
name="Gender">M   
<input type="radio" name="Gender" value="F">F</p>
<p>In what age group do you belong: <select size="1" name="Age">
  <option value="1">Younger than 18</option>
  <option value="2">18-26</option>
  <option value="3">27-45</option>
  <option value="4">46-65</option>
  <option value="5">Older than 65</option>
</select></p>
<p>Enter some general comments about what you think about ASP:</p>
<p><textarea rows="5" name="Comments" cols="50"></textarea></p>
<p align="center"><input type="submit" value="Submit" name="B1"></p>
</form>

</body>

</html>
```

Figure 3.3 shows how this form appears.

Now see how this code is processed via the form collection of the Request object. Listing 3.5 illustrates a page that processes the information entered into the form of the page shown in Figure 3.3 by using the Request object's form collection.

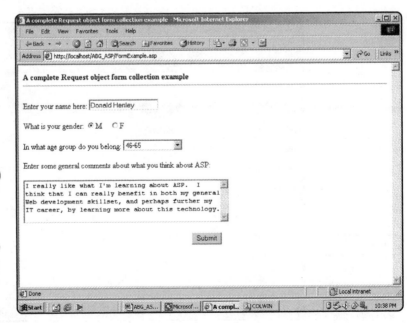

FIGURE 3.3

A typical HTML form, with several types of form elements (a one-line text box, a scrolling text box, radio buttons, and the like).

Listing 3.5 FormExample_Process.asp

```
<html>

<head>
<title>A complete Request object form collection example</title>
</head>

<body>

<p><b>A complete Request object form collection example - -</b>
</p>
<p><i>Utilizing the Request object form collection to read the data</i>
<hr>
<p align="left">Name of visitor to the Web page: <%=Request.Form("Name")%> </p>
<p align="left">Gender of the visitor: <%=Request.Form("Gender")%></p>
<p align="left">Age classification of the visitor: <%=Request.Form("Age")%></p>
<p align="left">Visitor comments:<p>
<i><%=Request.Form("Comments")%></i>
<p align="left"> </p>
</body>

</html>
```

Figure 3.4 shows this page as it processes the information entered in the form illustrated in Figure 3.3.

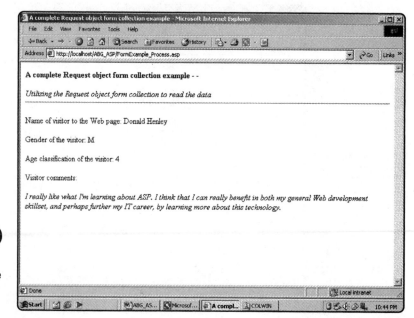

FIGURE 3.4

The form is processed using the Request object's form collection.

As you can see in Listing 3.5, the form collection can be used to read information from any form element (text box, radio button, and so on). Because forms and form processing are described in far greater detail in Chapter 6, for now you can familiarize yourself with how form data is being passed and then manipulated via the form collection of the Request object.

The Request Object QueryString Collection

The QueryString collection works nearly the same as the form collection, except that you append values to the URL of the user's request rather than use a form to capture and pass data.

To demonstrate this, let me refer you to Listing 3.5 in the preceding section. Say that after you pass the form information to the FormExample_Process.asp page, you want to pass that information to another page, this time using the QueryString collection, shown in Listing 3.6.

Listing 3.6 FormExample_Process2.asp

```
<html>

<head>
<title>A complete Request object querystring collection example</title>
</head>

<body>

<p><b>A complete Request object querystring collection example - -</b>
</p>
<p><i>Utilizing the Request object querystring collection
to read the data</i>
<hr>
<p align="left">Name of visitor to the Web page:
<%=Request.Querystring("Name")%> </p>
<p align="left">Gender of the visitor:
<%=Request.Querystring("Gender")%></p>
<p align="left">Age classification of the visitor:
<%=Request.Querystring("Age")%></p>
<p align="left">Visitor comments:<p>
<i><%=Request.Querystring("Comments")%></i><hr>

</body>

</html>
```

Figure 3.5 shows how this code appears when executed.

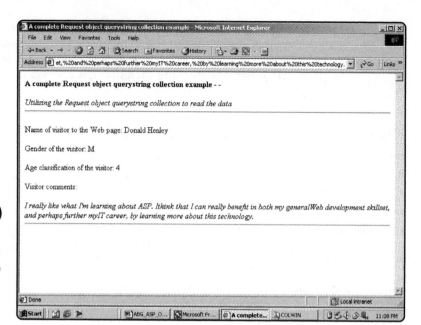

FIGURE 3.5

This page looks exactly the same as that shown in Figure 3.4, which uses the form collection of the Request object.

As you see, you get the same results using either the form or QueryString collection of the Request object. However, you should be aware of several issues when deciding which of these collections to use:

- Compare the URL in Figure 3.4 to the one in Figure 3.5. In Figure 3.4, there is no sign that any data has been passed. All the information entered by the user on the form is processed via the Request object form collection. Using the form collection is a more secure method of passing information; nothing is visible as it is passed.

- Depending on the type of Web browser being used (and, in some cases, the limitations of the Web server), there can be a limit on the size of the URL. For example, if you use the QueryString collection to pass an excessively large amount of information, not all of it may be transferred via the appended URL.

- The appended URL cannot contain any spaces. Spaces can result in errors when processing. Although Internet Explorer (usually) automatically converts a space to a + sign, other browsers might not be able to handle this type of advanced URL processing.

TRICK

For all the reasons listed here, you should always try to use the form collections and the POST method to pass information. You will be learning much more about processing forms (including the POST method) in ASP in Chapter 6, "Using Forms."

Introducing the File Object

The capability of your Web pages to write to a text file is a powerful attribute of ASP. Say that you have a Web-based survey (using a typical Web form) that asks visitors to analyze your Web site's design and functionality. After the form is completed and the user clicks the typical Submit button, you want the user's information to be saved to a text file so that you can review it later. Say that you own a small company that specializes in computer training. On your Web site, you have an online registration form that folks interested in taking your classes can complete, and it sends their registration information to them in a text file (so that they can print it out and bring it with them to class). The capability to write to a text file would be perfect for this example.

The possible uses of this capability go on and on. To understand the functionality of the File object (or the ASP object you use to access all this file manipulation capability), you will program the ASP MadLibs game in this chapter. Remember MadLibs? This is the word game that asks you to think of several verbs, nouns, and adjectives. Then, the seemingly innocent list of words you generate is inserted into a prefabricated story, often with very funny results. For example, say that you are asked for two nouns, two verbs, and two adjectives. Your list of words is then inserted into the following story:

> One day, (*noun*) was walking down the street. Suddenly, he (*verb*) the
>
> (*noun*) he was carrying and (*verb*) into the nearest store. All this
>
> activity gave him a/an (*adjective*) appearance, so he (*adverb*) walked to the
>
> nearest phone and called his mother!

As you can see, with the list of words you provide, this story can take on humorous connotations. You will learn how to program a Web-based version of this game, using the File object to create your final story. As a mechanism for requesting (and collecting) the various words, this is a preview of using forms in ASP.

Although the File object has several properties and characteristics, special focus in this chapter is on using the File object to

- Read from a text file.
- Write to a text file.

The File Object Properties

As you did with the Request and Response objects, you will begin by examining the specific properties of the File object:

- **Attributes.** Returns the various attributes of a file. Such attributes include whether the file is read-only and hidden, its name, and its location (in which folder it resides).
- **DateCreated.** Tells the date and time the file was created.
- **DateLastAccessed.** Tells when the file was last accessed.
- **DateLastModified.** Tells when the file was last modified.

TRICK

Remember that DateLastAccessed **and** DateLastModified **are quite different. When a file was last** *accessed* **means when it was last opened or examined.** DateLastModified **refers to the most recent date the file was** *altered,* **not simply opened or examined.**

- **Drive.** Tells you on which drive the file resides.
- **Name.** Returns the name of the file.

- `ParentFolder`. Tells you the folder in which the file resides.
- `Path`. Returns the absolute path of the file's location.
- `ShortName`. Tells the DOS-style name of the file.
- `ShortPath`. Shows the DOS-style path of the file.
- `Size`. Returns the size of the file in bytes.
- `Type`. Tells the file type (for example, .txt for a text file).

As you progress through the following sections (especially as you code the ASP MadLibs game example), you will see most of these properties in action.

The File Object Methods

The `File` object also has its own set of methods:

- `Copy`
- `Delete`
- `Move`
- `CreateTextFile`
- `OpenAsTextStream`

Of these methods, you are going to be looking specifically at the `CreateTextFile` and `OpenAsTextStream` methods because within your ASP code, they allow you to create a new file and then read from, write to, or otherwise append the file.

A File Object Example

Listing 3.7 gives a quick example of how to work with the `File` object, its properties, and its methods.

Listing 3.7 FirstFile.asp

```
<html>
<title>Working with the File Object</title>
<body>
<b>This is a first example of working with the File object!</b>
<hr>
<%
set TestFile=Server.CreateObject("Scripting.FileSystemObject")
set TFileStream=TestFile.CreateTextFile("c:\inetpub\wwwroot\ABG_ASP\
TestFile.txt")
TFileStream.WriteLine "Welcome to the File Object in ASP!"
TFileStream.Close
%>
</body>
</html>
```

To ensure that you understand everything in this code, go ahead and work with it directly now:

1. From the CD-ROM, open the file FirstFile.asp, and save it in your ABG_ASP folder within the wwwroot directory.

2. Open your Web browser of choice, and navigate to this file. When the page loads within your Web browser, it looks like Figure 3.6.

3. After the page loads, the text file you created via the VBScript code (I'll explain this in a moment) is created in your ABG_ASP folder. Navigate to that folder now, and find a text file named *TestFile.txt*. Open this file within Notepad (or your favorite text editor). It looks like Figure 3.7.

How does the code in Listing 3.7 work? Very simply, as you will see here:

1. An instance of the `File` object is created. This is done via the line

```
set TestFile=Server.CreateObject("Scripting.FileSystemObject")
```

Note that the `TestFile` name given to this particular instance is just a random name. You can call it anything you want, but it's a good idea to keep it as short as possible for easier manipulation within the rest of your code.

2. The file is created as you specify the exact path where you want the file created. This is done in the line

```
TFileStream=TestFile.CreateTextFile("c:\inetpub\wwwroot\ABG_ASP\TestFile.txt")
```

In this example, you are creating the file (*TestFile.txt*) directly within your ABG_ASP development folder, but note that you can create the file anywhere you

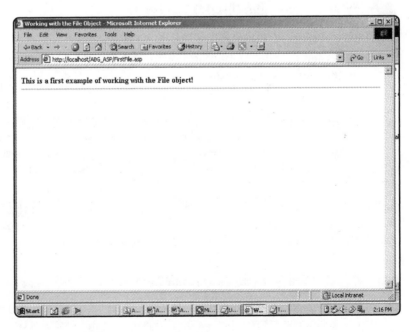

FIGURE 3.6

As with most ASP functionality, most of the exciting stuff—in this case, the VBScript code that manipulates the File object— occurs behind the scenes, with only simple HTML being output to the Web browser.

FIGURE 3.7

The line of text you asked to be included in this file has, indeed, been added.

like. However, you should decide where you will allow the file to be created or otherwise manipulated, according to the sensitivity of the information being passed and where within your system you want to allow this type of access.

3. After you create a file via the CreateTextFile method of the File object, you write to the newly created file. This is done in the line

```
TFileStream.WriteLine "Welcome to the File Object in ASP!"
```

As you see in Figure 3.7, this very line ("Welcome to the File Object in ASP!") is written to the *TestFile.txt* file. The WriteLine method is a method of the TextStream object, which is discussed in more detail in the following sections.

4. Finally, when the file manipulation is completed, this particular instance of the File object is closed in the line

```
TFileStream.Close
```

TRICK

Closing your objects when you are finished working with them is a good practice because it helps prevent coding errors and other problems. Leaving an object open after you are done with it is *not* a good programming practice.

This is a simple example to whet your appetite for working with the File object. Now that you have some idea of how it works, you can dive in to far more robust coding. The first step is a closer examination of the TextStream object.

Introducing the TextStream Object

The TextStream object is the heart of most of the file manipulation in ASP, as illustrated in Listing 3.7. There are three specific methods within the TextStream object: CreateTextFile, OpenTextFile, and OpenAsTextStream. In Listing 3.7, you use the CreateTextFile to create the file and the WriteLine method of the TextStream object to write to the newly created file.

The `TextStream` object has its own set of properties and methods. First, take a look at the `TextStream` object's properties:

- `AtEndOfLine`. Returns a value of `True` if the file *pointer* (the location of the response as the file is read) is at the end of a line in the file.

- `AtEndOfStream`. Returns a value of `True` if the file pointer is at the end of the file.

- `Column`. Depending on the current character being read within the file, returns the column number of this character, starting from 1.

- `Line`. Depending on the current line number being read within the file, returns this line number, starting from 1.

You will see many of the `TextStream` object's methods in action in the listings and the ASP MadLibs game:

- `Close`. Closes an open file.

- `Read` *(a number)*. Reads a specific number of characters from the file. For example, `Read(20)` reads the first 20 characters within the file being examined.

- `ReadAll()`. Reads the entire file and places it within a text string. (For more information on text strings, see Chapter 2, "Programming ASP Web Pages with VBScript.")

- `ReadLine()`. Reads a single line from the file and places it within a text string.

- `Skip` *(a number)*. Skips over a specific set of characters from the file being examined.

- `SkipLine`. Skips a line when reading from the file being examined.

- `Write` *(a string)*. Writes a specified string to the file being examined. For example (as shown in Listing 3.7), the line

```
TFileStream.WriteLine "Welcome to the File Object in ASP!"
```

writes the line `Welcome to the File Object in ASP!` to the specified text file (as specified by the `CreateTextFile` method, by the way).

- `WriteLine` *(a string)*. Writes a string to the file being examined and then writes a newline character within the file.

- `WriteBlankLines` *(a number)*. Writes the specified number of blank lines to the file being examined.

Although these methods are self-explanatory, it is easier to understand them if you see them in action. The following sections give examples of how to use these various methods of the `TextStream` object.

Writing to a Text File

Although Listing 3.7 gives you a simple example of how to create and write to a text file, as well as read from a file, Listing 3.8 is a more substantial demonstration of how to write to a text file.

Listing 3.8 SecondFile.asp

```
<html>
<title>Working with the File Object</title>
<body>
<b>A second example of working with the File object!</b>
```

```
<hr>
<%
set TestFile=Server.CreateObject("Scripting.FileSystemObject")
set TFileStream=TestFile.CreateTextFile("c:\inetpub\wwwroot\ABG_ASP\
Test2File.txt")
TFileStream.WriteLine "Welcome to the File Object in ASP!"
TFileStream.WriteBlankLines(3)
TFileStream.WriteLine "Between this line and the opening line are
three blank lines.  These blank lines were inserted using the
WriteLine method of the TextStream object.  Now, let's write three
more blank lines before the next section of text is inserted."
TFileStream.WriteBlankLines(3)
TFileStream.WriteLine "Okay, that's better--three more blank lines
have just been inserted!  I think you probably get the idea of how to
use the WriteLine method, so let's move on to more interesting things."
TFileStream.Close
%>
</body>
</html>
```

Now, follow these steps to see this code in action:

1. From the CD-ROM, open the file *SecondFile.asp*, and save it in your ABG_ASP folder within the wwwroot directory.

2. Open your Web browser of choice, and navigate to this file. When the page loads within your Web browser, it looks like Figure 3.8.

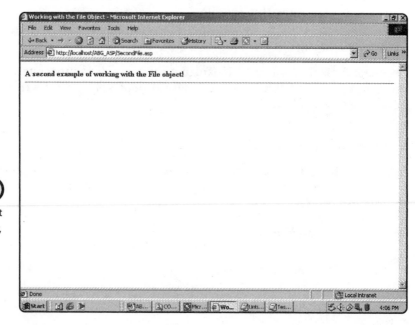

FIGURE 3.8

Not much to look at within the browser, but this doesn't mean that nothing is happening underneath the hood!

FIGURE 3.9

All the text you asked to be inserted, including the blank lines, is included within this file.

3. After the page loads, the *Test2File.txt* file is created within your ABG_ASP folder. Navigate to that folder now, and open this file. It looks like Figure 3.9.

You probably have the hang of writing to a text file. It's a simple process: Create an instance of the File object, define the file path where you want the file to be created, and write to the file with whatever text you want to include. Now you will move on to reading directly from a file into your ASP Web pages.

TRICK

The information you write to a text file doesn't have to be static text. You can define and assign specific values to variables (which you learned how to do in Chapter 2, "Programming ASP Web Pages with VBScript") and then, as a result of your own code processing, insert dynamic values into the text files. For example, you ask visitors to your Web site to enter specific information. Then, you have your code process that information and write the results of that processing to a text file.

Come to think of it, this is exactly the type of processing the ASP MadLibs game performs. Stay tuned for a complete File object example later in this chapter.

Reading from a Text File

Reading from a file is also very straightforward via the power of the TextStream object. See how this is done in Listing 3.9 with some of the TextStream object's properties and methods.

Listing 3.9 ThirdFile.asp

```
<html>
<title>Working with the File Object</title>
<body>
```

```
<b>A third example of working with the File object!</b>
<hr>
<%
set TestFile=Server.CreateObject("Scripting.FileSystemObject")
set TFileStream=TestFile.OpenTextFile("c:\inetpub\wwwroot\ABG_ASP\
Test2File.txt")
TextFormat=TFileStream.ReadLine
%>
<p>
<font face="Century Gothic" size="5" color="#008000">
<i>
<%=TextFormat%></i>
</font></p>
</body>
</html>
```

As with the other examples, save this file (it is named *ThirdFile.asp* on the CD-ROM) into your ABG_ASP folder. Then open it in a Web browser. It looks like Figure 3.10.

As you can see in Figure 3.10, the code from Listing 3.9 first opens the Test2File for reading. Then (through the power of the ReadLine method) the code reads the first line of text from this file, Welcome to the File Object in ASP!. Remember from the description of the ReadLine method, the data returned is set to a string. Keeping this in mind, you set the value of the ReadLine method to the variable TextFormat. Finally, before outputting the contents of this variable to the screen (via the line <%=TextFormat%>), you apply some general HTML formatting. I set the font to Century Gothic, assigned a bigger font size, and italicized it. This formatting gives the text (as read from the file) its unique appearance (refer to Figure 3.10).

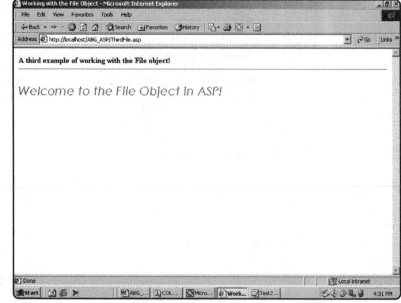

FIGURE 3.10

The capability to read from an existing text file enables you to draw on all kinds of additional information resources when developing in ASP.

ASP MadLibs—Working with ASP Objects

You have learned how to work with the Request, Response, and File objects and have explored their respective methods and properties. You had a preview of working with forms and QueryStrings and now understand how to create a text file and have your ASP pages write to and read information from these pages.

With all these skills under your belt, you are ready to program ASP MadLibs. This game draws on all three objects in this chapter and gives you yet another preview of working with forms, as well as a hint of how your ASP pages can interact with a database, such as Microsoft Access. Speaking of integrating your ASP pages with Microsoft Access, you will learn how to do just that in Chapter 5, "Database Access with ADO." Stay tuned for more exciting programming via the power of ASP.

The ASP MadLibs game is composed of the following three steps:

1. A typical HTML form is used to gather the required information from the user (more on what this information entails in just a moment) and pass it to the (ASP) page that processes the data.

2. The page that processes the user information displays the resulting MadLib and presents the user with options (play again, save the MadLib, and so on).

3. A text file is created that allows the user to save his or her unique MadLib creation as a text file, using a name the user specifies.

Sound cool? It should be, when everything is working. Let's get to it.

The Game Data Input Form

The first part of the ASP MadLibs game is to build the form that gathers the information from the user. Figure 3.11 illustrates this form.

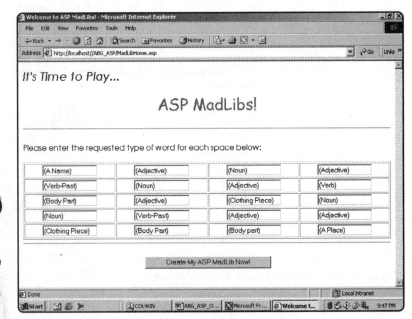

FIGURE 3.11

This form is used to gather the required information from the user so that a unique ASP MadLib can be created.

This is a simple HTML form (with the 20, one-line, text box form elements placed into a table for a cleaner appearance). The code for this page is in Listing 3.10. Note the form attributes. The ACTION attribute is set to *MadLibProcess.asp*—the page that will generate the MadLib, based on the information entered on this form. Also, notice that each one-line text box is numbered and named sequentially (Word1, Word2, Word3, and so on).

Listing 3.10 MadLibHome.asp

```
<html>

<head>
<title>Welcome to ASP MadLibs!</title>
</head>

<body>

<p><font face="Century Gothic" size="5"><i>It's Time to Play...</i></font></p>
<p align="center"><font face="Comic Sans MS" color="#FF0000" size="6">ASP
MadLibs!</font></p>
<hr>

<p align="left"><font face="Century Gothic">Please enter the requested type of
word for each space below:</font></p>
<form method="POST" action="MadLibProcess.asp">
<p>
<table border="1" width="100%" height="139">
  <tr>
    <td width="25%" align="center" height="23"><input type="text"
    name="Word1" size="15" value="(A Name)"></td>
    <td width="25%" align="center" height="23"><input type="text"
    name="Word2" size="15" value="(Adjective)"></td>
    <td width="25%" align="center" height="23"><input type="text"
    name="Word3" size="15" value="(Noun)"></td>
    <td width="25%" align="center" height="23"><input type="text"
    name="Word4" size="15" value="(Adjective)"></td>
  </tr>
  <tr>
    <td width="25%" align="center" height="23"><input type="text"
    name="Word5" size="15" value="(Verb-Past)"></td>
    <td width="25%" align="center" height="23"><input type="text"
    name="Word6" size="15" value="(Noun)"></td>
    <td width="25%" align="center" height="23"><input type="text"
    name="Word7" size="15" value="(Adjective)"></td>
    <td width="25%" align="center" height="23"><input type="text"
    name="Word8" size="15" value="(Verb)"></td>
  </tr>
```

```
<tr>
   <td width="25%" align="center" height="23"><input type="text"
   name="Word9" size="15" value="(Body Part)"></td>
   <td width="25%" align="center" height="23"><input type="text"
   name="Word10" size="15" value="(Adjective)"></td>
   <td width="25%" align="center" height="23"><input type="text"
   name="Word11" size="15" value="(Clothing Piece)"></td>
   <td width="25%" align="center" height="23"><input type="text"
   name="Word12" size="15" value="(Noun)"></td>
</tr>
<tr>
   <td width="25%" align="center" height="23"><input type="text"
   name="Word13" size="15" value="(Noun)"></td>
   <td width="25%" align="center" height="23"><input type="text"
   name="Word14" size="15" value="(Verb-Past)"></td>
   <td width="25%" align="center" height="23"><input type="text"
   name="Word15" size="15" value="(Adjective)"></td>
   <td width="25%" align="center" height="23"><input type="text"
   name="Word16" size="15" value="(Adjective)"></td>
</tr>
<tr>
   <td width="25%" align="center" height="17"><input type="text"
   name="Word17" size="15" value="(Clothing Piece)"></td>
   <td width="25%" align="center" height="17"><input type="text"
   name="Word18" size="15" value="(Body Part)"></td>
   <td width="25%" align="center" height="17"><input type="text"
   name="Word19" size="15" value="(Body part)"></td>
   <td width="25%" align="center" height="17"><input type="text"
   name="Word20" size="15" value="(A Place)"></td>
</tr>
</table>
<hr>

<p align="center"><input type="submit" value="Create My ASP MadLib Now!"
name="B1"></p>

</form>
</body>

</html>
```

The MadLib Processing Page

Now that you have a method (the Web form) for gathering information from the user, it is time to create the page that takes that information and creates the ASP MadLib.

ASP Programming for the Absolute Beginner

The processing page for the game is named *MadLibProcess.asp*, and the code is in Listing 3.11.

Listing 3.11 MabLibProcess.asp

```
<html>

<head>
<title>Here's Your ASP MadLib!</title>
</head>

<body>

<p><font face="Century Gothic" size="5"><i>Thank you!  And now, here is
your </i></font></p>
<p align="center"><font face="Comic Sans MS" color="#FF0000" size="6">ASP
MadLib!</font></p>
<hr>

<p align="left"><font face="Comic Sans MS" size="3">Dear <font
color="#FF0000"><%=Request.Form("Word1")%> ,</font></p>
<p align="left"><font face="Comic Sans MS" size="3">I am having the most
interesting vacation.  I've seen so many strange things.  Upon my
arrival at the airport, a <font color="#FF0000"><%=Request.Form("Word2")%>
</font>
man and I
mixed up our luggage.  At the hotel, I opened his suitcase to find three
<font color="#FF0000"><%=Request.Form("Word3")%>s</font>
and a <font color="#FF0000"><%=Request.Form("Word4")%></font>
toothbrush.  I nearly
<font color="#FF0000"><%=Request.Form("Word5")%></font> out of there when
I discovered a
<font color="#FF0000"><%=Request.Form("Word6")%></font>
wrapped in tissue paper.  I took the
<font color="#FF0000"><%=Request.Form("Word7")%></font> man's luggage
down to the hotel clerk.  The clerk began to
<font color="#FF0000"><%=Request.Form("Word8")%></font> when I told him
about the mix-up.  He pointed his
<font color="#FF0000"><%=Request.Form("Word9")%></font> at a
<font color="#FF0000"><%=Request.Form("Word10")%></font>
man standing in the
lobby, wearing my <font color="#FF0000"><%=Request.Form("Word11")%></font>
on his head!</font></p>
<p align="left"><font face="Comic Sans MS" size="3">After straightening out the
luggage mix-up, I decided to do some sight-seeing.  I hardly had made it
out of the hotel when I immediately noticed the sky darkening, and it began to
```

```
rain <font color="#FF0000"><%=Request.Form("Word12")%>s</font>. 
I ran for cover into the closest <font color="#FF0000">
<%=Request.Form("Word13")%></font>
I could
find, but I <font color="#FF0000"><%=Request.Form("Word14")%></font> into an
<font color="#FF0000"><%=Request.Form("Word15")%></font>
group of school children.  They began laughing and pointing at me. 
</font></p>
<p align="left"><font face="Comic Sans MS" size="3">I checked my reflection in
a storefront window, only to discover I had the
<font color="#FF0000"><%=Request.Form("Word16")%></font>
man's <font color="#FF0000"><%=Request.Form("Word17")%></font> hanging from my
<font color="#FF0000"><%=Request.Form("Word18")%></font>!  Wow! 
I've only been
<font color="#FF0000"><%=Request.Form("Word19")%></font> for three hours
and I'm ready
for a vacation from my vacation!  I figure it can't get much worse. 
Oh, no!  It seems the stamp I wanted to use to mail this letter is stuck
to my <font color="#FF0000"><%=Request.Form("Word20")%></font>!</font></p>
<HR>

<p align="left"><font face="Comic Sans MS" size="3">Would you like to save this
ASP MadLib to a text file?</font></p>
<form method="POST" action="MadLibSave.asp">
  <p align="left">Please enter a name for this file: <input type="text"
name="MadLibName" size="20"></p>
  <p align="center"><input type="submit" value="Save this ASP MadLib!"
name="B1"></p>
  <input type="hidden" name="Word1" value="<%=Request.Form("Word1")%>"><input
type="hidden" name="Word10" value="<%=Request.Form("Word10")%>">
<input type="hidden" name="Word11"
value="<%=Request.Form("Word11")%>"><input type="hidden" name="Word12"
value="<%=Request.Form("Word12")%>"><input type="hidden" name="Word13"
value="<%=Request.Form("Word13")%>"><input type="hidden" name="Word14"
value="<%=Request.Form("Word14")%>"><input type="hidden" name="Word15"
value="<%=Request.Form("Word15")%>"><input type="hidden" name="Word16"
value="<%=Request.Form("Word16")%>"><input type="hidden" name="Word17"
value="<%=Request.Form("Word17")%>"><input type="hidden" name="Word18"
value="<%=Request.Form("Word18")%>"><input type="hidden" name="Word19"
value="<%=Request.Form("Word19")%>"><input type="hidden" name="Word2"
value="<%=Request.Form("Word2")%>"><input type="hidden" name="Word20"
value="<%=Request.Form("Word20")%>"><input type="hidden" name="Word3"
value="<%=Request.Form("Word3")%>"><input type="hidden" name="Word4"
value="<%=Request.Form("Word4")%>"><input type="hidden" name="Word5"
value="<%=Request.Form("Word5")%>"><input type="hidden" name="Word6"
```

```
value="<%=Request.Form("Word6")%>"><input type="hidden" name="Word7"
value="<%=Request.Form("Word7")%>"><input type="hidden" name="Word8"
value="<%=Request.Form("Word8")%>"><input type="hidden" name="Word9"
value="<%=Request.Form("Word9")%>">
</form>
<hr>
<p align="left"><font face="Comic Sans MS" size="3">
<a href="http://localhost/ABG_ASP/MadLibHome.asp">
No thanks, I want to generate another ASP MadLib!</a></font></p>

</body>

</html>
```

After the information on the first page is entered and submitted, this page processes the information to generate a unique (and usually funny) ASP MadLib. Figure 3.12 shows an example of such a MadLib.

On this page, you have the option of creating another MadLib or saving the one you created, giving it a special name. If you choose the save option, you use the `File` object to write your unique ASP MadLib to a text file, the name of which you specify. Figure 3.13 displays this option.

The following section describes the save feature of the ASP MadLibs game.

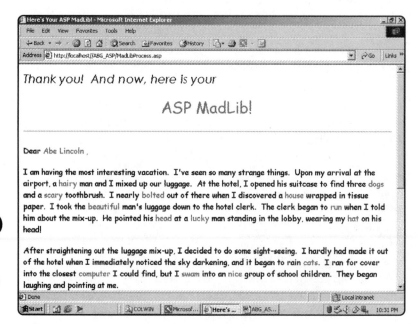

FIGURE 3.12

By using the form collection of the Request object, the ASP MadLib is created.

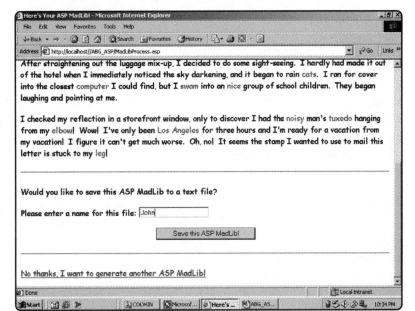

FIGURE 3.13

If you really like a
particular ASP
MadLib, you can
save it for posterity
by writing it to a text
file. If you don't like
the MadLib you just
created, note the
hyperlink below to
return to the data
input page.

The Save Feature: Storing Your ASP MadLibs to a Text File

You can easily save your favorite generated MadLibs to a text file (which is stored on the
server, by the way, and not the client machine). If you enter a name for the text file to
be created and click the Save this ASP MadLib! button (refer to Figure 3.13), you are
directed to the *MadLibSave.asp* page. The code appears in Listing 3.12.

Listing 3.12 MadLibSave.asp

```
<html>

<head>
<title>Saving your ASP MadLib!</title>
</head>
<body>
<%
set TestFile=Server.CreateObject("Scripting.FileSystemObject")
set TFileStream=TestFile.CreateTextFile
("c:\inetpub\wwwroot\ABG_ASP\"&Request.Form("MadLibName")&".txt")
TFileStream.WriteLine "Dear "&Request.Form("Word1")& ","
TFileStream.WriteBlankLines(2)

TFileStream.WriteLine "I am having the most interesting vacation!
```

```
I've seen so many strange things! Upon my arrival at the airport, a
"&Request.Form("Word2")& " man and I mixed up our luggage.  At the hotel,
I opened his suitcase to find three "&Request.Form("Word3")& "s and a
"&Request.Form("Word4")&" toothbrush.  I nearly "&Request.Form("Word5")& "
out of there when I discovered a "&Request.Form("Word6")& " wrapped in
tissue paper.  I took the "&Request.Form("Word7")&" man's luggage down to
the hotel clerk.  The clerk began to "&Request.Form("Word8")& " when I told
him about the mix-up.  He pointed his "&Request.Form("Word9")&" at a lucky
"&Request.Form("Word10")&" standing in the lobby, wearing my
"&Request.Form("Word11")&" on his head!"
TFileStream.WriteBlankLines(2)
TFileStream.WriteLine "After straightening out the luggage mix-up, I
decided to do some sight-seeing.  I hardly had made it out of the hotel
when I immediately noticed the sky darkening, and it began to rain
"&Request.Form("Word12")& "s.  I ran for cover into the closest
"&Request.Form("Word13")&" I could find, but I "&Request.Form("Word14")&"
into a "&Request.Form("Word15")&" group of school children.  They began
laughing and pointing at me."
TFileStream.WriteBlankLines(2)
TFileStream.WriteLine "I checked my reflection in a storefront window,
only to discover I had the "&Request.Form("Word16")&" man's
"&Request.Form("Word17")&" hanging from my "&Request.Form("Word18")&"!
Wow!  I've only been in "&Request.Form("Word19")&" for three hours and I'm
ready for a vacation from my vacation!  I figure it can't get much worse!
Oh, no! It seems the stamp I wanted to use to mail this letter is stuck to my
"&Request.Form("Word20")&"!"
%>


<p><font face="Century Gothic" size="5"><i>Thanks for playing...</i></font></p>
<p align="center"><font face="Comic Sans MS" color="#FF0000" size="6">ASP
MadLibs!</font></p>
<p align="center"> </p>
<p align="left"><font face="Century Gothic" size="5">Your ASP MadLib has been
saved for future reference.  Be sure and play again very soon!</font></p>


</html>
```

Note that this page pulls only the individual, one-line, text box form elements from the *MadLibHome.asp* page via the Request object. Then each of the words entered by the user is inserted into the story.

If the user decides to save the story to a text file, he or she is asked to provide a name for the file. Each of the form fields is assigned as a hidden field (more on this in Chapter 6) and passed to the *MadLibSave.asp* page. Very similar to displaying the story on screen within the Web browser, each of the form elements is again inserted into the

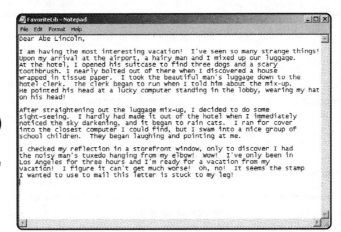

FIGURE 3.14

Using the `File`
object, you can save
your favorite ASP
MadLibs for later
viewing in a typical
text file.

story, with the final story being saved to the text file under the name provided by the
user. This is accomplished in the following line:

```
TFileStream=TestFile.CreateTextFile("c:\inetpub\wwwroot\ABG_ASP\
"&Request.Form("MadLibName")&".txt")
```

In this line, note the path where you save the file. After the ABG_ASP folder, the line
uses the `Request` object again to retrieve the name the user wants to assign to the soon-
to-be-generated text file (the one-line, text box form element used to gather the name
of this file is named *MadLibName*—refer to Listing 3.12 for *MadLibProcess.asp*).

Summary

This chapter introduces you to the concept of ASP objects, including the `Request`, `Response`,
and `File` objects. You learned how to use the `Request` object to process form data and how
to pass information via a QueryString. Then, moving on to the `File` object, you studied
several examples of how to write and read information to a text file via your ASP pages.
Finally, you programmed the ASP MadLibs game, which is a complete demonstration of
how to use the `Request`, `Response`, and `File` objects to produce an entertaining game.

EXERCISES

Try out these exercises to improve your understanding of the Request, Response, and File objects:

1. Design a form for a fictional Web site that asks visitors to provide their name, address (including city, state, and ZIP), telephone number, and e-mail address. Then, have another page process this information, formatting each element in a different way (for example, bold and italicize the name, underline the address, and so on).

2. Repeat exercise 1, but rather than use the forms collection of the Request object, pass the information to the processing page via a QueryString.

3. Create a text file with three or four paragraphs of text. Using the methods and properties of the File object, read the information in this file into an ASP Web page, formatting the text (boldface, italic, different fonts, and so on) as the file is read.

4. Modify the ASP MadLibs game so that on the *MadLibProcess.asp* page, the words to be inserted into the story are formatted in a different fashion than they appear in the original code (for example, change their font size, color, style, and so on).

5. Write your own ASP MadLibs. When you have a good story (with appropriate blanks for inserting words provided by the player), create the form to gather these words, and also create a page to display the story via a Web browser. Finally, just like the game in this chapter, give players the ability to save their story to a text file.

CHAPTER

Working with ASP Components

I n this chapter, you will

- **Review where ASP components are installed on your computer and how to access them.**

- **Learn how to implement the various components into your ASP Web pages, seeing first-hand the potential functionality, convenience, and ease of use they bring to your programming.**

- **Learn the limitations of components and when to consider using an alternative to achieve the functionality they present.**

Ah, the infamous TV dinner. Food for millions of bachelors and otherwise challenged cooks throughout this country and the world at large. From meatloaf to chicken nuggets, the variety of dinners you can nuke in your microwave is seemingly endless.

You will notice throughout this book that I have a habit of introducing ASP topics by developing an analogy to strange topics (I think that the one I'm making here is probably the weirdest). These wacky comparisons always (I hope) make the subject under discussion easier to understand.

Okay, enough justification. Just what *do* TV dinners have in common with ASP components? Think of a typical TV dinner and why you buy it. Assuming (and this is admittedly an assumption, but just go with it for a moment) that you like the taste of the things, what do they have to offer? Well, within that fancy cardboard tray, you are presented with an assortment of food you would otherwise have to buy and prepare yourself. In a typical TV dinner, you get convenience, everything in one place and without your having to put in the work.

Such is the case with ASP components. Instead of your having to program on your own, the components do the work for you. Also, they offer you tremendous convenience by easily plugging in to your ASP Web pages. They load automatically with Internet Information Server, so you get all this functionality in one place, too.

Now that you know what TV dinners and these components have in common(!), you are ready to begin work with the components.

What Are ASP Components?

The key benefit of using components is that they present, in an easy-to-use, accessible package, a lot of functionality you would otherwise have to program on your own. If there is one rule of programming I like to live by, it's this: If you find an easy way to do something, don't hesitate to use it! If that sounds deceptively simple, you are right. Oftentimes, as you develop with ASP (and any programming or scripting language), you struggle for many hours (days?!?) trying to find a solution to a particular problem. What makes this task equally rewarding and frustrating is that, nine times out of ten, your final solution is so darn simple (and often, elegant) you can't believe that you worked so hard to get there. That said, always keep the components in the back of your mind as you develop your pages. They can save you a tremendous amount of time (and aspirin, for your headaches).

In this chapter, you're going to look at four of the ASP components:

- **Content Linking component.** This component allows you to add a table of contents (or just contents) page into your site. After this is established, you can link back and forth to all the pages within your site. Then, when you need to make changes (add or remove pages and links), you just edit the text file from which this component runs rather than go through each and every page of your site, making individual changes.

- **Ad Rotator component.** This component brings the functionality of rotating graphics to your ASP pages each time a page is loaded. I'm sure that you've seen this type of advertisement during your surfing adventures on the Web; each time you visit a page, the advertisements are different. With the Ad Rotator component, you can easily add this functionality to your own pages.

- **Content Rotator component.** Similar to the Ad Rotator component, the Content Rotator component allows you to rotate various text and HTML information on your pages.
- **Page Counter component.** Use this component to track the number of visitors to your Web site.

TRAP

You should note that not all of the components load "at the same time." In other words, depending on the specific configuration of your system, you may not have access to every ASP component. For example, if you use FrontPage, you will gain access to some different components (sometimes referred to as WebBots) that you would otherwise not have access to. For more information on the FrontPage WebBot issue, see Chapter 10, "ASP and HTML Scripting with FrontPage 2000."

There is one other ASP component, the ActiveX Data Object component (*ADO* for short). I discuss this in Chapter 5, "Database Access with ADO." Because of the tremendous functionality and power of ADO, I devote an entire chapter to it.

TRICK

Various third-party ASP components are available for free download via the Web. Please refer to the enclosed CD-ROM for a sampling of some of these components.

The best way to understand the functionality of the components is to see them in action. I will get straight to that by describing each component and providing an example of it in action.

Working with the Content Linking Component

As your Web sites grow beyond a few pages, ensuring that all the hyperlinks on these pages point to the correct location becomes more of a priority (and more of a burden). You use the Content Linking component to assist you in this important task.

Imagine that you have the URLs in Listing 4.1 on a number of pages within your Web site.

Listing 4.1 URL Listing

```
<a href="home.asp">ABC Company Home Page</a href>
<a href="guest_services.asp">Guest Services</a href>
<a href="order_form.asp">Order Form</a href>
<a href="order_catalog.asp">Order Catalog</a href>
<a href="feedback_form.asp">Feedback Form</a href>
<a href="account_status.asp">Account Status</a href>
<a href="copyright_info">ABC Company Copyright</a href>
```

Say that the number of pages that contain these links totals around 50 within your site. What happens if, for some reason, the location of one of these links changes? For example, what if the link to the order form page changes from *order_form.asp* to just *orderform.asp*? You have to go through each page in your site and manually make this change.

However, if you use the Content Linking component to create the list, you can make a change in one place, and that change will be updated in all the pages in your Web site. Sound useful? It is!

The Content Linking component uses a text file to store all the links you want to include on your pages. For example, using the links in Listing 4.1, the text file might look like Listing 4.2.

TRAP When creating your text files for use with the Content Linking component, be sure that you tab between the URL, the description, and the optional comment. If you just use the spacebar, you will receive errors when using this file with the Content Linking component.

Listing 4.2 Contents.txt

```
home.asp       Home page of the ABC Company      Our window to the world
guest_services.asp      Listing of all the services we offer
order_form.asp     Main order form for our catalog      Can access directly
feedback_form.asp      Customer comment line      Checked on a daily basis
account_status.asp     View all account information
copyright_info.asp     Copyright for use of ABC name      Updated yearly
```

Each listing in a text file has the following format:

- The URL of the page
- The description of the page
- An optional comment line for the page (no comment for the *guest_services.asp* and *account_status.asp* pages in Listing 4.2)

As you learned in Chapter 3, "Working with ASP Objects," each object has a specific member listing. Such is the case with these components. For the Content Linking component, its members are

- GetListCount. Returns the number of items in the text file containing all the URLS of the pages to which you want to link
- GetListIndex. Returns the index (or number) of the current page being viewed, as it is listed in the text file
- GetNextURL. Retrieves the next URL in the list, as listed in the text file
- GetNextDescription. Retrieves the next description in the list, as listed in the text file
- GetPreviousURL. Retrieves the previous URL in the list, as listed in the text file
- GetPreviousDescription. Retrieves the previous URL in the list, as listed in the text file
- GetNthURL. Retrieves a specific URL in the text file
- GetNthDescription. Retrieves a specific description in the text file

The Content Linking Component—An Example

Listing 4.3 is an example of the Content Linking component in action. In this example, you'll see how the Content Linking component can read from an existing text file (in this case, *Contents.txt*) to display the results on-screen.

Listing 4.3 Content_Linking.asp

```
<html>
<head>
<title>Working with Content Linking Component</title>
</head>
<body>
<b>This page will display the links in the Content.txt file</b>
<hr>
<%
Set Num_of_links=Server.CreateObject("MSWC.NextLink")
LinkNum=Num_of_links.GetListCount("Contents.txt")
For i=1 to LinkNum
%>
<table border="1" width="38%">
  <tr>
    <td width="100%">
      <ul>
        <li>
        <a href="<%=Num_of_links.GetNthURL("Contents.txt", i)%>">
        <%=Num_of_links.GetNthDescription("Contents.txt", i)%></a>
        </li>
      </ul>
  </td>
</tr>
<% Next %>
</table>
</body>
</html>
```

Using the text file described in Listing 4.2 (see the file named *Contents.txt* on the CD-ROM) in conjunction with the code from Listing 4.3, when this page is loaded into a browser, it looks like Figure 4.1.

 TRAP

Make sure that the text file you create for use with the Content Linking component is in the same Web folder as the page that calls it.

Here is how this code works:

1. As you learned in Chapter 3, the object is called and defined. In this case, you are naming your instance of the object `Num_of_Links`.

2. A simple `For...Next` loop is used to dynamically run through each URL listed in the text file and display it on-screen.

3. Finally, as each of the lines is read from the text file, the URL and its description are output to the screen. If you look at the status bar of the browser in Figure 4.1, you can see how the URL is dynamically created.

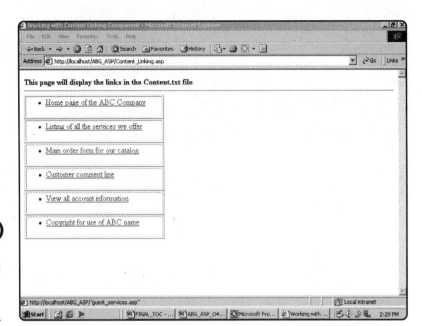

FIGURE 4.1

Each respective URL is bulleted and placed within a unique row of a typical HTML table.

If you're confused about the `For...Next` business in step 2, stay with me. You will be learning all about loops and how to use them in the coming chapters. The important thing at this point is that you understand how the Content Linking component works with a text file to read information from that text file into a Web page.

Working with the Ad Rotator Component

You use the Ad Rotator component to mimic the action you see on numerous Web pages where various advertisements are rotated each time the page is loaded into your Web browser. Even if you don't have traditional advertisements (that is, you're not trying to sell anything), you can use this component to rotate through any set of images. For example, you might have four or five business graphics representing various assets of your company. Even if only your employees see these graphics, using the Ad Rotator component makes for an attractive, easy method of displaying information.

Like the Content Linking component, the Ad Rotator component has specific members. These are

- `GetAdvertisement` **method.** Uses the information found in the related Ad Rotator file. (I'll talk about this file in a moment. It is similar in function to the text file you used when working with the Content Linking component.) This is the only method of the Ad Rotator component.

- `Border` **property.** Indicates the thickness of the border that should appear around the advertisement image.

- `Clickable` **property.** Determines whether the image displayed should also serve as a hyperlink. Normally, this is the case so that when you click an image, you are taken to that advertiser's Web site.

- `TargetFrame` **property.** Determines which frame to load the page that is linked to the image, if you are using frames on the page where you display the advertisement. I talk more about frames and other HTML formatting in Chapter 9, "Formatting Processed Output."

As already mentioned, the Ad Rotator component also reads from a text file to retrieve important information on how the specific advertisements should be displayed. Take a look at the sample text file in Listing 4.4, which I'll explain in the example of working with the Ad Rotator component.

Listing 4.4 Rotator.txt

```
WIDTH 137
HEIGHT 180
BORDER 1
*
2h.gif
http://www.premierpressbooks.com
Link to Premier Press, Inc.
2
9d.gif
http://www.premierpressbooks.com
Link to Premier Press, Inc.
2
```

The Ad Rotator Component—An Example

Before I explain how the text file in Listing 4.4 works, Listing 4.5 shows it in action, along with a page that uses the Ad Rotator component.

Listing 4.5 Ad_Rotator.asp

```
<html>
<head>
<title>Working with the Ad Rotator Component</title>
</head>
<body>
<%
Set objRotate=Server.CreateObject("MSWC.AdRotator")
objRotate.Border=0
objRotate.Clickable=True
RotateHTML=objRotate.GetAdvertisement("Rotator.txt")
Response.Write(RotateHTML)
%>
</body>
</html>
```

When this page is loaded in a Web browser, the result looks like Figure 4.2.

FIGURE 4.2

Depending on the specifications you list in the corresponding text file, different images or advertisements appear. The displayed text is for the sake of browsers that do not support graphics. Also, in this example, the images are hyperlinked to a Web site (http://www.premierpressbooks.com).

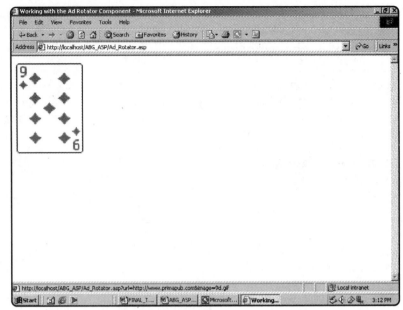

Take a closer look at all of this to be sure that you understand what is happening. First, you need to understand how the corresponding text file works and what information is stored within it (refer to Listing 4.4):

- The first part of the text file (everything above the * mark in Listing 4.4) indicates the size of the image to be displayed and whether it should have a border. You specify zero for no border.
- Underneath the * mark are the attributes for each specific ad image.

1. The first line (2h.gif) is the image file. In this case, the image file is in the same directory as the rest of your Web pages, so all you have to do is list the file name. If it is in a different directory, you add this information to the front of the image file name: /some_directory/another_directory/2h.gif.

2. The second line indicates the URL to which you want the image to link. In the case of the *Rotator.txt* file used here, both the images link to the Premier Press home page (http://www.premierpressbooks.com).

3. The third line indicates the text that should appear when the cursor hovers over the image or the text to be displayed if the Web browser cannot support images. Again, in the case of these two images, the text to display is Link to Premier Press, Inc.

4. The fourth line is more complicated. Depending on the number of ads represented in the file (in this case, two: 2h.gif and 9d.gif), the number on the fourth line is a *weight* for how many times an image should be displayed. This number, also called the *impression*, is roughly equivalent to the percentage of times each image will appear. For example, if there are three images, the first image has its impression value set to 3, the second has its value set to 5, and the third set to 1. This translates to the first image being displayed 30 percent of the time, the second 50 percent, and the third 10 percent.

In Listing 4.5, look at the code that calls the Ad Rotator component:

```
<%
Set objRotate=Server.CreateObject("MSWC.AdRotator")
objRotate.Border=0
objRotate.Clickable=True
RotateHTML=objRotate.GetAdvertisement("Rotator.txt")
Response.Write(RotateHTML)
%>
```

1. As with all components, the particular component is created and named first (in this case, `objRotate`).
2. The specific properties of the Ad Rotator component are defined. In this case, it is given no border (`obj.Border=0`), and the images are made clickable (`objRotate.Clickable=True`).
3. The text file is called (`RotateHTML=objRotate.GetAdvertisement("Rotator.txt")`), as described in the preceding list.

Working with the Content Rotator Component

The Content Rotator component is very similar to the Ad Rotator component and is just as useful. By using the Content Rotator component, you can quickly insert uniform text into any Web page. Also, like the Content Linking component, you can change the information in the text file and see those changes immediately reflected in all pages that use the component (rather than go through each individual page and change the content).

The following two methods are used by the Content Rotator component:

- `GetAllContent`. Retrieves and makes available all the content in the associated text file (more about this text file in a moment)
- `ChooseContent`. Allows you to get the next string from the text file but does not display it

As with the Content Linking component, a text file is used with the Content Rotator component. Listing 4.6 is an example of such a text file.

Listing 4.6 ContentRotator.txt

```
%% 4 // The following is the usual welcome message
Welcome to ASP Programming for the Absolute Beginner. We hope that you
find it enjoyable and useful in your learning to program with ASP!
%% 2 // The following is the link to Premier Press
For more information on Premier Press, visit http://premierpressbooks.com
%%3 // The following is an example of some formatted HTML text
<b>Within the text file, you can also include HTML formatting</b>
<hr>
<center>Welcome to the exciting world of the Content Linking component!</center>
```

How does this text file work?

1. Each line of text begins with `%%`.

2. The number that follows is similar to the expression number in the Ad Rotator component in that it corresponds (roughly) to a percentage of how often that particular line of text will display.

3. The information that follows the // is an optional comment.

4. The line of text is inserted. As you can see in the third line of text in Listing 4.6, you can also include HTML formatting directly within this text file.

The Content Rotator Component—An Example

Listing 4.7 is an example of the Content Rotator component in action. Note that the *ContentRotator.txt* file reference is the same sample text file described in Listing 4.6.

Listing 4.7 ContentRotator.asp

```
<html>
<head>
<title>Working with the Content Rotator Component</title>
</head>
<body>
<%
Set CRotator=Server.CreateObject("MSWC.ContentRotator")
RotatorContent=CRotator.GetAllContent("ContentRotator.txt")
Response.Write RotatorContent
%>
</body>
</html>
```

When this page is loaded into a Web browser, it looks like Figure 4.3.

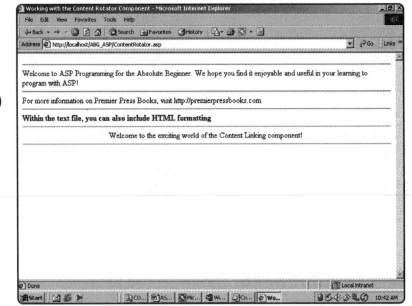

FIGURE 4.3

Notice how you can include HTML tags within the text file and it will display the formatting on screen when the text file is read— very similar to the Ad Rotator component and its corresponding text file.

Working with the Page Counter Component

I'm sure that you have seen the various page counters on different Web pages. Perhaps they have corresponding text that reads something like `You are the (number) person to visit this Web site`. By using the Page Counter component, you can add this functionality to your ASP pages as well.

The Page Counter component has the following three methods:

- `Hits`. Returns the number of hits (or number of times the page has been accessed) for either a specified page or the current page.
- `PageHit`. Increases the hit count for the current page.
- `Reset`. Returns the hit count for the specified page to zero. If such a page is not indicated, the current page has its hit count returned to zero.

The Page Counter Component—An Example

Listing 4.8 is an example of the Page Counter component. This component is particularly useful in providing an easy, yet effective, way of tracking and displaying the number of visitors to your Web site.

Listing 4.8 PageCounter.asp

```
<html>
<head>
<title>Working with the Page Counter Component</title>
</head>
<body>
<%
Set PageCount=Server.CreateObject("MSWC.PageCounter")
Response.Write('You are the ' & PageCount.PageHit & ' person to visit
this page')
%>
</body>
</html>
```

When this page is loaded into a Web browser, it looks like Figure 4.4.

Summary

This chapter gives you a brief overview of some of the more common, easy-to-use ASP components. Many of these components use a simple text file to store essential information that helps to drive their functionality. Within these text files, you can also include HTML and other scripting information, which is then executed in the ASP page on which the component resides. Finally, you assign and call components in the same way you learned how to work with other objects in Chapter 3, "Working with ASP Objects."

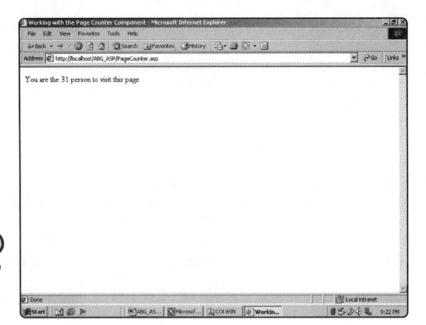

You are the 31 person to visit this page

FIGURE 4.4

Each time the page
is visited, the
number shown
increases by one.

EXERCISES

This chapter presents a cursory overview of components. You can increase your understanding by performing the following exercises:

1. Create a new page that makes use of the Page Counter component. Design the page (using standard HTML) so that the Page Count listing appears in the center of your page (perhaps use a table to make this appear neatly formatted).

2. Pull some images or graphics from your personal files and integrate them into the Ad Rotator component example.

3. Develop a text file for use with the Content Linking component that uses at least five URLs for your favorite Web sites.

4. Utilizing the Ad Rotator component, set at least one of the image/advertisements so that the URL contained within it points to one of your favorite Web sites.

5. Finally, develop a page of your own that integrates all the components described in this chapter.

Database Access with ADO

I n this chapter, you will

- Learn the fundamentals of ADO, the heart of this Web page database connectivity in ASP.

- Learn how to configure your databases so that they can be used in conjunction with your Web pages.

- Learn the major Structured Query Language (SQL) statements that you will use in your ASP code to work with information in your databases via your Web pages.

- Experiment with different kinds of data access within your ASP Web pages so that you can see the power of a dynamic, database-driven Web page (compared to a static Web page without this type of access).

I think that I was about twelve or thirteen when my parents bought me my first component stereo system for Christmas. Up to that point, I had always received my older sister's hand-me-down stereos. (At that time, we weren't talking CD player, 200-watt surround sound! No, it was more like a turntable and an 8-track player.) I was really excited to have, finally, a stereo worthy of my ever-growing record collection. At any rate, my parents bought the stereo well before Christmas, and given that it came in seven or eight (very big) boxes, there was no way to hide it. I was obviously well beyond the Santa Claus years, but my Mom insisted that I not see what was inside the boxes until Christmas morning (even though I knew, of course, what sonic delights awaited me inside those boxes). Fortunately, my Dad was still a big kid at heart, and he didn't see any harm in "just opening the boxes" so that I could view the goods. This, of course, turned into "Well, we'll put the rack together for the stereo, but we won't add any components," which then turned into "Well, now that we've got the rack together, we might as well put the components in, but we won't hook them up." Things progressed until my Mom finally put her foot down and made me wait until Christmas morning to hear the thing.

What does this story have to do with database access with ASP? Think of my unconnected stereo system as a Web page without any access to a data source. Yes, it's very pretty to look at (and perhaps impressive, on a superficial level), but it doesn't do anything! Without giving your Web pages a means of interacting with data (and thus making them dynamic, versus static), you are very limited in not only the types of information you can display, but also—and more importantly—the type of interaction you can provide to your users. Fortunately, as with most things involving ASP, providing your Web pages with this database interaction is quite easy—and that, loyal reader, is the focus of this chapter.

Understanding ADO

Imagine a world where every type of car, regardless of the make and model, ran on a different kind of gasoline, or, instead of having one standard for recording and playback, there were twenty-five types of compact discs. In both scenarios, it would be very difficult to achieve any type of standard because so many people could be (potentially) using so many things. The undeniable result: confusion, frustration, and a major lack of productivity.

So it was before ADO and the effort in accessing information from a database. (Okay, maybe it wasn't that bad, but it was at the very least more complicated.) With ADO (short for *ActiveX Data Objects*), programmers have a way to access information easily from a database via the Web.

However, ADO isn't the full story. In the early 1990s, Microsoft created a standard known as the *Open Database Connectivity* standard (ODBC). Using this technology, you can connect to data regardless of where it is stored, that is, in an Access database, in Oracle, you name it. This worked (and worked well), but the question then became how to access information that *isn't* stored in a database, for example, in an Excel worksheet. The next iteration of ODBC was OLE-DB, short for *Object Linking and Embedding Database*, which allows this kind of data retrieval from an information source other than a database.

Yikes, you are probably saying at this point. What do all these confusing terms mean, and why should you worry about them? What does any of this have to do with ADO (which is, if you've forgotten, the title of this section)? In reality, you don't have to be overly concerned with the history of this topic as long as you understand the importance of ADO, especially in relation to your work with ASP. In short, ADO represents a collection of objects that, via ASP, you can easily manipulate to gain incredible control over the information stored in your data source (be it an Access database, an Excel spreadsheet, and so on).

The ADO Object Collection

You're probably getting annoyed with me at this point (and if so, I don't blame you) for introducing all these terms (and very quickly). Now I've gone and added yet another term, *objects*, to the mix. Stay with me, though. With objects, you've reached the important point of this discussion of ADO. (Put simply, I'm not going to hit you with any more confusing terms, at least not for the moment.)

Objects represent relationships between other objects in that some objects have to be created before other objects can be used. Moreover, each object represents a unique part of the interaction that occurs between your ASP Web pages and your data source. Within ADO are three major objects, which I'll discuss in this book:

- **Connection object.** Used to do just that—create a connection to the data source.

- **Command object.** Allows you to program commands to access the information stored in the data source. These commands are created using the Structured Query Language (*SQL* for short, pronounced *See-Quell*). I'll be talking a lot about SQL in this and subsequent chapters because it provides the primary mechanism for accessing and manipulating data in a database.

- **Recordset object.** Comes in handy because it serves as a repository of information returned from the execution of the command objects. Think of the recordset objects as the results of your actions. Through the power of recordsets, you can create your own unique view of the information stored in a database.

To understand how these three objects work together, think of ordering a new computer. When you place the order on-line, you are presented with an order form that lists all the options available for each component of the computer (memory, hard disk size, and the like). As you go through the form, you specify exactly which options you want, and the result of all this specification is a computer unique to your needs.

In comparing this with the ADO objects, think of the process this way:

- When you go on-line and access the form, you are creating a link to the manufacturer's stored information. This is like the connection object because you are establishing the connection to the data source.

- When you start to configure your specific requirements, you are commanding the manufacturer's information to produce the computer that meets your specific needs. In a Web page utilizing SQL, you are reaching into the database and commanding that specific information be returned to you.

- Finally, based on the specifications you provide, a unique computer is built for you. In ADO, this corresponds to the recordset object: You have established a connection, have commanded (or to use the SQL-specific terminology, *queried*) the database to return unique information, and now, via the recordset object, have access to that unique information.

Are you still with me? Again, my goal is to familiarize you with the three major objects of ADO because you will consistently use them in your ASP programming. Although the history of ADO development is important, the real issue is understanding the power of ADO and how you can best exploit it. That is the focus of this chapter, so let's jump into some examples now.

Creating a Data Source Name (DSN)

Before you can begin using your database in your ASP Web page, you have to create the appropriate connection to the database. By creating this connection, you are creating a Data Source Name (*DSN* for short).

HINT

Before creating your first DSN, you should have some type of Web server installed on your computer. If you haven't installed a Web server as instructed in Chapter 1, "Preparing to Work with ASP," you should do that now.

HINT

You might have noticed my seemingly interchangeable use of the terms *data source* and *database*. Specifically, a *data source* is any type of information store that has information you want to retrieve, so a data source can include a database, a Word or an Excel document, and so on. Moving forward, however, when I write about data sources, I am specifically referring to a database. Moreover, I am referring to Microsoft Access databases.

Now you will create a DSN for the *Music.mdb* Access database found on the enclosed CD-ROM:

1. Before you do anything else, copy the *Music.mdb* file from the CD-ROM to your ABG_ASP directory, in the wwwroot directory of the Inetpub folder.

2. Navigate to the ODBC Data Source Administrator dialog box, using one of the following paths, and click the System DSN tab (see Figure 5.1):

   - For Windows 9x, click Start, Settings, Control Panel, and then the 32-bit ODBC icon.

   - For Windows 2000 (from which these screens are captured), click Start, Settings, Control Panel, Administrative Tools, and then the Data Sources (ODBC) icon.

TRICK

Depending on which version of Windows you are running (Windows 9x or 2000), getting to the ODBC Data Source Administrator dialog box (refer to Figure 5.1), involves two slightly different paths. Note, however, that after you arrive at the dialog box, the process for establishing a DSN is the same, regardless of which version of Windows you are running.

3. Click the Add button. The Create New Data Source dialog box opens (see Figure 5.2). Scroll down the list, and select the Microsoft Access Driver (*.mdb*) option.

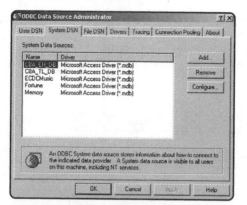

FIGURE 5.1

Click the System
DSN tab to begin
the configuration
process of creating
a DSN.

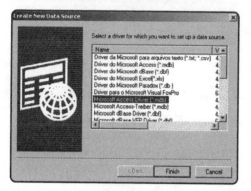

FIGURE 5.2

Note the list of
available drivers.
ADO/ODBC can
integrate with a
variety of data
sources.

4. Click the Finish button. The ODBC Microsoft Access Setup dialog box opens (see Figure 5.3).

5. In the Data Source Name field, type **Music**.

6. In the Description field, type **This is the DSN that is used with Chapter 5 of the book**.

7. In the Database section, click the Select button. The Select Database dialog box opens (see Figure 5.4). Navigate to the ABG_ASP folder in the wwwroot directory of the InetPub folder to find the *Music.mdb* file. Select it, and then click OK.

FIGURE 5.3

You select the data
source for which
you want to create
a DSN.

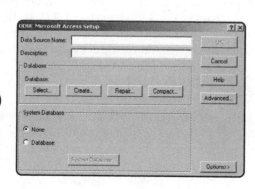

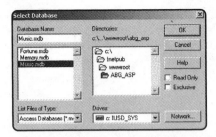

FIGURE 5.4

You select the database file that will be used with the Music DSN you are creating.

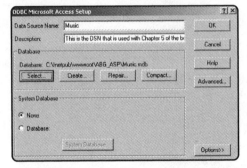

FIGURE 5.5

With the ODBC Microsoft Access Setup dialog box completed, you have provided all the information necessary to create a DSN.

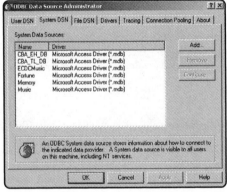

FIGURE 5.6

With the Music DSN created, you are ready to access the *Music.mdb* database from within your ASP Web pages.

8. Your screen should look like Figure 5.5. Click OK. You will be returned to the ODBC Data Source Administrator dialog box (refer to Figure 5.1). Note that your *Music.mdb* file has been added as a System Data Source (see Figure 5.6).

This process for creating a DSN is repeated several times in this book because you will work with different Access databases (all included on the CD-ROM). Although this process might seem complicated now, it will soon become second nature. The next section allows you to test your newly created DSN and introduces you to the power of SQL.

Introducing SQL

Now that you've created a DSN, you can begin working with the *Music.mdb* database within your ASP pages. If you recall, from the discussion of ADO objects at the beginning of the chapter, SQL is the primary mechanism for retrieving and manipulating data from within your database via your ASP pages. It's time to introduce you to SQL and show you how this method makes your Web pages come alive.

TRICK Although it is best to learn how to code by hand before moving to any type of HTML/ scripting editor, in the future you will find that the use of such an application has distinct advantages. Not the least of these is the time saved by automating routine, mundane tasks. That said, I will return to many concepts presented in this chapter (especially the discussion of the various SQL statements) in Chapter 10, "ASP and HTML Scripting with FrontPage 2000." Although you might be tempted to move ahead to that chapter now, resist the temptation! By reading this chapter first, you will gain a far greater fundamental understanding of these important database concepts than those who rely heavily on a tool such as FrontPage without first gaining an understanding of how things work.

TRICK A full discussion of SQL is well beyond the scope of this book. You will learn how to work with the four major SQL statements that, combined with a little creativity on your part, allow you to do all kinds of wonderful database interactions in conjunction with ASP. However, if you are interested in learning more about SQL, be sure to check out *Microsoft SQL Server 7 Administrator's Guide* (Premier Press).

What is SQL? Again, this term is short for *Structured Query Language*, which was developed to serve as a universal method of manipulating information in a database. By using SQL (via ADO) within ASP Web pages, you can do some amazing things. This chapter will whet your SQL whistle (so to speak!), with later chapters building on the foundation you learn here.

You can use SQL to test whether the DSN configuration you created is working properly. You will create a Web page to do just that:

1. In Notepad, open the file *SQL_Test.asp* on the CD-ROM, and immediately save it (keeping the name *SQL_Test.asp*) to your ABG_ASP folder.
2. Open this page in a Web browser. If everything is configured properly, your screen should look like Figure 5.7.

TRAP A common mistake in establishing a DSN is not referring to it properly with your ASP pages. If you see the following error message,

Error Type:

```
Microsoft OLE DB Provider for ODBC Drivers (0x80004005)
[Microsoft][ODBC Driver Manager] Data source name not found
and no default driver specified
```

then you probably have misspelled the DSN reference within your code or not properly referenced the DSN within your code.

Take a look at the code for this page to see everything that is happening:

Listing 5.1 SQL_Test.asp

```
<HTML>
<HEAD>
```

```
<TITLE>ADO First Test</TITLE>
<BODY>
<B>Here is a listing of all the records in the Catalog table of the
Music.mdb database!</B>
<HR>
<%
Set Catalog=Server.CreateObject("ADODB.Recordset")
Catalog.open "SELECT * FROM Catalog", "DSN=Music"
Do WHILE NOT Catalog.EOF
Response.Write Catalog("Title") & "<p>"
Catalog.MoveNext
Loop
Catalog.Close
Set Catalog=Nothing
%>
</BODY>
</HTML>
```

Note in Code Listing 5.1 the following lines:

```
Catalog.Close
Set Catalog=Nothing
```

These lines do two important things, which you should be careful to include in all of your code that utilizes ADO: the first line literally closes the connection to the data source (which is important because keeping a connection open can cause application errors, performance loss on the server, and so on). The second line, then, erases any lingering association with the connection to the variable name (in this case, Catalog).

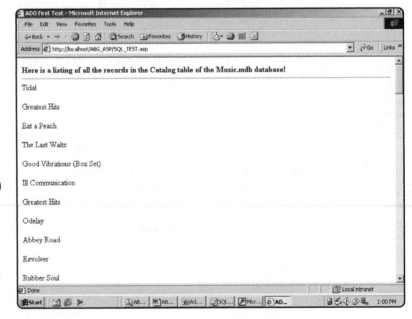

FIGURE 5.7

If your DSN is configured properly, your SQL_Test.asp page will display information from the *Music.mdb* database.

What's happening with Code Listing 5.1? It's really not that complicated if you take a moment to follow the programming logic to see how the page functions:

- First, some simple HTML formatting is provided, including giving the page a title (`ADO First Test`).

- The script section begins with the usual `<%` identifier.

- Next, a connection is made to the Music database via the recordset object. This connection is given the name *Catalog*. Note that you can name these connections whatever you want. However, it is usually a good idea to keep them simple and in some sense descriptive of what the connection represents. The `"DSN=Music"` portion is used as an indicator, letting your code know which DSN you are interested in using.

- When the connection is made, the connection is then opened (`Catalog.open`), and the SQL query is performed. In this case, the query asks for all records in the Catalog table to be returned. (I explain this and other SQL statements in much more detail later in this chapter.)

- Next, the line `Do WHILE NOT Catalog.EOF` instructs the script to run through each record in the returned recordset. The *returned recordset* is all the records generated by the SQL query—in this case, all the records in the Catalog table of the database. *EOF* is short for *End of File*, so, in essence, this script will execute (or loop) until the last record in the Catalog table is returned.

- The next line, `Response.Write Catalog("Title") & "<p>"`, instructs the code to write to the screen the current value being returned for the Title field of the Catalog table. Remember, the script is looping through all the records in the Catalog table, so the current value is whatever value, at that point in the loop, is present in the Title field.

- The next two lines, `Catalog.MoveNext` and `Loop`, instruct the code to do just that: Move to the next record, and then continue looping through the returned recordset (until the EOF value is reached).

- Finally, the lines `Catalog.Close` and `Set Catalog=Nothing` close all connections to the database. You should always perform this step in all ADO scripts because this ensures that no connections are maintained past the point you need them. More important, this helps to prevent unwanted and frustrating errors.

Clear as proverbial mud, right? It's not that difficult if you view the code logically and take the statements at face value (meaning that their functioning is very similar to the simple meaning they imply).

Although I talk more about all the components of this code throughout the chapter, take a closer look now at the SQL statement:

```
SELECT * FROM Catalog
```

This statement is simple, but (as with all things SQL) deceptively so. The SELECT statement is perhaps the primary SQL statement because it is used in various permutations to select or "read" data from a table. The information that follows it (in this case, the * symbol) modifies it to the level of specificity in which you are interested. Put simply, you first invoke the SELECT statement and then tell it how "selective" you want it to be in retrieving records from the specified table (in this case, the Catalog table of the Music.mdb database). In this statement, you can interpret it in plain English as saying, "Please return all the records and fields from the Catalog table to me."

Besides the SELECT statement, there are three basic SQL commands you will learn how to use in this chapter. If you master these simple commands and use your creativity, you can use SQL to manipulate data very powerfully within your ASP Web pages. The three additional statements you will be zeroing in on include

- INSERT
- UPDATE
- DELETE

The following sections examine each of these statements, presenting code examples showing how they work with ADP and ASP.

The SELECT Statement

In the preceding section, you saw a simple use of the SELECT statement. This is all fine and good, but on many occasions you won't need to return all the records in a specific table. You might be looking for a specific record or for records that fall within a given range. All these data query options are possible via the SELECT statement by increasing the level of selectivity in which the statement is executed.

Here are a few examples to demonstrate these concepts:

1. Load the file *SELECT_A.asp* from the CD-ROM, and save it inside your ABG_ASP folder.

2. Open the page in your Web browser. Note that this page (like all examples in this chapter) accesses the *Music.mdb* database, so you need to ensure that you've created a working DSN connection to this database, as described earlier in this chapter. Your Web browser should look similar to Figure 5.8.

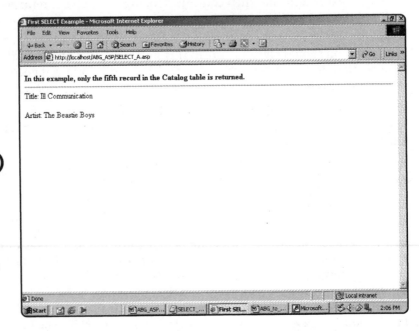

FIGURE 5.8

By modifying a typical SELECT statement with a WHERE clause, you gain far more precise control on the data returned via your SQL queries.

How does this work? As usual, take a look at the code.

Listing 5.2 Select_A.asp

```
<HTML>
<HEAD>
<TITLE>First SELECT Example</TITLE>
<BODY>
<B>In this example, only the fifth record in the Catalog table is returned.</B>
<HR>
<%
Set Catalog=Server.CreateObject("ADODB.Recordset")
Catalog.open "SELECT * FROM Catalog WHERE ID=5", "DSN=Music"
Response.Write "Title: " & Catalog("Title") & "<p>"
Response.Write "Artist: " & Catalog("Artist")
Catalog.close
Set Catalog=Nothing
%>
</BODY>
</HTML>
```

The following is an explanation of this code. It's not terribly different from the preceding listing, but the biggest difference is in the SELECT statement:

- As before, a connection is established to the Music database. This connection is given the name *Catalog*. Remember, you can name these connections whatever you want.

- Next, the SQL command is executed. In this example, you are instructing the code to return only the fifth record in the Catalog table. This is indicated via the WHERE clause: WHERE ID=5.

- How do you know what the fifth record is? Open the Music database in Access, and view the Catalog table, shown in Figures 5.9 and 5.10.

FIGURE 5.9

The Music database, consisting of three tables. If you are using an older version of Access, these screens may appear slightly different.

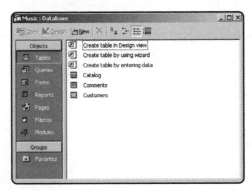

FIGURE 5.10

The Catalog table, illustrating the fifth record. Note the use of the ID field as an Autonumber field (see Appendix C, "Access Essentials," for more information).

ID	Artist	Title	Price
1	Fiona Apple	Tidal	$10.99
2	The Allman Brothers Band	Eat a Peach	$8.99
3	The Band	The Last Waltz	$17.99
4	The Beach Boys	Good Vibrations (Box Set)	$42.99
5	The Beastie Boys	III Communication	$10.99
6	Blondie	Greatest Hits	$8.99
7	Beck	Odelay	$10.99
8	The Beatles	Abbey Road	$12.99
9	The Beatles	Revolver	$12.99
10	The Beatles	Rubber Soul	$12.99
11	The Beatles	Let it Be	$11.99
12	Big Star	Radio City	$9.99
13	David Bowie	ChangesBowie (Greatest Hits)	$11.99
14	James Brown	Live at the Apollo	$10.99
15	The Byrds	The Byrds (Box Set)	$39.99
16	Johnny Cash	Live at Folsom Prison	$13.99
17	The Cars	Greatest Hits	$10.99
18	Eric Clapton	Eric Clapton's Rainbow Concert	$10.99
19	The Cowboy Junkies	The Trinity Sessions	$10.99
20	Crosby Stills and Nash	CSN	$10.99
21	Depeche Mode	Violator	$11.99
22	Bob Dylan	Blood on the Tracks	$9.99

Record: 5 of 82

HINT

What is the Music database? For illustrative purposes in this chapter (as well as Chapter 10, "ASP and HTML Scripting with FrontPage 2000"), imagine this database as the central repository for a small record store. The owners have decided to place all their inventory information (the Catalog table), as well as information about their customers (the Customers table), into an Access database. Perhaps they (like you) are also interested in integrating their database with ASP and creating an e-commerce Web site where their customers can place orders on-line. All these things are possible through ADO and ASP.

- As you see in Figure 5.10, the fifth field corresponds to the ID field where the value is 5.
- Finally, utilizing the response object, the values of both the Artist and Title fields are written to the screen. Then, the Catalog connection is closed and set to nothing.

This WHERE clause example is fine, but what if you want to add an even greater level of specificity regarding which record is returned? Take a look at another example:

1. Load the file *SELECT_B.asp* from the CD-ROM, and save it inside your ABG_ASP folder.
2. Open the page in your Web browser. It should look like Figure 5.11.

Take a look at the following code to see what is happening:

Listing 5.3 Select_B.asp

```
<HTML>
<HEAD>
<TITLE>Second SELECT Example</TITLE>
<BODY>
<B>In this example, the only record that is returned is the first record
```

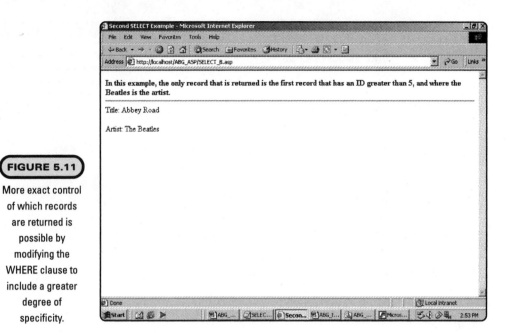

FIGURE 5.11

More exact control of which records are returned is possible by modifying the WHERE clause to include a greater degree of specificity.

```
that has an ID greater than 5, and where the Beatles is the artist.</B>
<HR>
<%
Set Catalog=Server.CreateObject("ADODB.Recordset")
Catalog.open "SELECT * FROM Catalog WHERE ID > 5 AND ARTIST='The Beatles'",
"DSN=Music"
Response.Write "Title: " & Catalog("Title") & "<p>"
Response.Write "Artist: " & Catalog("Artist")
Catalog.close
Set Catalog=Nothing
%>
</BODY>
</HTML>
```

This code is very similar (indeed, nearly identical) to the preceding listing, with the exception of the SQL statement. Note that in this example you are instructing the code to return the first record that has an ID greater than 5 and where the Artist field has a value of The Beatles.

You should note at this point that, depending on the level of specificity of the returned data, your SQL statements can become quite long. To demonstrate this, here is yet another example of the WHERE clause:

1. Load the file *SELECT_C.asp* from the CD-ROM, and save it to your ABG_ASP folder.

2. Open the page in a Web browser. It should look like Figure 5.12.

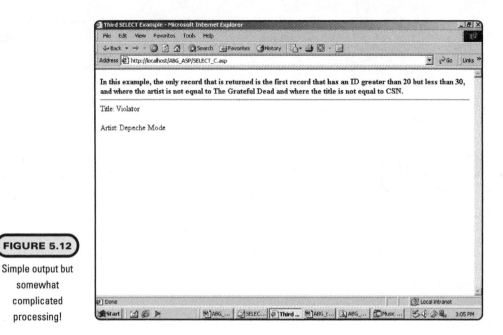

FIGURE 5.12

Simple output but somewhat complicated processing!

The code listing for the *SELECT_C.asp* page is shown here:

Listing 5.4 Select_C.asp

```
<HTML>
<HEAD>
<TITLE>Third SELECT Example</TITLE>
<BODY>
<B>In this example, the only record that is returned is the first record
that has an ID greater than 20 but less than 30, and where the artist is not
equal to The Grateful Dead and where the title is not equal to CSN.</B>
<HR>
<%
Set Catalog=Server.CreateObject("ADODB.Recordset")
Catalog.open "SELECT * FROM Catalog WHERE ID > 20 AND ID < 30 AND ARTIST <>
'The Grateful Dead' AND TITLE <> 'CSN'", "DSN=Music"
Response.Write "Title: " & Catalog("Title") & "<p>"
Response.Write "Artist: " & Catalog("Artist")
Catalog.close
Set Catalog=Nothing
%>
</BODY>
</HTML>
```

Again, the only difference between this code listing and the preceding two is the SQL statement. Note how, by adding qualifiers to the SQL statement, you can instruct the code to return a very specific record.

As you move through the rest of the book, you will see many examples of the WHERE clause being used to return a specific record. For now, you might want to experiment with the three examples listed here, modifying the SQL statements to return different values, depending on the level of specificity your SQL statement calls for.

The INSERT Statement

Although the SELECT statement is the core statement of SQL, it can take you only so far. What happens when, for example, you want to insert information into a database as it is provided by visitors to your Web site or as a result of the processing of your code? That is where the INSERT statement comes in handy.

Here is an example:

1. Load the *INSERT_A.asp* file from the CD-ROM, and save it to your ABG_ASP folder.
2. Open the page in a Web browser. It should look like Figure 5.13.

Examine the following code listing to see how things are working:

Listing 5.5 Insert_A.asp

```
<HTML>
<HEAD>
<TITLE>First INSERT Example</TITLE>
<BODY>
<B>If you are viewing this code, then the following information has been
inserted into the Customer table of the Music database.</B>
```

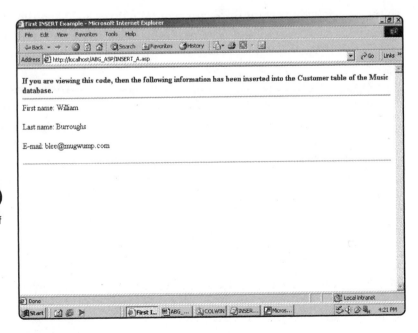

FIGURE 5.13

A simple example of using the SQL INSERT statement to add information to a database via your ASP Web pages.

```
<HR>
First name: William<p>
Last name: Burroughs<p>
E-mail: blee@mugwump.com<p>
<hr>
<%
Set Catalog=Server.CreateObject("ADODB.Recordset")
Catalog.open "INSERT INTO CUSTOMERS (LastName, FirstName, Email) VALUES
('william', 'Burroughs', 'blee@mugwump.com')", "DSN=Music"
%>
</BODY>
</HTML>
```

In this example, the INSERT statement is used to insert information into three specific columns (FirstName, LastName, and Email) of the Customers table of the database. This table is illustrated in Figure 5.14.

The INSERT statement isn't difficult to master, although you have to be careful with the syntax. Note the use of the parentheses around the table field names, as well as the values inserted into these field names. Other than this, the INSERT statement is easy to use. Throughout the other chapters in this book, you will see more examples of how this powerful statement can be used, especially in the next chapter, where information gathered directly from a Web form is inserted into a database.

Ensuring Proper Database Permissions

Unlike the SELECT statement, which simply reads data, the INSERT statement (and the UPDATE and DELETE statements, discussed later in this chapter) requires that proper permissions be set on the database.

This is especially important if you are using Windows 2000 and the Internet Information Server (IIS) because the security is much more robust, thus requiring more attention on your part. If you don't set the security levels correctly, your code can generate errors.

Now you will set these security levels on the Music database and ensure that the permissions are set properly on your ABG_ASP folder.

1. Navigate to where you have saved the *Music.mdb* file (this should be in your ABG_ASP folder). Select the file, and then right-click. From the pop-up menu, select Properties.

2. In the properties dialog box that opens, click the Security tab. Then, in the Name section, click Everyone (see Figure 5.15).

FIGURE 5.14

The Customers table of the Music database.

ID	LastName	FirstName	Email
17	Gosney	John	jgosney@youbet.net
18	Richards	Sally	srich@abcd.net
19	Thompson	Martin	mtom@someplace.com
25	william	Burroughs	blee@mugwump.com

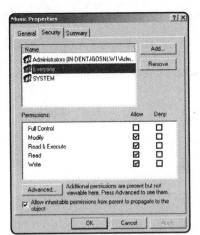

FIGURE 5.15

Setting specific
security levels for
your databases is
critical to proper
functioning
with ASP.

3. For this example (and all other databases you will be working with in this book),
be sure that all the checkboxes—with the exception of Full Control—are checked
in the Permission area of the dialog box (refer to Figure 5.15).

4. Now that you've set the database permissions, it's time to ensure that the permissions are set properly on the ABG_ASP folder in which you are placing all
your ASP pages. Navigate to that folder, select it, and right-click. From the pop-up
menu, select the Properties option, and click the Security tab. The properties
dialog box opens (see Figure 5.16).

5. Set the permissions for Everyone to include everything except the Full Control
option. Then click Apply.

The UPDATE Statement

The UPDATE statement is similar to the INSERT statement in that both statements alter the
information in your database. However, the key difference between the two is that with
UPDATE, you can make modifications to a specific record (or records) that already exists.

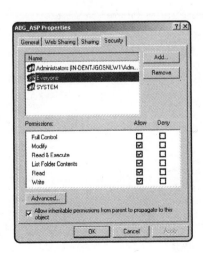

FIGURE 5.16

The permission
settings for your
ABG_ASP Web
folder should be the
same for everyone
as they are for your
databases.

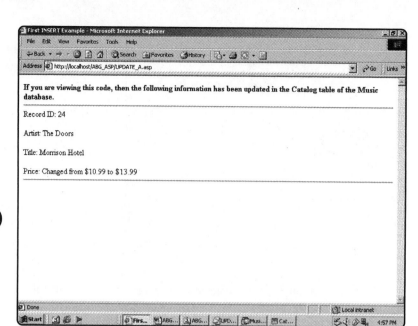

FIGURE 5.17

Similar to INSERT, the UDPATE statement allows you to modify existing database records.

As always, an example is in order:

1. Load the *UPDATE_A.asp* file from the CD-ROM, and save it to your ABG_ASP folder.

2. Open the file in your Web browser. Your screen should look like Figure 5.17.

This is the code for *UPDATE_A.asp*:

Listing 5.6 Update_A.asp

```
<HTML>
<HEAD>
<TITLE>First UPDATE Example</TITLE>
<BODY>
<B>If you are viewing this code, then the following information has been
updated in the Catalog table of the Music database.</B>
<HR>
Record ID: 24<p>
Artist: The Doors<p>
Title: Morrison Hotel<p>
Price: Changed from $10.99 to $13.99
<hr>
<%
Set Catalog=Server.CreateObject("ADODB.Recordset")
Catalog.open "UPDATE Catalog SET Price='$13.99' WHERE ID=24", "DSN=Music"
%>
</BODY>
</HTML>
```

The critical thing you need to remember when using the UPDATE statement is that you must be sure to specify *which* record (or records) is to be updated. Take another look at the SQL statement in the preceding listing, and compare it to the following SQL statement:

```
UPDATE Catalog SET Price='$13.99'
```

In this example, there is no WHERE clause. Can you guess what would happen if this statement was executed? If your guess is that all the records in the Catalog table would have their price set to $13.99, you are exactly right. Unless this type of global change is what you have in mind, be very careful when using the UPDATE statement so that you update only the records that need to have their information changed.

Another example of the UPDATE statement follows:

1. Load the *UPDATE_B.asp* file from the CD-ROM, and save it in your ABG_ASP folder.
2. Load the page in a Web browser. Your screen should look like Figure 5.18.

Here is the code:

Listing 5.7 Update_B.asp

```
<HTML>
<HEAD>
<TITLE>Second UPDATE Example</TITLE>
<BODY>
<B>If you are viewing this code, then all records in the Catalog table
with an ID greater than 30 but less than 40, and with a price equal to
$9.99 have had their price updated to $15.99</b>
<HR>
<%
```

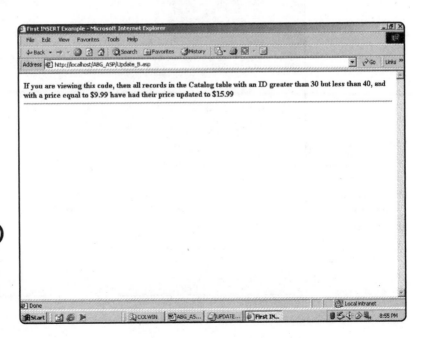

FIGURE 5.18

Another UPDATE example, this time with an even more specific WHERE clause.

```
Set Catalog=Server.CreateObject("ADODB.Recordset")
Catalog.open "UPDATE Catalog SET Price='$15.99' WHERE ID > 30 AND ID < 40
AND PRICE='$9.99'", "DSN=Music"
%>
</BODY>
</HTML>
```

Again, this code should look familiar. The only difference is the use of a more specific WHERE clause, which is updating the price field to $15.99 in only those records that have an ID in the range of 30–40 and a price of $9.99.

The DELETE Statement

So far, you've learned how to read, insert, and update information in a database. Through ADO and ASP, I hope that you are finding this experience very easy and that it is giving you ideas about how to create even more dynamic, exciting Web pages.

You've learned a lot about basic SQL, but there is still one more fundamental statement you need to learn. This is the DELETE statement.

Consider the following example:

1. Load the file *DELETE_A.asp* from the CD-ROM, and save it in your ABG_ASP folder.

2. Load the page in a browser. Your screen should look just like Figure 5.19.

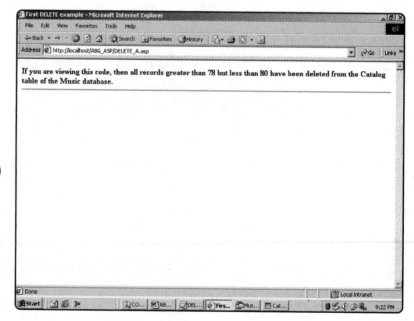

FIGURE 5.19

Deleting records from a database. As with the UPDATE statement, you need to be careful about clearly specifying which records you want to delete.

Here is the code:

Listing 5.8 Delete_A.asp

```
<HTML>
<HEAD>
<TITLE>First DELETE example</TITLE>
<BODY>
<B>If you are viewing this code, then all records greater than 78 but
less than 80 have been deleted from the Catalog table of the Music database.
</b>
<HR>
<%
Set Catalog=Server.CreateObject("ADODB.Recordset")
Catalog.open "DELETE * FROM Catalog WHERE ID > 78 AND ID < 80", "DSN=Music"
%>
</BODY>
</HTML>
```

After the code is run, if you look in the Catalog table of the Music database, you will see that record 79 has been deleted (see Figure 5.20).

The Counting Magician: Working with Recordsets

You now understand the essential components of database access via ADO and ASP, you know how to create a DSN connection so that your databases can be accessed via your ASP Web pages, and you've experimented with the core statement of SQL.

Whew! That's a lot of material. Before I close out this chapter, take just one more look at the issue of recordsets and how you can manipulate them.

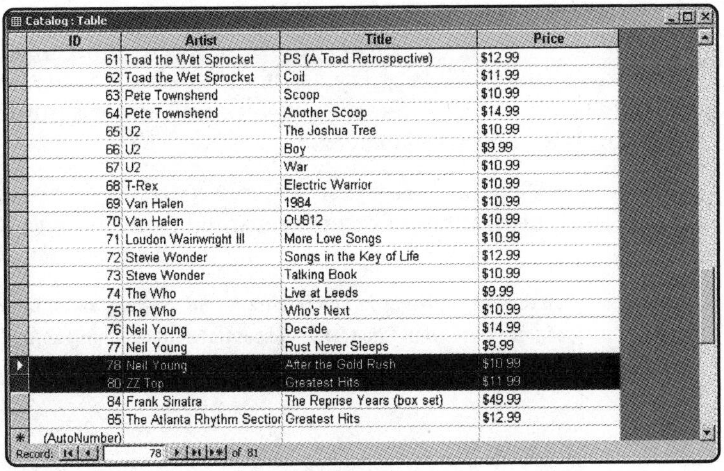

Catalog : Table

ID	Artist	Title	Price
61	Toad the Wet Sprocket	PS (A Toad Retrospective)	$12.99
62	Toad the Wet Sprocket	Coil	$11.99
63	Pete Townshend	Scoop	$10.99
64	Pete Townshend	Another Scoop	$14.99
65	U2	The Joshua Tree	$10.99
66	U2	Boy	$9.99
67	U2	War	$10.99
68	T-Rex	Electric Warrior	$10.99
69	Van Halen	1984	$10.99
70	Van Halen	OU812	$10.99
71	Loudon Wainwright III	More Love Songs	$10.99
72	Stevie Wonder	Songs in the Key of Life	$12.99
73	Stevie Wonder	Talking Book	$10.99
74	The Who	Live at Leeds	$9.99
75	The Who	Who's Next	$10.99
76	Neil Young	Decade	$14.99
77	Neil Young	Rust Never Sleeps	$9.99
78	Neil Young	After the Gold Rush	$10.99
80	ZZ Top	Greatest Hits	$11.99
84	Frank Sinatra	The Reprise Years (box set)	$49.99
85	The Atlanta Rhythm Sectior	Greatest Hits	$12.99
(AutoNumber)			

Record: 78 of 81

FIGURE 5.20

By utilizing a typical WHERE clause with the DELETE statement, you have pinpoint control over which records you want to delete from a database.

ASP Programming for the Absolute Beginner

To illustrate this, let me refer you to the first listing in this chapter, repeated here:

Listing 5.9 Counting_Magic.asp

```
<HTML>
<HEAD>
<TITLE>ADO First Test</TITLE>
<BODY>
<B>Here is a listing of all the records in the Catalog table of the
Music.mdb database!</B>
<HR>
<%
Set Catalog=Server.CreateObject("ADODB.Recordset")
Catalog.open "SELECT * FROM Catalog", "DSN=Music"
Do WHILE NOT Catalog.EOF
Response.Write Catalog("Title") & "<p>"
Catalog.MoveNext
Loop
Catalog.Close
Set Catalog=Nothing
%>
</BODY>
</HTML>
```

If you recall, when this code is executed, the result is a simple dump of all values contained in the Title field of the Catalog table for each record in the table (refer to Figure 5.7). In the chapters that follow, you will learn all kinds of nifty ways to format your returned recordsets (dynamically populating form drop-down menus, creating tables on-the-fly, and so on). For now, however, you will stick to something simple: the recordset Counting Magician.

In the preceding code (and as described earlier in the chapter), you know that a DO WHILE loop is executed so that all the records are returned from the SQL query. In the case of the SQL statement illustrated in this code listing, this accounts for all the records in the Catalog table because there is no WHERE clause to specify individual records. Although dumping all the results of this query as this loop executes to the screen might be useful, it would be even more interesting if you could have a running tally of the total number of records as they are displayed.

Enter the Counting Magician. With just a simple Response.Write statement, you can see how you can count the number of records returned from the SQL query.

TRICK

You will be working in much more detail with DO WHILE **loops and other essential program control in Chapter 7, "Essential Programming Logic."**

Consider the following code, which includes just a minor change from the preceding listing:

Listing 5.10 Counting_Magic_B.asp

```
<HTML>
<HEAD>
<TITLE>The Counting Magician</TITLE>
<BODY>
<B>Here is a listing of all the records in the Catalog table of the
Music.mdb database!</B>
<HR>
<%
Set Catalog=Server.CreateObject("ADODB.Recordset")
Catalog.open "SELECT * FROM Catalog", "DSN=Music"
DIM counter
counter = 0
Do WHILE NOT Catalog.EOF
counter=counter+1
Response.Write Catalog("Title") & "<p>"
Response.Write "This is record count number " & counter & "<p>"
Catalog.MoveNext
Loop
Catalog.Close
Set Catalog=Nothing
%>
</BODY>
</HTML>
```

To see this code in action, do the following:

1. Open the file *Counting_Magic_B.asp* from the CD-ROM, and save it in your ABG_ASP folder.

2. Open the file in a Web browser. Your screen will look like Figure 5.21.

Again, in later chapters, you will be manipulating to a much greater degree the recordsets returned by various SQL queries. For now, just start thinking about how you might dynamically export to a Web page the information returned from a SQL query. As you will see later (especially in Chapter 9, "Formatting Processed Output," and Chapter 10, "Advanced Output Processing"), you can do some amazing things via ADO and ASP. Some real fun is in store for you.

Summary

You have covered much ground in this chapter. Specifically, you've learned

• The essentials of ADO, including its developmental history and how it integrates with ASP.

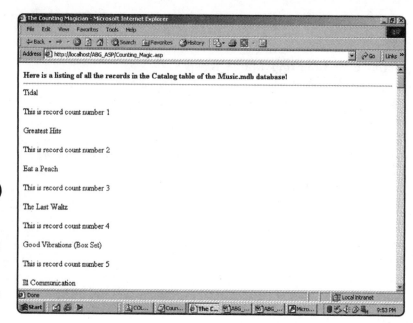

FIGURE 5.21

By adding a simple variable, you can utilize the DO WHILE loop to count the number of records being returned from your recordset.

- How to create a Data Source Name (DSN) connection, which is the essential first step in making your databases accessible to your ASP Web pages.

- The four fundamental SQL statements: SELECT, INSERT, UPDATE, and DELETE. You've seen examples of how to use them alone and in conjunction with WHERE clauses, an important element in gaining exact control over how your queries are executed.

- How to use a DO WHILE loop to run through a complete recordset, as returned from a SQL query. You will be working with this type of data manipulation at a much higher level in later chapters.

EXERCISES

Work through the following exercises to increase your understanding of the concepts presented in this chapter:

1. Create a new Access database, name it *MyDatabase*, and then establish a DSN connection to it.

2. Create in your database a table named *Address_Book* that has the following fields. Make all of them text fields, with the exception of the ID field. Make this field an Autonumber field.

   - ID
   - FirstName
   - LastName
   - Street
   - City
   - State
   - Zip

   After you create this table, add five or ten unique records so that each field in each record has something in it.

3. Using the Address_Book table, write an ASP page that reads all the records from the table and displays them, one after the other.

4. Using the Address_Book table, write an ASP page that selects and displays only those records in which the ID field is greater than 3 but less than 6.

5. Using the Address_Book table, write an ASP page that inserts the following new record into the table:

   First Name: Donald

   Last Name: Fagen

   Street: 123 Green Flower

   City: Aja

   State: California

   Zip: 90104

6. Create an ASP page that deletes at least one record from the Address_Book table, based on a WHERE clause you specify.

7. Create an ASP page that updates at least one record from the Address_Book table, based on a WHERE clause you specify.

CHAPTER

6

Using Forms

I n this chapter, you will

- Work with the ASP response and request objects to learn the fundamentals of working with forms in ASP.

- Immediately start building simple forms in your Web pages that allow visitors to enter information and have it processed and/or manipulated to display results on another Web page.

- Learn how to use forms to store information in a database as users enter it on your Web pages.

- Program the Memory Game, which highlights all the ASP form functionality just mentioned, including how to display form-manipulated data results on your Web pages.

Undoubtedly, making your way across the vast expanse of the Internet, you have encountered what is perhaps the greatest functional asset of the Web: the skillful and practical use of forms. Forms contribute to the Web's unique level of usability and are the centerpiece of much of what the Web has to offer. For example, you can search for information, enter pertinent order information for an electronic purchase, upload information about yourself to an on-line dating service—the list goes on. In the past (before Active Server Pages), the use of forms was complicated and not something to be undertaken by the novice programmer. With the power of ASP, you can learn how to use—and begin implementing—forms within your Web pages in a matter of minutes.

The Memory Game

As I'm fond of admitting, I'm a victim of '70s popular culture. Having spent the formidable years of my childhood watching such television programs as *The Bionic Man*, *S.W.A.T.*, and *Charlie's Angels*, not to mention listening to '70s popular music (I promise not to sneak in a veiled reference to "The Piña Colada Song," maybe), the zeitgeist of that period is always haunting my thoughts in one way or another. That said, another big pop culture influence of that time (and of the early '80s, too, for younger readers) is the infamous game show. Ultimately going by the wayside, in favor of talk shows, game shows were big business not that long ago, and everyone has a favorite.

Among my favorite game shows was *Concentration*. Do you remember that show? The object of the game was to guess the meaning of a pictograph. For example, they would show pictures of a man with the word *Don* above his head, then a plus sign, and then a skeleton key. The answer to this pictograph was *donkey*. However, this pictograph was hidden behind a game board made up of numbered squares. Behind each square was one half of a "match," usually some common object, such as a household item, an animal, and the like. As the players called out a numbered square and its contents were revealed, they had to find its corresponding match on the game board. As matches were made, these squares were removed to display the hidden pictograph. As more and more matches were made, more of the pictograph was revealed, making it easier to guess the meaning of the pictograph and thus win the game. The game was called *Concentration* because, when the contents of a square were revealed, you had to remember where its corresponding match was located on the game board.

For this chapter, you will program a game similar in scope to *Concentration*. Although your game won't have a pictograph hidden underneath the squares (with more time devoted to programming the game, you could do such a thing), it will mimic the matching aspect of the original *Concentration*. Players will be presented with a game board composed of 16 squares corresponding to eight matches. The object of the game is to match all eight matches in the shortest number of guesses. Figure 6.1 shows the Memory Game board in action.

Before you start building the Memory Game, you need to learn some basics of working with forms in ASP. This involves an understanding of the response and request objects, which happen to be the focus of the next section. The code for the Memory Game will also draw heavily on the ADO skills you learned in Chapter 5, "Database Access with ADO," because the game has interaction with a Microsoft Access database as an essential component.

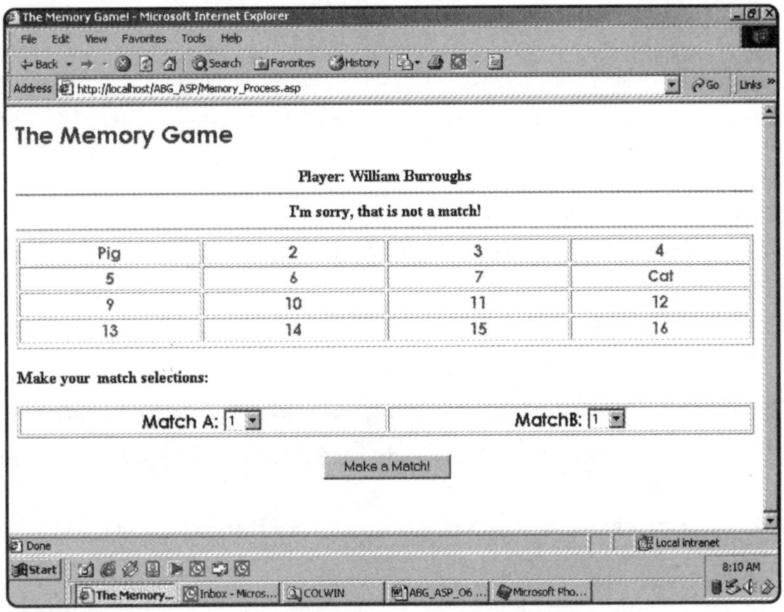

FIGURE 6.1

The Memory Game highlights essential form functionality, including how to build on this functionality by integrating with a database.

Form Essentials: The Response and Request Objects

When I started working with ASP, the promise of easy form functionality was something I couldn't resist. Having struggled with CGI programming for too long, the idea that I could develop a simple form and immediately have the information that was entered into it processed by another page, let alone stored in a database, seemed too good to be true. Fortunately, I was not disappointed. Working with forms in ASP is incredibly easy. Best of all, with this ease of use comes no loss in functionality or overall programming power. Who says you can't have it all?!?

For this chapter, I'm assuming that, although you might never have worked with processing forms, you do have some understanding of the various form elements, for example, text box, radio button, and the like. These represent a fundamental component of basic HTML. However, if you aren't familiar with the form elements, you will be exposed to nearly all of them in this chapter.

Also, many HTML editing programs have extensive, built-in form functionality. One of these programs, Microsoft FrontPage 2000, is discussed in Chapter 10, "ASP and HTML Scripting with FrontPage 2000."

To begin the discussion of forms, why don't I show you a simple form example so that you, too, can share the excitement of this powerful feature of ASP. Take a look at the following code:

Listing 6.1 FirstForm.asp

```
<HTML>
<TITLE> My first ASP Form </TITLE>
<BODY>
```

```
<B> My first ASP Form! </B>
<HR>
<FORM METHOD="POST" ACTION="FormRead.asp">
What is your first name? <input type="text" name="FirstName" size="20">
<P>
What is your last name? <input type="text" name="LastName" size="20">
<HR>
<input type="submit" value="Submit this data!" name="B1">
</FORM>
</BODY>
</HTML>
```

Before you start exploring this code, take the following actions:

1. Either enter the preceding code into Notepad, or open it in Notepad from the CD-ROM.
2. After you have the code in Notepad, save it in your ABG_ASP directory with the name *FirstForm.asp*.
3. After you save the page, open it in your Web browser. It should look similar to Figure 6.2.

Although this page is very basic HTML, take a look at the code to make sure that you understand the form-specific elements at work here.

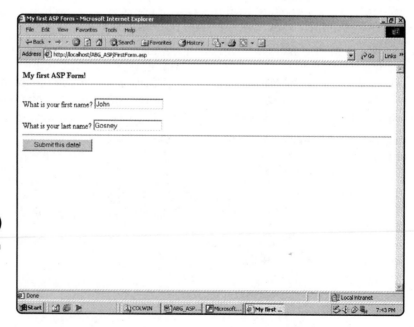

FIGURE 6.2

A simple HTML form but one that demonstrates the power of working with forms in ASP.

Begin by examining the line `<FORM METHOD="POST" ACTION="FormRead.asp">`. This line performs a few form-specific tasks:

- First, it tells the Web browser that the code that follows (until the `</FORM>` tag is encountered) is part of a form.
- Second, it defines the type of METHOD that will be used to send the data entered on the form.
- Finally, it indicates to which page the data should be directed (that is, ACTION="FormRead.asp"). Note that you can use various METHOD types to post data (depending on the type of data you are sending). In this book, I will stick with the POST method.
- The next section of code defines two text box form elements. Be sure to note the name given to each text box ("FirstName" and "LastName") because this will be critical when you process the information entered into these form elements.
- Finally, a Submit button form element is defined and given the label Submit my data!. When users click this button, displayed in their Web browser, the data they entered into the FirstName and LastName text boxes is posted to the *FormRead.asp* page, which I'll discuss next.

All in all, a simple HTML form. Now you will see how the data entered into this form (specifically, the first and last name of a user) can be processed or otherwise manipulated on another Web page.

Reading and Manipulating Form Data

A form doesn't do you much good unless you can read or manipulate the data you capture. As I've said already, and it bears repeating again, ASP makes it extremely easy to work with form data.

The real magic of this ASP functionality is the request object. Before I lead you into a discussion of what this is, why don't you create a Web page that reads and manipulates the data entered on the *FirstForm.asp* page created in the preceding section:

Listing 6.2 FormRead.asp

```
<HTML>
<TITLE> Reading Form Input with ASP </TITLE>
<BODY>
<B> Reading Form Input with ASP! </B>
<%
FirstName=Request.Form("FirstName")
LastName=Request.Form("LastName")
<HR>
<B><font face="Century Gothic" color="#008000">
<%=Response.Write(FirstName)%>  

<%=Response.Write(LastName)%></font></color></B>
<HR>
```

ASP Programming for the Absolute Beginner

Welcome to the exciting world of ASP forms!
```
</BODY>
</HTML>
```

Go ahead and enter this code into Notepad:

1. Either enter the code into Notepad or open it in Notepad from the CD-ROM.
2. When you have the code in Notepad, save it in your ABG_ASP directory with the name *FormRead.asp*.
3. After you save the page, open your Web browser and open the *FirstForm.asp* page. Enter your first and last name; then click the Submit This Data! button. Your screen should look something like Figure 6.3.

The *FirstForm.asp* and *FormRead.asp* pages are very simple illustrations of how to read form data using ASP. Don't let that simplicity fool you. Within this simple code lies the foundation of much more powerful and functional ASP programming. Take a look at the key elements of the *FormRead.asp* page, most notably, the request and response objects:

- The first major programming in this page is the assignment of the FirstName and LastName variables. Because you were introduced to these crucial ASP elements in Chapter 3, "Working with ASP Objects," you will probably use the response and request objects more than any other objects as you learn ASP programming. In the first lines of code for the *FormRead.asp* page, you use the request object literally to request the data entered in the two text box form fields on the *FirstForm.asp* page.

TRICK

Note that the two variables, FirstName and LastName, are named to correspond to the text box form field names on the *FirstForm.asp* page. Giving the variables you set the same names as the form fields is a convenient way to remember which data you are manipulating and to make your code, in general, easier to debug and read later.

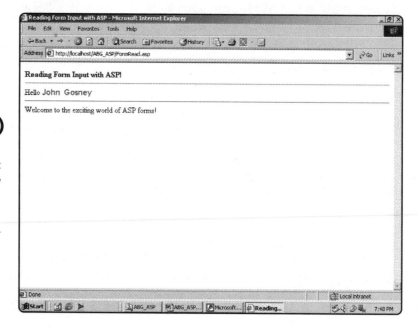

FIGURE 6.3

The names you entered on the first page are "read" by the *FormRead.asp* page. Note how, using simple HTML formatting, your name is in a different font and color and is boldface.

TRICK

You don't have to define these two variables to retrieve your form data. For example, you can place the request object directly within your HTML. Take another look at the preceding code, and consider the following:

```
<B><font face="Century Gothic" color="#008000">
<%=Request.form("FirstName")%> nbsp;
<%=Request.form("LastName")%>
<font></color></B>
```

In this example, you call the request object directly within the HTML. In other words, rather than use the response object, you don't define the FirstName **and** LastName **variables first, as done in the preceding code listing. Either way works, but it is good programming practice to define your variables first to make your code easier to understand and debug.**

- The rest of the code for the *FormRead.asp* page is straight HTML. I added extra formatting—a different font, a different color, and boldface—to highlight the information being read from the *FirstForm.asp* page, but all in all, this is a very simple page.

You have examined some simple form processing and been introduced to important concepts regarding the use of forms. Now you will move on to programming the Memory Game. This will highlight several aspects of form functionality, including manipulation of data on-screen, the use of form data in code processing, and the use of forms as a method of integrating your collected information with a database.

The Memory Game: A Design Overview

If you recall from the beginning of the chapter, I asked you to take a little trip down memory lane and come up with your favorite game show. Hopefully, you have a favorite show—after all, game shows are the ambrosia of any healthy pop culture diet! If you don't, you're going to get a chance to program your own game show in this chapter. It's called the *Memory Game*, and you're going to build it now.

Several facets of the Memory Game enhance what you've learned so far and introduce you to new areas of ASP programming:

- Building on what you learned in Chapter 5 about ADO, the Memory Game utilizes a Microsoft Access database as its central functionality component.
- To gather information from users, the Memory Game presents players with form fields so that they can enter their match choices.
- Simple HTML formatting, combined with the VBScript RND function, makes the game new and challenging each time it is played.
- The Memory Game gives you a preview of advanced program decision making via IF...THEN statements and tools you will learn more about in Chapter 7, "Essential Programming Logic," and Chapter 8, "Essential Programming Logic, Part II."

Like the other game examples in this book, the Memory Game is simple in its programming code but powerful in its execution. If you haven't noticed yet, this combination of (relatively) easy programming and powerful functionality is a key component of ASP and what makes it such a popular Web scripting language for both beginners and professionals.

ENSURING THAT FORM DATA IS PROVIDED

If you have ever ordered anything on the Web or been asked to complete a questionnaire, survey, and the like, you've probably seen some type of marking on the form to indicate that certain fields are required. Perhaps you ignored these required fields, leaving them blank, and tried to submit the form without providing any data.

More than likely, if you were using a well-designed form, you were presented with a message announcing that you failed to provide required data and are being returned to the form to enter this information. This type of form data verification can be done in a variety of ways and is critical to ensuring that all the data you want to collect via a form is, indeed, collected.

Fortunately, because of the increasing power of HTML editing programs such as Microsoft FrontPage or Macromedia HomeSite, you don't have to know any special programming to build this type of form verification into your Web pages. In fact, you can do simple form data verification by using ASP. (I'll show you an example of this later in this chapter, as well as in later chapters.) If you use an application like FrontPage (don't forget that you're going to be taking a look at FrontPage in Chapter 10, "ASP and HTML Scripting with FrontPage 2000"), automated tools allow you to customize the type of verification you want to perform on form data. For example, you can

- Verify the type of data being entered into the form field (letters, digits, white space, and the like).
- Verify the length of the data string being entered into the form field. You can set a minimum or maximum number of characters that must be entered into a specific field for the form to be processed. This type of form field verification is especially useful when you are capturing such information as a social security number, in which case, you'd set the minimum and maximum data string lengths to 9.
- Verify a range within which the form field data must fall. For example, you can require it to be greater than or equal to a specific value.

In short, form field verification is yet another tool for ensuring the overall integrity, usability, and functionality of your Web pages. There is nothing worse than your users trying to access your Web site, but through no fault of their own—such as entering information into a form field that falls outside your desired range—the page crashes or does not function as you intended.

Are you ready to build the Memory Game? Let's get started, then, with the design of the Memory database.

The Memory Database

The Memory Game database is a Microsoft Access database and consists of two primary tables: History and MatchData (see Figure 6.4):

- MatchData is used as a transient storage table to capture data specific to each game. Figure 6.5 illustrates the MatchData table in Design view. As you start to program the Memory Game code, you will review this table in detail.

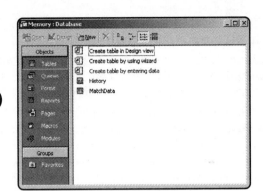

FIGURE 6.4

The *Memory.mdb* database, consisting of two tables: History and MatchData.

- History is used to store information about each game for future reference (see Figure 6.6). Specifically, this table stores the player's name, the date he or she played the game, and the number of guesses it took to correctly make all the matches.

Install the *Memory.mdb* database by following these instructions. If you are using Windows 9x, open the Control Panel, and click the ODBC icon to perform these steps. Although the dialog boxes look slightly different, the process of establishing the ODBC connection is nearly identical to that of Windows 2000.

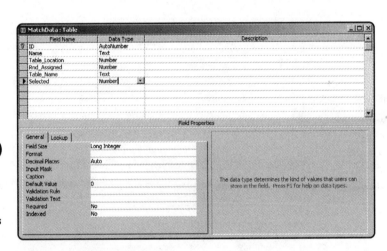

FIGURE 6.5

The MatchData table is used to store information about each game as it is being played.

ID	Name	Guesses
1	Jim Morrison	5
2	William Burroug	8
3	George Harrisor	9
7	Melissa Gosney	7
(AutoNumber)		0

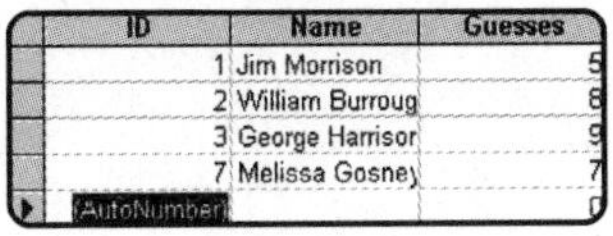

FIGURE 6.6

As with many electronic games, the History table serves as a repository of high (and low!) scores for later review (and possibly gloating over).

1. Locate the *Memory.mdb* database file on the enclosed CD-ROM, and copy it into your ABG_ASP folder in the Inetpub directory.

2. Create the ODBC connection to the database. From the Windows 2000 Control Panel, click the Administrative Tools icon, and then click the Data Sources (ODBC) icon. The ODBC Data Source Administrator dialog box opens (see Figure 6.7).

3. Click the System DSN tab, and then click Add to open the Create New Data Source dialog box (see Figure 6.8). Highlight the Microsoft Access Driver (*.mdb) option, and click Finish.

4. Complete the ODBC access setup process by clicking the Select button and selecting the *Memory.mdb* database file you copied into your ABG_ASP directory (see Figure 6.9).

5. As shown in Figure 6.9, you complete the Data Source Name field by entering **Memory.mdb**. Provide a short description in the Description field, and click the OK button. Figure 6.10 shows the *Memory.mdb* database added to your list of available System Data Sources.

You have now established an ODBC connection to the Memory database.

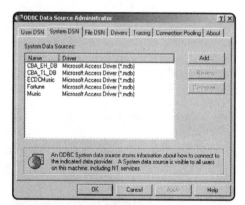

FIGURE 6.7

Select the System DSN tab to begin the ODBC connection process.

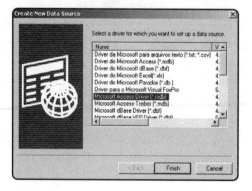

FIGURE 6.8

As mentioned in Chapter 5, note the different kinds of data source drivers available to you via ODBC.

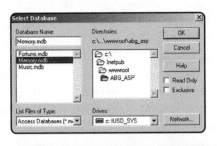

FIGURE 6.9

The ODBC setup is
nearly complete!

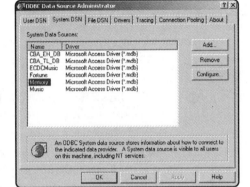

FIGURE 6.10

You should see the
Memory.mdb file in
the listing of System
Data Sources under
the System DSN tab.

Establishing Database Permissions with Windows 2000

If you are using Windows 2000 and Access 2000, you must establish the proper security setting on the database so that it will work properly with your ASP code:

1. Navigate to the *Memory.mdb* file, select it, and right-click. From the pop-up menu that appears, select the Properties option (see Figure 6.11).
2. The Memory Properties dialog box opens. Click the Security tab. In the Name section of the dialog box, select the Everyone listing. In the Permissions section, make sure that the Modify, Read & Execute, and Read and Write options are

FIGURE 6.11

If you are using
Windows 2000 and
Access 2000, you
must set the proper
security
permissions on the
Memory database
for it to work with
your ASP code.

selected; then click the Apply button. Your database is now ready to function properly with the Memory Game ASP code.

As you move through the programming of the Memory Game, you will come to understand in more detail how the Memory database and its tables fit into the functioning of the game. For now, be content in having established the ODBC connection and the proper security settings because these are critical "first things first" issues of programming a game.

Programming the Memory Game

Now that you have established the database, it's time to begin programming the Memory Game.

One of the key elements of the game is its capability to assign the matches randomly each time the game is played. In other words, the game board should never be the same configuration twice, to make it more difficult (and more fun) to guess where the matches are hidden.

Before you begin to build the game (including the HTML that will form the game board, as shown in Figure 6.1), I want to make sure that you understand the piece of code that randomly generates the game board each time it is played.

Random Number Generation, Part I

An essential element of any game is the ability to randomly generate numbers. This is used to add an element of chance to any game, and the Memory Game example in this chapter is no exception.

That said, let's take a moment to review a sample random number generator code that will, in turn, be used with the Memory Game.

1. Locate the *Random.asp* file on the enclosed CD-ROM, and copy it into your ABG_ASP folder in the Inetpub directory.

A LITTLE SECURITY IN AN INSECURE WORLD

Why bother with security? Although it's true that you don't have to worry about "unauthorized" access to data with the games in this book, in the real world you will undoubtedly want to limit access to your critical data. A full discussion of Windows security and permission settings is well beyond the scope of this book, but be aware that setting proper security on your systems (especially your Web sites, given that the porous nature of the Web provides an open invitation to would-be hackers) is an absolute requirement in today's world. There is no worse feeling of helplessness than when you realize that your Web site and related systems have been penetrated by unauthorized and often times malevolent intruders. Be cautious with both the design and placement of your critical data.

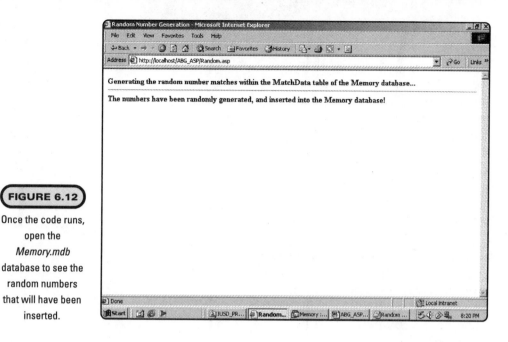

Generating the random number matches within the MatchData table of the Memory database...

The numbers have been randomly generated, and inserted into the Memory database!

FIGURE 6.12

Once the code runs, open the *Memory.mdb* database to see the random numbers that will have been inserted.

2. Open this page within a Web browser. After a few moments, the ASP code within this page will execute, and your screen will look like Figure 6.12. The ASP code within *Random.asp* takes a few moments to complete because it must perform certain conditional logic statements, as well as insert information into the Memory database each time the loop that makes up the code is executed.

3. Admittedly, the screen output isn't exciting, but the ASP code behind the scenes is doing some interesting things. Navigate to the Memory database, open it, and then open the MatchData table. Your MatchData table should look something like Figure 6.13.

The following code is for the *Random.asp* file. Take a look at it to see what you can figure out. Then I'll explain how the code works.

FIGURE 6.13

New, random numbers (1–16) are assigned to each record in the MatchData table every time the *Random_Code.asp* page is executed.

Microsoft Access - [MatchData : Table]

File Edit View Insert Format Records Tools Window Help

ID	Name	Table_Location	Rnd_Assigned	Table_Name	Selected
14	Sheep2	16	0	Sheep	1
11	Chicken1	15	0	Chicken	1
1	Dog1	14	0	Dog	1
9	Horse1	13	0	Horse	1
13	Sheep1	12	0	Sheep	1
12	Chicken2	11	0	Chicken	1
4	Cat2	10	0	Cat	1
6	Pig2	9	0	Pig	1
2	Dog2	8	0	Dog	1
10	Horse2	7	0	Horse	1
3	Cat1	6	0	Cat	1
15	Goat1	5	0	Goat	1
7	Cow1	4	0	Cow	1
16	Goat2	3	0	Goat	1
5	Pig1	2	0	Pig	1
8	Cow2	1	0	Cow	1
(AutoNumber)		0	0		

Listing 6.3 Random.asp

```
<HTML>
<TITLE>Random Number Generation</TITLE>
<BODY>
<B>Generating the random number matches within the MatchData table of
the Memory database...</B>
<HR>

<%

Dim CheckVar
For i=1 to 16

set DataCheck=Server.CreateObject("ADODB.Recordset")
sqlstmt="SELECT * FROM MatchData WHERE ID=" & i
DataCheck.Open sqlstmt, "DSN=Memory", 3, 3, 1
B=DataCheck("RND_Assigned")

IF B=0 THEN
CheckVar=0
ELSE
CheckVar=1
END IF

DO UNTIL CheckVar = 1
RANDOMIZE
RndCheck=INT((16-1+1) * RND + 1)

For Index = 1 to 750000
Next

set Datacheck2=Server.Createobject("ADODB.Recordset")
sqlstmt2="SELECT * FROM MatchData WHERE Table_Location="&RndCheck
DataCheck2.Open sqlstmt2, "DSN=Memory", 3, 3, 1

If DataCheck2.recordcount = 0 THEN
set InsertCheck=Server.Createobject("ADODB.Recordset")
sqlinsert="UPDATE MatchData SET Table_Location=" & RndCheck & " & "
WHERE ID="& i
InsertCheck.Open sqlinsert, "DSN=Memory"
CheckVar=1
END IF
DataCheck2.close
Set DataCheck2=nothing
LOOP
```

```
Datacheck.close
Set Datacheck=nothing
Next
%>


<B>The numbers have been randomly generated and inserted into the
Memory database!</B>
</BODY>
</HTML>
```

As mentioned before, a primary function of the Memory game is to generate numbers randomly from 1 to 16 so that each matching pair can be assigned a random location within the table every time the game is played. This is accomplished through the use of two `For...Next` loops. You were introduced to `For...Next` loops in Chapter 2, "Programming ASP Web Pages with VBScript." You will learn more about using loops in Chapter 7, "Essential Programming Logic," and you can also find a reference for this and other VBScript topics in Appendix A, "VBScript Variable Reference."

In essence, the two `For...Next` loops split this code into two parts. Take a look at each piece individually so that you can understand how everything fits together:

1. The line `For i=1 to 16` is, as you know, the beginning line of a `For...Next` loop. By beginning the loop at 1 and ending it at 16, you are telling the loop—you guessed it!—to repeat itself 16 times. Each time through the loop, the current number (1–16) is assigned to a variable so that you can tell within your code how far you are into the loop. In this case, I used the variable `i`, but you can call this variable anything you want.

2. The next part of the code establishes a connection to the Memory DSN you created. Note that, in the `SELECT` statement, the only record that is returned is the one that matches the current number of the loop. This is done by utilizing the `i` variable assigned to the loop. For example, the fifth time through the loop, the `SELECT` statement would read `SELECT * FROM MatchData WHERE ID=5`.

3. After this particular record is retrieved via the `SELECT` statement, a variable is created (`B`), and the value of the Selected field from the returned record is assigned to this variable. For example, if this is the fifth time through the loop, the `SELECT` statement reads the record from the MatchData table where the ID record equals 5. Then, the `B` variable is given the same value as the value in the Selected field of the returned record.

4. For the game to work properly, each matching pair should be assigned a unique number between 1 and 16. This enables each match (for example, Dog1, Cat2, Goat1, and so on) within the MatchData table of the database to have a unique number. That said, the next section of the code checks whether the record currently selected has already been assigned a number from 1 to 16. This is done using an `IF...THEN` statement (which you learned about in Chapter 2): If the variable `B` equals `0`, a new variable, `CheckVar`, is set to `0`. Otherwise, the `CheckVar` variable is set to `1`. The `CheckVar` variable is used to denote whether the *selected* record (the record currently being analyzed via the `For...Next` loop) has already been assigned a random number between 1 and 16.

Random Number Generation, Part II

In essence, the first part of the *Random.asp* code described in the preceding section just establishes the For...Next loop that will run for 16 times. Each time through, the MatchData table of the Memory database is queried, and, for the record returned, the value of the Rnd_Assigned field is checked. That value is assigned to the CheckVar variable.

Now the second part of the *Random.asp* code comes into play, depending on whether the value of the CheckVar variable is a 0 or a 1. First, examine the second part of the code when the CheckVar variable is set to 0:

1. When the CheckVar variable is set to 0, this denotes that the B variable has been set to 0. Take another look at the section of code that assigns the B variable: If the Rnd_Assigned field is 0, this means that a random number between 1 and 16 has yet to be assigned for the record being analyzed (the record being reviewed as the For...Next, 1–16 loop executes).

2. When CheckVar is set to 0, the next section of code, a DO loop, executes until CheckVar is set to 1 (the DO loop is denoted by the line DO UNTIL CheckVar=1). As you learned in Chapter 2, you can use a DO loop to execute a specific section of code until some variable evaluates to a value you specify. In this case, you want the DO loop to execute until the CheckVar variable is equal to 1.

3. After the DO loop is called, the first lines of code generate a random number between 1 and 16. The random number generated is assigned to the variable RndCheck. Then (similar to the first call to the Memory DSN in Part I of this code), a connection is set to the MatchData table (this connection is DataCheck2). In this case, the SELECT statement pulls the specific record from the MatchData table where the Table_Location field is set to the random number that has been generated. The Table_Location field is used to denote where on the game table this matching pair is to be located.

4. If the record count of this query is 0, no records were found in the MatchData table where the Table_Location record is equal to the RndCheck variable, and the next section of code executes. Again, a connection (InsertCheck) to the MatchData table is created. This time, an UPDATE statement is used to assign the value of the RndCheck variable to the Table_Location field of the record being analyzed. If the record count of the DataCheck2 connection is greater than 0, the random number that has been generated already has been assigned to some other record in the table, so the DO loop continues to execute. That is, another random number between 1 and 16 is generated, the DataCheck2 connection is established again, the record count is checked, and so on.

5. After the CheckVar variable is set to 1 (or after a unique random number between 1 and 16 has been generated and then inserted via the UPDATE statement into the database), the DO loop is terminated, and the next number in the FOR...NEXT loop is generated, with the entire process being repeated. To put all of this simply, each individual record in the MatchData table must be assigned a unique number between 1 and 16 to ensure that each record has a unique location on the game board.

6. Finally, when the FOR...NEXT loop is completed, the text you see in Figure 6.12 is output to the screen, indicating that the entire code has executed.

TRAP

You might (should!) have noticed that I didn't mention the following lines of code in my explanation of how the *Random.asp* code executes:

```
For Index = 1 to 750000
Next
```

As you already know, this code assigns a variable (`Index`) to the value of the `For...Next` loop each time it executes. This particular `For...Next` loop executes 750,000 times(!) but doesn't seem to do anything other than that. On the surface, at least, all this section of code seems to be doing is to pause the execution of the rest of the code. Before anything else can execute, this loop has to execute three-quarters of a million times! However, this pause is the whole point. Because of ADO's speed limitations when working with Access, it is sometimes necessary to include these code pauses. Otherwise, your code tends to jump ahead of itself, resulting in errors.

What do I mean? Try running the *Random.asp* code without this particular `For...Next` loop. Within the MatchData table, you will see the same random, 1–16 number being assigned to more than one record. The reason for this is that, because the `DataCheck2` and `InsertCheck` connections are established (and the specific SQL statements executed), the Access ADO driver can't keep up with the speed of the code execution. As the `DO` loop executes, this results in the `DataCheck2` connection being run before the `InsertCheck` is allowed to execute fully. The result of this overlap is that the `DataCheck2` record count returns an erroneous value. That is, what would otherwise return a record count greater than 1 returns as 0 because the `InsertCheck` connection has not been allowed to execute and thus update the MatchData table.

Long story short: When you are calling back-to-back connections to an Access database via ADO—especially if one of those connections is inserting or updating information into the database—it is wise to place one of the `For...Next` delays between the connections to ensure that your connections have a chance to *execute* (close) fully before the next connection is established and executed.

This code will become clearer as you study the rest of the code that comprises the Memory Game. For now, however, understand the following plain-English summary of how this section of code functions:

1. Hi, I'm the code for the Memory Game! For every matching pair (Cat1, Cat2, Dog1, Dog2), I need to assign a unique random number between 1 and 16. This random number will correlate to the location of each matching pair on the game board.

2. To do this, I use a `For...Next` loop that executes 16 times. Each time through the loop, I check the MatchData table of the database to see whether the record being analyzed (again, this record corresponds to each time through the `For...Next` loop) has already been assigned a random number. This random number will be the unique location on the game board for that matching pair.

3. If the random number generated has already been assigned, I keep generating a random number (1–16) via a `DO` loop. When I find a random number that has not already been assigned, I use the SQL `UPDATE` statement to assign this number to the record being analyzed (again, the record being analyzed corresponds to the 1–16 number currently being evaluated via the `For...Next` loop).

4. When all 16 records in the MatchData table are assigned a unique random number between 1 and 16, the code is complete.

Understanding the Entire Memory Game Code

Whew! Feeling overwhelmed by the *Random.asp* code discussion? Well, you can relax. The rest of the Memory Game code is quite easy to understand and highlights the ways you can use forms to gather, manipulate, and insert data, either directly on a Web page or in conjunction with a database connection.

The Memory_Home.asp Page

The Memory Game consists of two pages: *Memory_Home.asp* and *Memory_Process.asp*. *Memory_Home.asp* is the opening screen of the game, greeting the players and asking them to enter their name. Figure 6.14 illustrates this opening screen.

Take a moment to review the code for the *Memory_Home.asp* page. From the CD-ROM, open the file *Memory_Home.asp*. Here is the code for this page:

Listing 6.4 Memory_Home.asp

```
<html>
<head>
<title>The Memory Game!</title>
</head>
<%
'Reset the game database
Set GameReset=Server.CreateObject("ADODB.Recordset")
sqlstmt="UPDATE MatchData SET Table_Location=0, Rnd_Assigned=0, Selected=0"
GameReset.Open sqlstmt, "DSN=Memory", 3, 3, 1
%>
<body>
<p align="left"><font face="Century Gothic" color="#008000"><i>
<b>Welcome to...</b></i></font></p>
<p align="center"><font face="Century Gothic"><hr></font></p>
<p align="right"><b><font face="Century Gothic" size="5" color="#800000">The
Memory Game!</font></b></p>
<p><b>Let's
 Play!</b></p>
<form method="POST" action="Memory_Process.asp">
  <p>What is your name? <input type="text" name="Name" size="20"></p>
  <p align="center"><input type="submit" value="Submit your name,
and begin play!" name="B1"></p>
</form>
<p> </p>
</body>
</html>
```

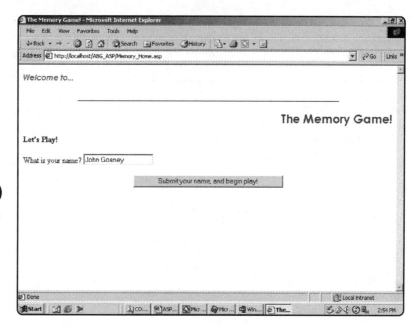

FIGURE 6.14

The opening screen of the Memory Game, utilizing a one-line text box form element to gather the user's name.

TRICK

Take a look at the code here, and notice the following line:

```
GameReset.Open sqlstmt, "DSN=Memory", 3, 3, 1
```

What does the 3, 3, 1 mean? This is a specific ADO configuration (where each number corresponds to a specific data access setting). For all the data access examples used within this book, don't forget to include this line of code, and leave it as 3, 3, 1.

Notice the ASP code at the beginning of this page. Every time this page loads, the MatchData table within the Memory database is reset, ready to begin another game. Take a look at the SQL statement in the GameReset connection. For each record in the database, the Rnd_Assigned and Selected fields are set to 0.

The rest of this page is straightforward HTML. In addition to minimal text formatting, a form is used to gather the player's name. Notice the action of the form (action = "Memory_Process.asp"), which points to the *Memory_Process.asp* page. This is where the real action is. Also notice the name given to the one-line text box used within the form (Name). This will be used on the *Memory_Process.asp* page so that the user's name can be both displayed on-screen and inserted into the History table of the database when the game is completed.

The Memory_Process.asp Page

After the user provides his or her name on the *Memory_Home.asp* page, the *Memory_Process.asp* page takes command, allowing the game to be played. Although the code for this page might seem overwhelming, it's quite easy to understand. Remember, too, that you already encountered the central—and most difficult—section of the *Memory_Process.asp* page when I discussed random number generation (the preceding code will be used verbatim in the *Memory_Process.asp* page).

Another interesting element of this page is that to provide the maximum amount of functionality with the minimum number of Web pages, the *Memory_Process.asp* page *submits to itself.* I'll explain this important concept of programming in a few moments.

For now, open the page within Notepad so that you can see the entire code:

Listing 6.5 Memory_Process.asp

```
<html>

<head>
<title>The Memory Game!</title>
</head>

<body>

<p align="left"><b><font face="Century Gothic" size="5" color="#800000">The
Memory Game</font></b></p>

<%
'Check to see if gameboard has been generated

IF Request.Form("GameStart")=1 THEN%>
<b><center>Player: <%=Request.Form("Player")%></center></b>
<%
'Add to the number of guesses
Guesses=Request.Form("Guesses")
Guesses=CInt(Guesses)
Guesses=Guesses+1

'Gameboard has been generated -- check for matches

Set MatchCheckA=Server.CreateObject("ADODB.Recordset")
sqlstmt="SELECT * FROM MatchData WHERE Table_Location="&Request.Form("MatchA")
MatchCheckA.Open sqlstmt, "DSN=Memory", 3, 3, 1
CheckA=MatchCheckA("Table_Name")

Set MatchCheckB=Server.CreateObject("ADODB.Recordset")
sqlstmt="SELECT * FROM MatchData WHERE Table_Location="&Request.Form("MatchB")
MatchCheckB.Open sqlstmt, "DSN=Memory", 3, 3, 1
CheckB=MatchCheckB("Table_Name")

'Check to see if a match has been made
IF CheckA=CheckB AND Request.Form("MatchA") <> Request.Form("MatchB") THEN

'A match is made -- update the MatchData table to reflect this

Set MatchInsert=Server.CreateObject("ADODB.Recordset")
```

```
sqlstmt="UPDATE MatchData SET Selected=1 WHERE Table_Name='" & CheckA & "'"
MatchInsert.Open sqlstmt, "DSN=Memory", 3, 3, 1


'Pause briefly to allow for update to be completed
FOR Z=1 to 750000
NEXT
%>
<hr>
<b><center>That's a match!</center></b>
<hr>
<table border="1" width="100%">
<tr>
<%
TableCount=0
FOR a=1 to 16
TableCount=TableCount+1
'Check to see if a match is made for this table location
Set TableDisplay=Server.CreateObject("ADODB.Recordset")
sqlstmt="SELECT * FROM MatchData WHERE Table_Location=" & a
TableDisplay.Open sqlstmt, "DSN=Memory", 3, 3, 1
%>
<td width="25%" align="center">
<%IF TableDisplay("Selected")=1 THEN%>
<p align="center"><font face="Century Gothic" color="#008000">
<b><%=TableDisplay("Table_Name")%></b></font>
</td>
<%ELSE%>
<p align="center"><font face="Century Gothic" color="#008000">
<b><%=a%></b></font>
</td>
<%END IF%>
<%
IF TableCount=4 THEN
TableCount=0
%>
</tr>
<tr>
<%
END IF
NEXT
%>
</table>


<%
```

```asp
ELSE
%>
<hr>
<b><center>I'm sorry, but that is not a match!</center></b>
<hr>
<table border="1" width="100%">
<tr>
<%
FormCheckA=Request.Form("MatchA")
FormCheckA=CInt(FormCheckA)
FormCheckB=Request.Form("MatchB")
FormCheckB=CInt(FormCheckB)

TableCount=0
FOR a=1 to 16
TableCount=TableCount+1
'Check to see if a match is made for this table location
Set TableDisplay=Server.CreateObject("ADODB.Recordset")
sqlstmt="SELECT * FROM MatchData WHERE Table_Location=" & a
TableDisplay.Open sqlstmt, "DSN=Memory", 3, 3, 1


%>
<td width="25%" align="center">
<%IF TableDisplay("Selected")=1 OR FormCheckA=a OR FormCheckB=a THEN%>
<p align="center"><font face="Century Gothic" color="#008000">
<b><%=TableDisplay("Table_Name")%></b></font>
</td>
<%ELSE%>
<p align="center"><font face="Century Gothic" color="#008000">
<b><%=a%></b></font>
</td>
<%END IF%>
<%
IF TableCount=4 THEN
TableCount=0
%>
</tr>
<tr>
<%
END IF
NEXT
%>
```

```
</table>


<%END IF
ELSE

'Execute the code to randomly build the matches
'Comment this
Guesses=0
Dim CheckVar
For i=1 to 16

set DataCheck=Server.CreateObject("ADODB.Recordset")
sqlstmt="SELECT * FROM MatchData WHERE ID=" & i
DataCheck.Open sqlstmt, "DSN=Memory", 3, 3, 1
B=DataCheck("Rnd_Assigned")

IF B=0 THEN
CheckVar=0
ELSE
CheckVar=1
END IF

DO UNTIL CheckVar = 1
RANDOMIZE
RndCheck=INT((16-1+1) * RND + 1)

For Index = 1 to 750000
Next

set Datacheck2=Server.Createobject("ADODB.Recordset")
sqlstmt2="SELECT * FROM MatchData WHERE Table_Location="&RndCheck
DataCheck2.Open sqlstmt2, "DSN=Memory", 3, 3, 1

If DataCheck2.recordcount = 0 THEN
set InsertCheck=Server.Createobject("ADODB.Recordset")
sqlinsert="UPDATE MatchData SET Table_Location=" & RndCheck & ",
Rnd_Assigned=1 " & " WHERE ID="& i
InsertCheck.Open sqlinsert, "DSN=Memory"
CheckVar=1
END IF
DataCheck2.close
Set DataCheck2=nothing
```

```
LOOP
Datacheck.close
Set Datacheck=nothing
Next
%>


<table border="1" width="100%">
<tr>
<%
TableCount=0
FOR a=1 to 16
TableCount=TableCount+1
%>
<td width="25%" align="center">
<p align="center"><font face="Century Gothic" color="#008000">
<b><%=a%></b></font>
</td>
<%
IF TableCount=4 THEN
TableCount=0
%>
</tr>
<tr>
<%
END IF
NEXT
%>
</table>
<%END IF%>


<%
'Now, scan the database to see if all matches have been made, and
'the game has been won
Set WinCheck=Server.CreateObject("ADODB.Recordset")
sqlstmt="SELECT * FROM MatchData WHERE Selected=1"
WinCheck.Open sqlstmt, "DSN=Memory", 3, 3, 1

IF WinCheck.Recordcount=16 THEN
'Insert player information into the database
Player=Request.form("Player")
Guesses=Guesses


sqlstmt="INSERT INTO History (Name, Guesses) VALUES
```

```
('"& Player & "'," & Guesses & ")"
Set GameInsert=Server.CreateObject("ADODB.Recordset")
GameInsert.Open sqlstmt, "DSN=Memory", 3, 3, 1
%>


<hr>
<b><center>YOU WIN THE GAME!</center></b><p>
You won the game in <%=guesses%> guesses!
<hr>
<form method="POST" action="Memory_Home.asp">
<center><input type="submit" value="Play again" name="b2"></center>
</form>
<%
ELSE
%>


<p><b>Make your  match selections:</b></p>
<form method="POST" action="Memory_Process.asp">
  <table border="1" width="100%">
    <tr>
      <td width="50%" align="center">
  <p><font face="Century Gothic" size="4"><b>Match A: <select size="1"
  name="MatchA">
  <%
  FOR i=1 to 16
  %>
  <option value="<%=i%>"><%=i%></option>
  <%
  NEXT
  %>
  </select></b></font></p>
      </td>
      <td width="50%" align="center">
      <font face="Century Gothic" size="4"><b>MatchB: <select size="1"
      name="MatchB">
    <%
    FOR i=1 to 16
    %>
    <option value="<%=i%>"><%=i%></option>
    <%
    NEXT
    %>
        </select></b></font></td>
    </tr>
```

```
    </table>
    <p align="center"><input type="submit" value="Make a Match!"
    name="B1"></p>
    <input type="hidden" name="GameStart" value="1">
    <input type="hidden" name="Guesses" value="<%=Guesses%>">
    <%
    IF Request.Form("GameStart")=1 THEN%>
    <input type="hidden" name="Player" value="<%=Request.Form("Player")%>">
    <%ELSE%>
    <input type="hidden" name="Player" value="<%=Request.Form("Name")%>">
    <%END IF%>
</form>
<p> </p>
<%END IF%>
</body>

</html>
```

I will explain this code in sections to ensure that you understand not only the basic script but also how it integrates with the Memory database, which it does extensively.

The Memory_Process.asp Page: Setting Up the Game

Take another look at the following excerpt:

```
<html>

<head>
<title>The Memory Game!</title>
</head>

<body>

<p align="left"><b><font face="Century Gothic" size="5" color="#800000">The
Memory Game</font></b></p>

<%
'Check to see if gameboard has been generated

IF Request.Form("GameStart")=1 THEN%>
<b><center>Player: <%=Request.Form("Player")%></center></b>
<%
'Add to the number of guesses
Guesses=Request.Form("Guesses")
Guesses=CInt(Guesses)
```

```
Guesses=Guesses+1

'Gameboard has been generated -- check for matches

Set MatchCheckA=Server.CreateObject("ADODB.Recordset")
sqlstmt="SELECT * FROM MatchData WHERE Table_Location="&Request.Form("MatchA")
MatchCheckA.Open sqlstmt, "DSN=Memory", 3, 3, 1
CheckA=MatchCheckA("Table_Name")

Set MatchCheckB=Server.CreateObject("ADODB.Recordset")
sqlstmt="SELECT * FROM MatchData WHERE Table_Location="&Request.Form("MatchB")
MatchCheckB.Open sqlstmt, "DSN=Memory", 3, 3, 1
CheckB=MatchCheckB("Table_Name")

'Check to see if a match has been made
IF CheckA=CheckB AND Request.Form("MatchA") <> Request.Form("MatchB") THEN

'A match is made -- update the MatchData table to reflect this

Set MatchInsert=Server.CreateObject("ADODB.Recordset")
sqlstmt="UPDATE MatchData SET Selected=1 WHERE Table_Name='" & CheckA & "'"
MatchInsert.Open sqlstmt, "DSN=Memory", 3, 3, 1

'Pause briefly to allow for update to be completed
FOR Z=1 to 750000
NEXT
%>
```

This initial section of code checks whether the game has already started, and if it has, checks to determine whether a match has been made. Remember how I said that the *Memory_Process.asp* page submits back to itself? When the game begins, the player selects two possible table locations for a match. When the player clicks Submit, the form has its action method set to *Memory_Process.asp*. This type of coding is convenient for keeping all the action confined to one place, so to speak, because you can put a lot of code in one container; that is, one Web page.

In the preceding code, the first task is to see whether the game board has been generated. The game board generation code is the random number generator code, as you will soon see. For each game, you want the game board to be generated only once, so the matching pairs are assigned a random number between 1 and 16—their unique hidden location on the game board—and they keep that location throughout the game. If the game has already started, the name of the player is captured, and the current guess is added to the overall number of guesses.

Assuming that the game board has been generated, which is determined by the IF Request.form ("GameStart") = 1 THEN) statement, the code checks whether a match has been made. The database is queried twice (note the connections MatchCheckA and MatchCheckB).

The variables CheckA and CheckB are set to the value of the Table_Name field from each respective query. If the CheckA and CheckB variables are equal (meaning that within the MatchData table of the database, the two matching pairs are equal), a match is indicated. When a match is made, the MatchData table is updated via the MatchInsert connection. Finally, as you saw in the random number generation code, a FOR...NEXT loop is inserted (FOR z=1 to 750000) to allow the database to be updated (again, the MatchInsert connection). If a match is made, the user is notified with the text That's a match!.

The Memory_Process.asp Page: Generating the Game Board and Playing the Game

The following section of code constitutes the second part of the Memory Game code. It is used to generate the board for each turn, and to display (where appropriate) all previous matches that have been made:

```
<table border="1" width="100%">
<tr>
<%
TableCount=0
FOR a=1 to 16
TableCount=TableCount+1
'Check to see if a match is made for this table location
Set TableDisplay=Server.CreateObject("ADODB.Recordset")
sqlstmt="SELECT * FROM MatchData WHERE Table_Location=" & a
TableDisplay.Open sqlstmt, "DSN=Memory", 3, 3, 1
%>
<td width="25%" align="center">
<%IF TableDisplay("Selected")=1 THEN%>
<p align="center"><font face="Century Gothic" color="#008000">
<b><%=TableDisplay("Table_Name")%></b></font>
</td>
<%ELSE%>
<p align="center"><font face="Century Gothic" color="#008000">
<b><%=a%></b></font>
</td>
<%END IF%>
<%
IF TableCount=4 THEN
TableCount=0
%>
</tr>
<tr>
<%
END IF
NEXT
%>
```

```
</table>


<%
ELSE
%>
<hr>
<b><center>I'm sorry, but that is not a match!</center></b>
<hr>
<table border="1" width="100%">
<tr>
<%
FormCheckA=Request.Form("MatchA")
FormCheckA=CInt(FormCheckA)
FormCheckB=Request.Form("MatchB")
FormCheckB=CInt(FormCheckB)

TableCount=0
FOR a=1 to 16
TableCount=TableCount+1
'Check to see if a match is made for this table location
Set TableDisplay=Server.CreateObject("ADODB.Recordset")
sqlstmt="SELECT * FROM MatchData WHERE Table_Location=" & a
TableDisplay.Open sqlstmt, "DSN=Memory", 3, 3, 1


%>
<td width="25%" align="center">
<%IF TableDisplay("Selected")=1 OR FormCheckA=a OR FormCheckB=a THEN%>
<p align="center"><font face="Century Gothic" color="#008000">
<b><%=TableDisplay("Table_Name")%></b></font>
</td>
<%ELSE%>
<p align="center"><font face="Century Gothic" color="#008000">
<b><%=a%></b></font>
</td>
<%END IF%>
<%
IF TableCount=4 THEN
TableCount=0
%>
</tr>
<tr>
<%
END IF
```

```
NEXT
%>
</table>
```

```
<%END IF
ELSE
```

The primary duty of this section of code is to redraw the game board to reflect all current matches and show the matching pairs associated with the numbers selected by the user from the two drop-down menus when he or she attempts to make a match.

The primary element of building the game board is the FOR...NEXT loop. Note that both loops (regardless of whether a match is made) are set from 1 to 16. Because there are 16 game pieces representing eight matching pairs, the number *16* should come as no surprise. Note, however, how the tables are built. By running the FOR...NEXT loop, creating a temporary variable named TableCount, and checking whether this variable is equal to 4, you can set the number of columns in the table. Basically, as the FOR...NEXT loop executes, the TableCount variable is increased by 1. Each time through the loop, this variable is checked to determine whether it is equal to 4. When it is, the </tr> tag is inserted, indicating that the fourth column has been reached and that a new table row should be started. When this happens, the TableCount variable is reset to 0, and the process begins again.

Also executing with this FOR...NEXT loop is the game's capability to determine whether each square of the game board has been matched. Notice the use of the TableDisplay connection, which queries the database based on the current number being evaluated via the FOR...NEXT loop, that is, the SQL statement "SELECT * FROM MatchData WHERE Table_Location=" & a, where a is the variable assigned to the FOR...NEXT loop. If the Selected field from this query is equal to 1, a match has been made on the specific matching pair, and its table name is displayed within the table, instead of the 1–16 number used to hide the contents of the square.

The Memory_Process.asp Page: Random Number Generation

The third section of code for the Memory Game is, in essence, the random number generator code described in the preceding section. For the game, this code is used to assign each matching pair a random number between 1 and 16, which, in turn, relates to the pair's 1–16 game board location. Remember from the beginning part of the *Memory_Process.asp* page, this random number generator code is executed only once, at the beginning of the game.

The Memory_Process.asp Page: Winning the Game

Here is the final section of code. It is used to track the results of each "turn" in the game and ultimately used to determine when the game is won:

```
<%
'Now, scan the database to see if all matches have been made, and
'the game has been won
```

```
Set WinCheck=Server.CreateObject("ADODB.Recordset")
sqlstmt="SELECT * FROM MatchData WHERE Selected=1"
WinCheck.Open sqlstmt, "DSN=Memory", 3, 3, 1


IF WinCheck.Recordcount=16 THEN
'Insert player information into the database
Player=Request.form("Player")
Guesses=Guesses


sqlstmt="INSERT INTO History (Name, Guesses) VALUES
('"& Player & "'," & Guesses & ")"
Set GameInsert=Server.CreateObject("ADODB.Recordset")
GameInsert.Open sqlstmt, "DSN=Memory", 3, 3, 1
%>


<hr>
<b><center>YOU WIN THE GAME!</center></b><p>
You won the game in <%=guesses%> guesses!
<hr>
<form method="POST" action="Memory_Home.asp">
<center><input type="submit" value="Play again" name="b2"></center>
</form>
<%
ELSE
%>


<p><b>Make your  match selections:</b></p>
<form method="POST" action="Memory_Process.asp">
  <table border="1" width="100%">
    <tr>
      <td width="50%" align="center">
  <p><font face="Century Gothic" size="4">
  <b>Match A: <select size="1" name="MatchA">
  <%
  FOR i=1 to 16
  %>
  <option value="<%=i%>"><%=i%></option>
  <%
  NEXT
  %>
  </select></b></font></p>
    </td>
    <td width="50%" align="center">
    <font face="Century Gothic" size="4"><b>MatchB:
```

```
       <select size="1" name="MatchB">
    <%
    FOR i=1 to 16
    %>
    <option value="<%=i%>"><%=i%></option>
    <%
    NEXT
    %>
        </select></b></font></td>
    </tr>
  </table>
  <p align="center"><input type="submit" value="Make a Match!"
  name="B1"></p>
  <input type="hidden" name="GameStart" value="1">
  <input type="hidden" name="Guesses" value="<%=Guesses%>">
  <%
  IF Request.Form("GameStart")=1 THEN%>
  <input type="hidden" name="Player" value="<%=Request.Form("Player")%>">
  <%ELSE%>
  <input type="hidden" name="Player" value="<%=Request.Form("Name")%>">
  <%END IF%>
</form>
<p> </p>
<%END IF%>
</body>

</html>
```

This final section of code checks, via the WinCheck connection, whether the game has been won. Through the use of the SQL query SELECT * FROM MatchData WHERE Selected=1, you ask the code to search through the entire MatchData table and return all records where the Selected field is equal to 1. (Remember, a value of 1 in this field indicates that a match has been made.) If the record count of this query is 16 (all the records in the MatchData table), all matches have been made, and the game won. An appropriate message is displayed, YOU WIN THE GAME!, and the option to play again is presented via a Submit button form element. If you look at the form in which this button resides, you will notice that the action attribute is set to return to *Memory_Home.asp*. This ensures that the code at the beginning of that page resets all the values in the MatchData table so that the game can be played again. If the game is won, note that within this section the user's name and the number of guesses it took to win the game are inserted into the History table of the database (via the GameInsert connection).

The other important element in this section of code is the presentation of the two drop-down menus, used by the players to select two numbers in search of a possible match. Similar to the dynamic rendering of the game board, note how a FOR...NEXT loop is used to build the values of the drop-down menus (again 1–16, to correspond to the number of squares on the game board). Finally, three hidden form fields are also included in the form that closes out this page (notice that the `action` attribute of the form is set to return to *Memory_Process.asp*). These three hidden form fields are

- **GameStart.** This form field is used to indicate that the game has already begun. Remember from the discussion on the first part of the code, if this form is detected and its value set to 1, the code knows that the game has already begun and therefore does not need to have the game board regenerated.
- **Guesses.** This form field is used to keep track of the number of guesses it takes the player to win the game. Each time through the code, the value of this form field increases by 1 to indicate that another guess has been made.
- **Player.** Finally, this form field is used to continue to pass the player's name each time the page resubmits back to itself. This value is originally captured on the *Memory_Home.asp* page, where users are asked to sign in and identify themselves.

Summary

You were presented with an incredible amount of information in this chapter, including how to capture and display form results and how to integrate form data into a SQL query of your database. Moreover, you saw how to use forms so that a page can submit to itself, thus saving valuable Web real estate and improving the efficiency of your code. Finally, via the Memory Game, you saw how you can use forms to capture information from players, enabling you to provide your Web pages with a dynamic interface. Depending on the information entered into the form fields, the page can react accordingly, often by querying a related database.

ASP Programming for the Absolute Beginner

EXERCISES

To continue your understanding and enjoyment of the use of forms within your ASP pages, try these exercises to improve the functionality and presentation of the Memory Game:

1. Rather than allow just one individual to play the game, rework the code so that it keeps track of two players, storing the results of each player's guess in the MatchData table and their game history in the History table.

2. Develop the dynamic presentation of the game board so that instead of showing (and continuing to show) all matches, you hide them when a match is made, by displaying a blank square where the match was made.

3. When the game is won, capture more than just the player's name and number of guesses in the History table. Also capture the date the game was played and perhaps a Comment field in which the players can enter remarks on how the game was played. This requires that you provide them with a form element to enter their comments after they receive the message that they have won the game.

4. Increase the number of possible matches to 32 instead of 16. In doing so, adjust not only the FOR...NEXT loops within the code, moving them from 1 to 32 instead of 1 to 16, but also the structure of the database. (You will need to come up with some more matching pairs.)

5. Finally, demonstrate how the *Memory_Process.asp* code could be divided into two or more Web pages. Rather than have the page submit to itself, see whether you can divide the code on this page into two separate Web pages. In other words, when the player clicks the Make a Match button, rather than resubmit to the *Memory_Process* page, have the game directed to another ASP Web page to process the form data and display the results.

6. On the *Memory_Home.asp* page, include a link that will display the stored game data in the History table of the database. Also, include a search form that allows players to look up their high scores, based on their name.

Essential Programming Logic, Part I

I n this chapter, you will

- **Work with the** If...Then **statement to add logic control to your ASP scripts.**

- **Learn how to integrate loops into your ASP scripts to avoid needless repetition in your programming, thus increasing the speed and power of your Web pages.**

- **Understand how to use this type of programming logic with your databases to gain more specific control over how your ASP Web pages integrate with them.**

- **Program the Fortune Teller game, in which users enter information via an ASP Web page and a unique fortune is returned, based on the information entered, the day of the month, and whether they have already received that fortune for the month.**

I've covered a tremendous amount of ground so far, introducing you to the power and complexity of ASP. Through the sample games and code, you are starting to see how easy (and fun!) it is to work with ASP and to integrate advanced Web development techniques such as form processing and database access. It's time to add some finesse to your ASP programming by learning to control how your code executes and performs. This is especially important when working with databases. For example, say that a visitor to your Web site wants to search for a specific record. You want to display only the record in which he or she is interested rather than return the entire recordset from your database. Implementing this type of exact control in your ASP pages makes your Web pages more functional and easy to use.

The Fortune Teller Game

To illustrate essential programming logic control best, I'll show you how to design and implement a Fortune Teller game. This game will highlight some basic functionality (much of which you've already seen in earlier chapters), but will touch on most of the inherent logic functionality in VBScript, including For...Next loops, If...Then statements, and integration with a datasource. First, though, I will talk a little about how the Fortune Teller game works.

The Fortune Wizard asks you to enter some basic information, such as your name and age. To make the resulting fortune seem more mystical and powerful, the wizard also asks you to enter a number between 1 and 20 (this number will be used in the processing of the fortune). Figure 7.1 shows the wizard's question page.

After information is entered and the user clicks the Unveil my Fortune! button, the wizard does its magic by processing the data with simple (but powerful) ASP script. Figure 7.2 shows the results.

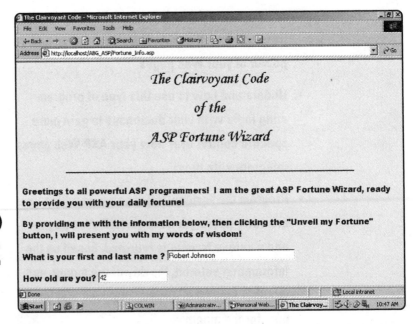

FIGURE 7.1

The Fortune Wizard asks for information before processing your clairvoyant code.

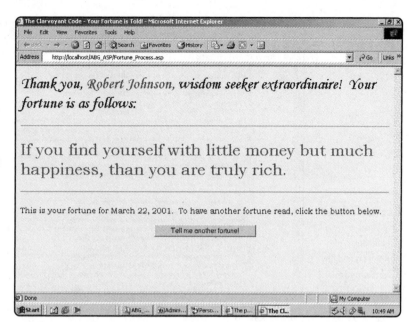

FIGURE 7.2

Based on the information provided by the user and whether the user has played the game before, a unique fortune is presented for each day of the month.

The user's fortune is personalized. Notice how the user's name, Robert Johnson, is also reflected on the results page, with the option to have another fortune read by clicking the Tell me another fortune! button. Because of the way the ASP code is written for this game (I'll discuss the code with you in just a moment), if a user enters the same name on the data entry screen (refer to Figure 7.1), the code checks the database to see whether the user has played the game before and which fortunes have already been presented to the user for that month.

Speaking of databases, the Fortune Teller game uses a simple Microsoft Access database as a place to store the 31 fortunes that make up the game and as a method of tracking the fortunes that have already been presented. Figures 7.3 and 7.4 illustrate the design of the *Fortune.mdb* database.

What gives real power to the Fortune Teller game is neither the database nor the way the fortunes are presented to the players but rather the internal programming logic. In conjunction with the information provided by the player, this ensures that each fortune presented to each player is random but also specific to each day of the month in which the player is playing. For the rest of this chapter, I'll show you how the Fortune Teller works its magic.

Fortune Teller Basics

Before you begin your exploration of the logic that drives the Fortune Teller, you must install and activate the *Fortune.mdb* database and build the data input page (refer to Figure 7.1) on which players provide basic information for the Fortune Wizard. The database for this chapter is named *Fortune.mdb* and can be found on the CD-ROM.

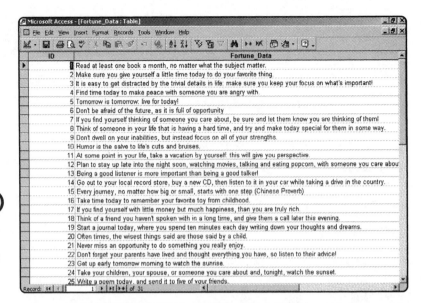

FIGURE 7.3

The Fortune_Data table stores the fortunes randomly presented to players.

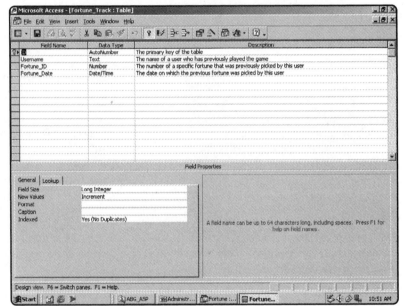

FIGURE 7.4

The Fortune_Track table, shown in Design view, stores specific player information, including the username and which fortune was displayed on a given date.

Creating an ODBC Connection for the Fortune.mdb Database

You learned how to create ODBC connections in Chapter 5, "Database Access with ADO." As you recall, the process for establishing this connection is quite easy, but in case you forgot or need a refresher, here are the steps for establishing the ODBC connection to the *Fortune.mdb* database.

TRICK Remember from Chapter 5, "Database Access with ADO," that the method of accessing the ODBC Data Source Administrator differs among Windows 95, 98, and 2000. After the Administrator is open, though, the steps for establishing the connection are the same.

1. Open the ODBC Data Source Administrator, using the steps specific to your operating system.
2. When the Administrator is open, from the list of User Data Sources, click the MS Access Database option, and click Add.
3. In the Create New Data Source dialog box, select Microsoft Access Driver (*.mdb) from the list, and click Finish.
4. In the ODBC Microsoft Access Setup dialog box, complete the fields as shown in Figure 7.5.
5. In the Data Source Name field, enter **Fortune**. Also, in the Database section, the path should be similar to what you see illustrated in Figure 7.5.

TRICK Depending on your specific development platform, the file path for the *Fortune.mdb* database will appear slightly different from what is shown in Figure 7.5 (C:\Inetpub\wwwroot\ABG_ASP\Fortune.mdb). Just be sure that you copied the *Fortune.mdb* database file within your ABG_ASP folder under your wwwroot folder.

6. When your ODBC Microsoft Access Setup dialog box looks like Figure 7.5, go ahead and click OK. You are returned to the ODBC Data Source Administrator dialog box. In the list of User Data Sources, you will see Fortune, as illustrated in Figure 7.6.

FIGURE 7.5

Complete the ODBC Microsoft Access Setup dialog box as shown here. Be sure to include a description of the data source so you can clearly identify it later.

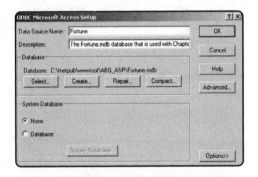

FIGURE 7.6

The *Fortune.mdb* database is successfully installed with an ODBC connection.

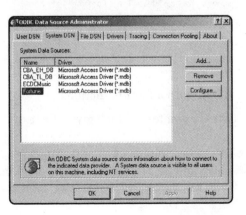

Creating the Fortune_Info.asp Data Input Page

Now that you've created the ODBC connection for the *Fortune.mdb* database, it's time to create the *Fortune_Info.asp* page (refer to Figure 7.1) for the players to provide necessary information to the Fortune Wizard. The *Fortune_Info.asp* file can be found within on the CD-ROM.

Within Notepad, enter the code in Listing 7.1 for the *Fortune_Info.asp* page, or load it directly from the CD-ROM.

Listing 7.1 Fortune_Info.asp

```
<html>
<head>
<title>The Clairvoyant Code</title>
</head>
<body bgcolor="#FFFF00">
<p align="center"><font face="Monotype Corsiva" size="6">
The Clairvoyant Code </font></p>
<p align="center"><font face="Monotype Corsiva" size="6">of the</font></p>
<p align="center"><font face="Monotype Corsiva" size="6">
ASP Fortune Wizard</font></p>
<hr>
<p align="left"><font face="Arial Black" size="3">Greetings to all powerful ASP
programmers!  I am the great ASP Fortune Wizard, ready to provide you with
your daily fortune!</font></p>
<p align="left"><font face="Arial Black" size="3">By providing me with the
information below, then clicking the &quot;Unveil my Fortune&quot; button, I
will present you with my words of wisdom!</font></p>
<form method="POST" action="Fortune_Process.asp">
  <p align="left"><font face="Arial Black">What is your first and last name ?
</font><input type="text" name="Name" size="40"></p>
  <p align="left"><font face="Arial Black">How old are you? <input type="text"
name="Age" size="20"></font></p>
  <p align="left"><font face="Arial Black">Pick a number between 1 and 20:
<input type="text" name="Number" size="20"></font></p>
  <p align="center"><input type="submit" value="Unveil my Fortune!"
name="B1"></p>
</form>
</body>
</html>
```

This page is straightforward HTML, with a few distinctions:

- Note the use of the Monotype Corsiva font, which gives the text a medieval, mystical quality.

- This page has three standard text box inputs: username, user age, and a field to enter a random number between 1 and 20. The form points to *Fortune_Process.asp*, where the Fortune Wizard does his stuff (I will discuss this page and the corresponding code shortly).

- Within the form section of the page, note the unique names of the three text box inputs: Name, Age, and Number.

TRICK

Admittedly, the formatting of this *Fortune_Info.asp* page is basic. Nevertheless, take advantage of even the simplest formatting (for example, the use of the MonoType Corsiva font) to give your pages easy-to-implement flair and style.

Working with the If...Then Statement

Now that you have established an ODBC connection to the *Fortune.mdb* database and have created the *Fortune_Info.asp* data input page, you are ready to begin exploring the ASP code that gives the Fortune Wizard his clairvoyant quality.

The Fortune Wizard draws much of his power from the use of the classic If...Then statement. This statement is perhaps the most famous of all programming statements because it allows the computer to make decisions, thus giving it a certain capability to think for itself. Of course, this (very) artificial intelligence is based solely on the rules you provide. The computer isn't thinking at all, but rather reacting to a series of rules. Consider the code in Listing 7.2.

Listing 7.2 Simple If...Then Example

```
<%
SomeNumber=56
UserNumber=<%=Request.form("Number")%>
IF UserNumber > SomeNumber Then
%>
<b> The number you entered is larger than the accepted maximum </b>
<%
End If
%>
```

To understand how the computer thinks through its processing of the code, look at what is happening here:

- The first two lines are defining the variables SomeNumber and UserNumber. Note that the UserNumber variable depends on what a user entered in a field named Number on a previous form.

- After the UserNumber variable is defined, the code makes a comparison of its value to the set value of the SomeNumber variable (which is 56). If the value assigned to the UserNumber variable is greater than 56, the text The number you entered is larger than the accepted maximum is displayed. If the value is less than 56, no special message is displayed.

Using the If...Then...Else Statement

If you think this example is simple, you're right—it is a basic example of the If...Then statement—and congratulations! You understand an essential element of programming logic, which you will use again and again when developing your ASP pages.

Because you obviously are staying right with me here, take a look at a more advanced example in Listing 7.3.

Listing 7.3 Simple If...Then...Else Example

```
<%
SomeNumber=56
UserNumber=<%=Request.form("Number")%>
IF UserNumber > SomeNumber Then
%>
<b> The number you entered is larger than the accepted maximum </b>
<% Else %>
<b> The number you entered is within the accepted range of values </b>
<%
End If
%>
```

Basically the same code, right? Take a closer look, and note the following, all-important line of code:

```
<% Else %>
```

By using the Else statement, you allow your code to consider more than one rule and thus "think" to a higher degree. In Listing 7.3, if the value assigned to UserNumber is greater than 56 (the value assigned to SomeNumber), the same message is still displayed (The number you entered is larger than the accepted maximum). However, in this example, you also provide another rule for the computer to consider as it processes the code: If the value assigned to SomeNumber is less than 56, the message The number you entered is within the accepted range of values is displayed. This capability to differentiate between presented messages is dependent on the Else statement, which gives the computer an option of which message to present if the SomeNumber variable is less than 56.

More Examples of If...Then...Else

The examples in the preceding sections compare one number to another to determine which message should be displayed to the user. However, you can also compare string values and time and even concatenate values for comparison. Take a look at Listing 7.4.

Listing 7.4 Comparing String Values with If...Then...Else

```
<%
SomeText="I am a great ASP Programmer"
UserText=<%=Request.form("DataText")%>
IF SomeText = UserText
%>
<b> You're exactly right!  You are a great ASP programmer!</b>
<% Else %>
<b> Ah, don't be so hard on yourself!  You really are a great ASP
programmer! </b>
<%
```

```
End If
%>
```

Rather than compare numbers, this code compares two string values (SomeText and UserText). Again, the UserText value is assigned from information entered within a DataText field on a previous form. If the user enters *I am a great ASP Programmer* in this DataText field, the encouraging message You're exactly right! You are a great ASP programmer is displayed. If not, the message Ah, don't be so hard on yourself! You really are a great ASP programmer! is displayed. Like the previous examples, the use of the If...Then...Else statement allows the computer to think through the information and respond according to the rules you've provided.

You can also use the If...Then...Else statement to *concatenate* (add together) values. By doing so, you can implement some advanced data manipulation within your ASP pages. Take a look at Listing 7.5.

Listing 7.5 Concatenating Values with If...Then...Else

```
<%
ValueA=20
ValueB=<%=Request.form("CheckValue")%> + 10
IF ValueA > ValueB THEN
%>
<b> The number you entered is too small!</b>
<% Else %>
<b> The number you entered is within the range of accepted value </b>
<%
End If
%>
```

In this example, the ValueB variable is defined by a number entered in a CheckValue field on a previous form. However, notice that in addition to this value, a value of 10 is added:

```
ValueB=<%=Request.form("CheckValue")%> + 10
```

After the ValueB variable is set, the If...Then statement checks whether it is greater than the defined ValueA variable (in this example, the ValueA variable is set to 20). If it is not, the message The number you entered is too small is displayed. Otherwise, the message The number you entered is within the range of accepted value is displayed.

Be sure to check out Appendix A, "VBScript Variable Reference," for general information on variable and evaluation syntax. This gives you more details on comparing and concatenating variables of different types (numeric, string, and so on).

Working with Loops

The If...Then...Else statement is powerful, and its uses are limited only by your imagination. As the basis of most of your coding (because the statement allows the computer to think by providing it with a set of rules), If...Then...Else can drive most of your code's decision-making abilities.

However, using the If...Then...Else statement is not always efficient. Take a look at Listing 7.6.

Listing 7.6 Non-efficient Programming

```
<html>
<body>
<%
RightValue = 5
TestValue=1
If TestValue=RightValue Then %>
That is the right answer <p>
<%Else%>
That is the wrong answer <p>
<%End If %>
<%TestValue=2%>
If TestValue=RightValue Then %>
That is the right answer <p>
<%Else%>
That is the wrong answer <p>
<%End If %>
<%TestValue=3%>
If TestValue=RightValue Then %>
That is the right answer <p>
<%Else%>
That is the wrong answer <p>
<%End If %>
<%TestValue=4%>
If TestValue=RightValue Then %>
That is the right answer <p>
<%Else%>
That is the wrong answer <p>
<%End If %>
<%TestValue=5%>
If TestValue=RightValue Then %>
That is the right answer <p>
<%Else%>
That is the wrong answer <p>
<%End If %>
</body>
</html>
```

When this code is executed within a Web browser, the output looks like Figure 7.7.

If you look at Listing 7.6, you can see that nothing complicated is going on. Using a typical If...Then...Else statement, the code is processed until the variable RightValue (which has been set to 5) equals the variable TestValue, which is increased by increments of 1. However, despite the simplicity of this process, it takes nearly 40 lines of code to achieve it! Now take a look at Listing 7.7.

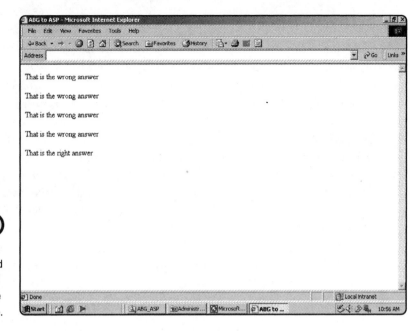

FIGURE 7.7

That is the wrong answer is displayed until the TestValue variable equals the RightValue variable.

Listing 7.7 Efficient Programming Using Loops

```
<html>
<body>
<%RightValue = 5%>
<%FOR TestValue = 1 to 5
%>
<% IF TestValue = RightValue THEN %>
That is the right answer <p>
<% ELSE %>
That is the wrong answer <p>
<% END IF %>
<%NEXT%>
</body>
</html>
```

As you can see, Listing 7.7 is much shorter than Listing 7.6 but accomplishes the same thing. Through the power of looping, you have to provide your evaluation rule only once (IF TestValue = RightValue THEN...). Each time the code *loops* (evaluates the TestValue variable in increments of 1, starting with 1 and running through 5), it automatically generates the specific rules you hard-coded in Listing 7.6. This type of calling is a FOR...NEXT loop and is extremely convenient when you need to evaluate large sets of values and compare them to other values. As you will see in the Fortune Teller example, this type of looping makes quick work of evaluating a returned database recordset, determining whether a specific record matches set rules or criteria you've defined with various If...Then...Else statements.

Building the Fortune Teller Wizard

Before programming the Fortune Teller Wizard, here is a review of the type of functionality the wizard (in other words, your ASP code) has to perform:

1. The wizard gathers all information from the user. This includes first and last name, age, and a number between 1 and 20. All this information is captured using the *Fortune_Info.asp* page (refer to Figure 7.1).

2. The wizard takes the user's information provided and processes it via the *Fortune_Process.asp* page (you will program this page in this chapter).

3. The wizard presents the user a fortune, based on the code processing done via ASP. Note that, as a critical part of this code processing, the wizard reads information from the *Fortune.mdb* database to determine the fortunes the user has already received and retrieves the appropriate fortune (via the Fortune_Data table) from the *Fortune.mdb* database.

Now you will program the clairvoyance into the Fortune Teller Wizard.

Creating the Fortune_Process.asp Page

If you refer quickly to Listing 7.1 (for the *Fortune_Info.asp* page), you will see that the page posts its information to a *Fortune_Process.asp* page:

```
<form method="POST" action="Fortune_Process.asp">
```

You have basically three pieces of information to work with in processing a user's fortune: the name, age, and "secret" number (between 1 and 20) they provide.

The HTML formatting to display the fortune is simple. I will get to that in a moment, but for now, I want to show you how to get the fortune, or put simply, how to program the wizard:

1. If Notepad isn't already open, open it and enter the following basic HTML code:
   ```
   <html>

   <head>
   <title>The Clairvoyant Code - Your Fortune is Told!</title>
   </head>

   <body bgcolor="#FFFF00">
   ```
   This is standard HTML code. Note the title you are giving to this page ("The Clairvoyant Code - Your Fortune is Told!") and the body background color you are assigning.

2. Save your page. Remember to save it with the *.asp* extension (you should be saving this page as *Fortune_Process.asp*).

3. Enter the rest of the code for the *Fortune_Process.asp* page as shown in Listing 7.8. I'll discuss each section in just a moment.

Listing 7.8 Fortune_Process.asp

```
<%
set FortuneTrack=Server.CreateObject("ADODB.Recordset")
FortuneTrack.Open "SELECT * FROM Fortune_Track WHERE Username='" &
Request.Form("Name") & "'", "DSN=Fortune"


Dim PrevFortune
PrevFortune = 0


Do While NOT FortuneTrack.EOF
PrevFortune = PrevFortune + FortuneTrack("ID")
FortuneTrack.MoveNext
Loop


FortuneTrack.Close
Set FortuneTrack=nothing


MagicNumber = PrevFortune + Request.Form("Age") + Request.Form("Number")
IF MagicNumber > 100 THEN
RANDOMIZE
NewFortune=INT((15 - 1 + 1) * RND + 1)
ELSE
RANDOMIZE
NewFortune=INT((31 - 16 + 1) * RND + 16)
END IF
UserName=Request.form("Name")


Set InsertFortune=Server.CreateObject("ADODB.RecordSet")
InsertFortune.Open "INSERT INTO Fortune_Track (Username, Fortune_ID)
 VALUES ('" & Username & "', " & NewFortune &
, "DSN=Fortune"


set TodayFortune=Server.CreateObject("ADODB.Recordset")
TodayFortune.open "SELECT * FROM Fortune_Data WHERE ID=" &
NewFortune, "DSN=Fortune"
%>


<p align="left"><font face="Monotype Corsiva" size="6">Thank you,
<font color="#0000FF">
<%=Request.Form("Name")%>,</font> wisdom seeker extraordinaire! 
Your fortune is as follows:</font></p>
<hr>
<p align="left"><font size="6" face="Bookman Old Style"
```

```
color="#0000FF"><%Response.Write
TodayFortune("Fortune_Data")%></font></p>
<hr>
<p align="left"><font face="Bookman Old Style" size="3">This is your
fortune for
<%=FORMATDATETIME(DATE,vbLongDate)%>. To have another fortune read,
click the button

below.</font></p>
<form method="POST" action="Fortune_Info.asp">
  <p align="center"><input type="submit" value="Tell me another fortune!"
name="B1"></p>
</form>
</body>
</html>
```

If Listing 7.8 seems complicated, don't fret. It's actually very straightforward and builds on skills you learned in the previous chapters. I'll go through each section of this code one chunk at a time, and you will soon see that this page is quite simple.

Fortune_Process.asp—Defining the Page Header Information

The first section of this code is straightforward HTML. All you are doing is defining the background (in this case, yellow) and giving the page a title:

```
<html>

<head>
<title>The Clairvoyant Code - Your Fortune is Told!</title>
</head>

<body bgcolor="#FFFF00">
```

Again, very simple. Other than the catchy page title (`The Clairvoyant Code - Your Fortune is Told!`), nothing special is happening in this section of the code.

Fortune_Process.asp—Reading Previous Fortune Entries

The next section of code scans the Fortune_Track table to determine (based on the username) how many fortunes have already been given to the user. Remember, every time a fortune is presented, information on the fortune seeker is inserted into the Fortune_Track table of the database.

```
<%
set FortuneTrack=Server.CreateObject("ADODB.Recordset")
FortuneTrack.Open "SELECT * FROM Fortune_Track WHERE Username='" &
```

```
Request.Form("Name") & "'", "DSN=Fortune"

Dim PrevFortune
PrevFortune = 0

Do While NOT FortuneTrack.EOF
PrevFortune = PrevFortune + FortuneTrack("ID")
FortuneTrack.MoveNext
Loop

FortuneTrack.Close
Set FortuneTrack=nothing
```

Take a closer look at what's going on here to understand this critical section of the code:

1. The first part of this section opens a connection to the database. The SELECT statement gathers all records within the Fortune_Track table where the Username field matches the name provided by the user on the *Fortune_Info.asp* page.

2. The variable PrevFortune is declared and initially set to zero. This variable records how many previous fortunes have been read (and subsequently recorded in the database) for a specific user.

3. Finally, the DO WHILE loop runs through all the return records, as gathered by the SELECT statement. As each record is returned, the values of the Fortune_ID fields are added together. The code will use this number for generating a new fortune.

HINT

In essence, the PrevFortune **variable is the sum of all the specific Fortune_ID values recorded in the Fortune_Track table. For example, if user Sally Jones has three entries in the Fortune_Track table (meaning that she has had her fortune read three times), the** PrevFortune **adds all the values contained in the Fortune_ID field. Note that the Fortune_ID field corresponds to the ID field of the Fortune_Data table. When a fortune is delivered to a user, the unique identifier of that fortune (the ID field in the Fortune_Data table) is recorded in the Fortune_ID field of the Fortune_Track table.**

Fortune_Process.asp—Generating the Magic Number for the New Fortune

The next section of code is where the clairvoyance of the code comes into play. This mystical power is compliments of the RANDOMIZE function within VBScript, as well as the If...Then statement.

```
MagicNumber = PrevFortune + Request.Form("Age") + Request.Form("Number")
IF MagicNumber > 100 THEN
RANDOMIZE
NewFortune=INT((15 - 1 + 1) * RND + 1)
ELSE
RANDOMIZE
```

```
NewFortune=INT((31 - 16 + 1) * RND + 16)
END IF
```

What's happening with this section of your code? The `MagicNumber` variable is used ultimately to pick a new fortune from the Fortune_Data table of the database.

1. The value of the `PrevFortune` variable (calculated in the first part of your code) is added to the `Age` and `Number` values entered by the user on the *Fortune_Info.asp* page.

2. The `RANDOMIZE` function is called to pick a fortune ID (again, corresponding to the ID field of the Fortune_Data table), depending on the ultimate value of the `MagicNumber` variable. If the `MagicNumber` variable is greater than 100, the `RANDOMIZE` function is called to select a random number between 1 and 15 (including 1 and 15). If the `MagicNumber` variable is less than 100, the `RANDOMIZE` function is called to select a random number between 16 and 31 (including 16 and 31). Again, you randomly select a number between 1 and 31 because this range corresponds to the ID field in the Fortune_Data table of the database.

3. This number is assigned to the variable `NewFortune`, which correlates to a specific ID within the Fortune_Data table.

Fortune_Process.asp—Displaying a New Fortune

After this processing is done, the only thing left to do is display the code. This is done via the following code:

```
UserName=Request.form("Username")

Set InsertFortune=Server.CreateObject("ADODB.RecordSet")
InsertFortune.Open "INSERT INTO Fortune_Track (Username, Fortune_ID) VALUES
('" & Username & "', " & NewFortune & ")""DSN=Fortune"

set TodayFortune=Server.CreateObject("ADODB.Recordset")
TodayFortune.open "SELECT * FROM Fortune_Data WHERE ID=" & NewFortune,
"DSN=Fortune"
%>

<p align="left"><font face="Monotype Corsiva" size="6">Thank you, <font
color="#0000FF">
<%=Request.Form("Name")%>,</font> wisdom seeker extraordinaire!  Your
fortune is as
follows:</font></p>
<hr>
<p align="left"><font size="6" face="Bookman Old Style"
color="#0000FF"><%Response.Write
TodayFortune("Fortune_Data")%></font></p>
<hr>
<p align="left"><font face="Bookman Old Style" size="3">This is your
```

```
fortune for
<%=FORMATDATETIME(DATE,vbLongDate)%>. To have another fortune read, click the
button
below.</font></p>
<form method="POST" action="Fortune_Info.asp">
  <p align="center"><input type="submit" value="Tell me another fortune!"
name="B1"></p>
</form>
</body>
</html>
```

Look at the specific features of this code:

1. After the `NewFortune` variable is defined (per the preceding section of code), it is inserted into a typical `SELECT` statement, which reads from the Fortune_Data table.

2. To record which fortune is given to the user, an `INSERT` statement is used to store the specific fortune ID, the username, and the current data into the Fortune_Track table of the database.

3. Regular HTML formatting (font, color, and so on) is used to present the fortune to the user. Note the use of `Response.Write` to display the name and the fortune.

4. A typical form (with a submit button labeled *Tell me another fortune*) is presented. When users click this form, they are returned to the *Fortune_Info.asp* page, where they can enter information again and have a new fortune read.

Summary

Through the Fortune Teller game, you have learned essential elements of programming ASP pages. You learned how to use the `If...Then` statement to add programming logic to your code You were introduced to the concept of loops in your code and saw how they greatly reduce the length of your code, as well as add tremendous functionality, especially in looping through records from a database. Building on the material you learned in Chapter 5, "Database Access with ADO," and Chapter 6, "Using Forms," you learned how to gather information from a user, integrate it with information being read from a database, and then store the information (via a simple `INSERT` statement) back into the database. Finally, by using even basic HTML formatting, you learned how to spice up your Web pages, especially when integrating dynamic information read from a database.

EXERCISES

Try these exercises to strengthen your understanding of the concepts presented in this chapter:

1. Although not a specific subject discussed in this chapter, create a new Access database and establish a DSN connection to it. (It never hurts to review this important concept!) Once this is done, create a few simple ASP pages that reference some information in the database, and in turn display it on-screen.

2. Create a Web page that asks the user to enter her age. Then, create another Web page that, utilizing the information provided by the user (you'll need to be comfortable with forms to work with this exercise), displays one message if the user is under 50 years of age, and another message if the user is over 50 years of age.

3. Similar to exercise #2 above, add a third message. For example, have your page display one message if the user is under 30 years of age; display a second message if he is 31-50 years of age; then, display a third message if he is over 50 years of age.

4. Create a Web page that asks the user to enter some number from one to ten. Then, pass that information to a form "processing" page and, utilizing a Loop, increment by one the number provided by the user. Display these new numbers on-screen, and "loop" (displaying each number for each iteration of the loop) until the loop reaches 50.

5. Develop a Web page that utilizes an If...Then, If...Then...Else and loop. If possible, have the page read/write information to an Access database, too.

Essential Programming Logic, Part II

I n this chapter, you will

- Learn how to use arrays to streamline your programming and to serve as useful containers for a wide range of values within your code.

- Work with various VBScript functions, including mathematical, date, and time functions, to add easy functionality to your ASP Web pages.

- Develop a game that uses many concepts you've learned so far, especially in Chapter 7— including integrating with a database and working with forms.

In Chapter 7, "Essential Programming Logic, Part I," you were introduced to fundamental programming concepts within VBScript, including the IF...THEN statement and basic loops. In this chapter, you will build on these essential concepts by learning more about VBScript functionality and, in the process, working more with loops, using arrays, and again integrating your Web pages with a Microsoft database. Finally, especially as you develop the game for this chapter, you will get a preview of more advanced HTML formatting possible with VBScript (you will be learning more about formatting your dynamic VBScript output in Chapter 9, "Formatting Processed Output").

Introducing Arrays: Why Do You Need Them?

To describe the concept of an array best, think of—what else—an egg carton. That's right, an egg carton (because eggs and ASP have so much in common). A typical egg carton has two rows, each containing six slots. If, for some reason, you felt compelled to do so, you could use a felt-tip marker and number the eggs 1 through 12.

Now, before you start defacing eggs in your local supermarket, do a little more visualization. Rather than number the eggs themselves, you number each slot in which the eggs rest. Then you color each egg a different color so that each egg has its own unique color (perhaps it's Easter time).

You're probably wondering where I'm going with this (as I am). Seriously, if you can imagine a typical egg carton with 12 uniquely colored eggs, you understand the basic concept of an *array*. An array is a variable in and of itself. However, unlike a typical variable, an array can store multiple values (usually, values that are related in some way). Consider the code in Listing 8.1.

Listing 8.1 Coding without Arrays

```
<%
DIM EggCarton(12)
        EggCarton(1)="Red"
        EggCarton(2)="Blue"
        EggCarton(3)="Yellow"
        EggCarton(4)="Brown"
        EggCarton(5)="Green"
        EggCarton(6)="Black"
        EggCarton(7)="Gold"
        EggCarton(8)="Silver"
        EggCarton(9)="Purple"
        EggCarton(10)="Orange"
        EggCarton(11)="Violet"
        EggCarton(12)="White"
%>
The color of the egg in slot 7 is <%=EggCarton(7)%>, but the color of
the egg in slot 10 is <%=EggCarton(10)%>.
```

As you can probably see in Listing 8.1, you are working with an array named EggCarton. This array has 12 slots, each of which corresponds to a specific egg. When the line of code is executed underneath the array, it reads like this:

```
The color of the egg in slot 7 is Gold, but the color of the egg in slot
10 is Orange.
```

What's happening here is that the EggCarton array is used to store the specific, related values (colors) of the 12 eggs. Although this is a simple example, you can already see how, by using arrays, you can easily group together related values for easy reference, retrieval, and manipulation within your code.

Arrays can also be multidimensional. What this means is that you can store more than one piece of information within each slot because within each position are subslots. For example, Listing 8.2 shows the EggCarton array as it would appear were it multidimensional.

Listing 8.2 Defining Elements in an Array

```
<%
DIM EggCarton(12,1)
        EggCarton(0,0)="Egg 1"
        EggCarton(0,1)="Red"
        EggCarton(1,0)="Egg 2"
        EggCarton(1,1)="Blue"
        EggCarton(2,0)="Egg 3"
        EggCarton(2,1)="Yellow"
        EggCarton(3,0)="Egg 4"
        EggCarton(3,1)="Brown"
        EggCarton(4,0)="Egg 5"
        EggCarton(4,1)="Green"
        EggCarton(5,0)="Egg 6"
        EggCarton(5,1)="Black"
        EggCarton(6,0)="Egg 7"
        EggCarton(6,1)="Gold"
        EggCarton(7,0)="Egg 8"
        EggCarton(7,1)="Silver"
        EggCarton(8,0)="Egg 9"
        EggCarton(8,1)="Purple"
        EggCarton(9,0)="Egg 10"
        EggCarton(9,1)="Orange"
        EggCarton(10,0)="Egg 11"
        EggCarton(10,1)="Violet"
        EggCarton(11,0)="Egg 12"
        EggCarton(11,1)="White"
%>
The egg in slot #4, <%=EggCarton(7,0)%>, has the color <%=EggCarton(7,1)%>
```

Another way to think of these multidimensional arrays is in terms of a table. Specifically, the first number (or index) in the array corresponds to the row of the table, and the second number (index) is the column.

TRICK

Visualizing arrays as tables is an excellent way of comprehending their layout and quickly understanding the values of each position.

Again, you will find that arrays are very useful for grouping together and categorizing related sets of information. Also, because you can dynamically define the values placed into them, they prove to be incredibly powerful tools for storing variable values that are determined as your code executes.

What do I mean by that? If you recall from examples in this book, you can assign values to variables on-the-fly. Consider the example in Listing 8.3.

Listing 8.3 First Array Example

```
DIM ScoreArray(5)
For i=1 to 5
Value="Score"&i
        ScoreArray(i)=Value
Next
```

When this code executes, the following actions occur:

1. An array by the name of ScoreArray is defined via the DIM statement.
2. A simple For...Next loop is begun. In this instance, the loop runs five times.
3. A variable named Value is set each time the loop executes. The value assigned to this Value variable is dynamically generated: It is a combination of the word *Score* and the current value of the i variable as it corresponds to the For...Next loop. Therefore, the first time through the loop, the Value variable has a value equal to Score1.
4. The Value variable is assigned to a specific position within the ScoreArray. Again, because this is dynamic code, the first time through the loop, the code executes as ScoreArray(1)="Score" (as the current value of i is evaluated).

Zero-Based Arrays

Zero-based indicates that all arrays have one more element than it would appear. In the array SomeArray(7), there are actually eight elements because the array is zero-based. Basically, this means that the zero position is a viable position for storing data within the variable, so the SomeArray(7) variable can have its elements defined as in Listing 8.4.

Listing 8.4 Example of Zero-Based Arrays

```
SomeArray(0)="Los Angeles"
SomeArray(1)="Boston"
SomeArray(2)="Chicago"
SomeArray(3)="Dallas"
```

```
SomeArray(4)="Denver"
SomeArray(5)="Indianapolis"
SomeArray(6)="Houston"
SomeArray(7)="New York"
```

As you can see, there are eight elements in the SomeArray(7) array, because of the existence of the zero position. Don't let this confuse you. Just remember that you always have that extra element (the zero position) to work with.

TRAP

Remember not to exceed the maximum number of elements within an array. In the SomeArray **example, if you tried to assign a value to element** SomeArray(8), **you would receive an error. Even though there are eight elements in this array, the zero element counts as the first position, so the highest element number is still 7.**

Useful Array Functions

VBScript presents many useful functions for working with arrays. In this section, I will describe a few of these and show how you can use them to your advantage within your ASP Web pages.

UBOUND()

The first function, UBOUND(), allows you to retrieve the size of an array quickly. For example, take a look at Listing 8.5.

Listing 8.5 Example of UBOUND() Function

```
DIM JohnArray(23, 34)
UBOUND(JohnArray)
UBOUND(JohnArray, 1)
UBOUND(JohnArray, 2)
```

What is displayed when this code executes? Each UBOUND() function call returns a unique value:

1. UBOUND(JohnArray) returns the value of 23. Why 23 and not 34 (or some other answer)? If you just place the array name within the UBOUND function, it automatically returns the highest value of the array's first dimension. In this case, the highest value possible in the first dimension is 23.

TRICK

Don't let all this talk of multidimensional arrays throw you. Think of a table, and visualize rows and columns so that you can see the different dimensions of the array and the values they contain.

2. In UBOUND(JohnArray, 1), the value of 23 is again returned. You are specifically asking for the upper limit of the first dimension of the array, which is 23.

3. In UBOUND(JohnArray, 2), the value of 34 is returned. You are asking for the upper limit of the second dimension to be returned, which is 34.

ERASE()

The second array function I want to discuss is the ERASE() function. Not surprisingly, you use this array to clear away the values stored in an array. Look at the code in Listing 8.6.

Listing 8.6 Example of ERASE() Function

```
<%
DIM JackArray(5)
JackArray(1)="Bob the Builder"
JackArray(2)="Blue's Clues"
JackArray(3)="Rugrats"
%>
The value of the second position of the array is <%=JackArray(2)%><p>
<%
ERASE JackArray
%>
The value of the first position of the array is <%=JackArray(1)%>
```

When this code is executed, the following output is presented:

```
The value of the second position of the array is Blue's Clues
The value of the first position of the array is
```

As you can see, the first statement has the value of the second position dynamically inserted (via the statement <%=JackArray(2)%>). However, the second statement has a blank spot where the value of the first position should be inserted, because the ERASE function was called right before this line is executed.

ISARRAY()

The final array-specific function I want to discuss is the ISARRAY() function. This function returns a value of true or false, depending on whether the variable being evaluated is an array. Consider Listing 8.7.

Listing 8.7 Example of ISARRAY() Function

```
<%
DIM GennaValue(5)
GeorgeValue
%>
Is GennaValue an array?  The answer is <%=ISARRAY(GennaValue)%><p>
Is GeorgeValue an array?  The answer is <%=ISARRAY(GeorgeValue)%>
```

When this code executes, the following is output to the screen:

```
Is GennaValue an array? The answer is TRUE
Is GeorgeValue an array? The answer is FALSE
```

Useful VBScript Functions

From IF...THEN statements to For...Next loops, arrays, and other variables, you have quite a bit of VBScript under your belt and, along with it, the knowledge to make your Web pages sing and dance by using VBScript with ASP. For more information on various facets of VBScript, be sure to review Chapter 2, "Programming ASP Web Pages with VBScript," Chapter 7, "Essential Programming Logic, Part I," and Appendix A, "VBScript Variable Reference."

In this section, you will take a look at a few more useful VBScript functions that will make your programming life much easier and your Web pages more exciting. This is a good overview of the functions available with VBScript, but not an exhaustive list.

The Convert Functions

Several functions available with VBScript enable you to convert a value to a specific subtype variant (for example, a date subtype and currency subtype):

- CCur(). Converts an expression to a variant of the subtype currency
- CDate(). Converts an expression to a variant of the subtype date
- Chr(). Converts ANSI code to the matching keyboard character
- CInt(). Converts an expression to a variant of the subtype integer

As I write this, I hear you asking me, "Why, John, would I want to use these functions?" Although they might seem boring and simple, they are very, very powerful. You will find that as you dynamically generate and assign values to variables within your code, you will want to turn around and manipulate those new values in a specific way, as in Listing 8.8, for example.

Listing 8.8 ConvertFunctions.asp

```
<head>
<title>Example of the CDate() Function</title>
</head>
<html>
<body>
<%
For i = 1 to 5
      DynamicDate=i&"/"&i&"/"&i
      DynamicDate=CDate(DynamicDate)
      DynamicDate=FORMATDATETIME(DynamicDate, vbLongDate)
%>
Date number <%=i%> is: <%=DynamicDate%><p>
<%
Next
%>
</body>
</html>
```

When this code is executed within a Web browser, it looks like Figure 8.1.

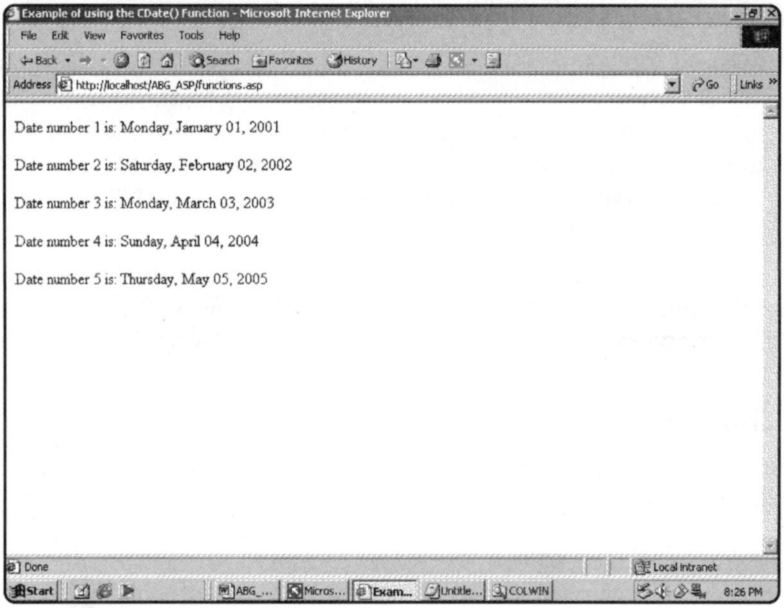

FIGURE 8.1

An example of using the CDate( ) function to convert a dynamically generated variable into a variant of the date subtype.

As you can see from the code, you are using another simple For...Next loop to provide a variable, i, that increases by a value of 1 each time through the loop. Using this variable, the DynamicDate variable is built (DynamicDate=i&"/"&i&"/"&i). After this variable is built, it is converted to a date subtype, by using the CDate( ) function, so that it can be further formatted, using the FORMATDATETIME function.

You can use the other conversion functions in the list to manipulate variables in the same way, so that their values can be converted to current, integer, or ANSI character subtypes.

Mathematical Functions

I admit it—I was never a math whiz. Calculus was a real struggle for me. However, I have always been fascinated with mathematical concepts and theories, even though I don't have a clue what any of them mean.

If you, too, are mathematically challenged, you will be glad to know that, for your computational pleasure, VBScript presents a wide assortment of trigonometric functions:

- Atn( ). Returns the arctangent of a number
- Cos( ). Returns the cosine of a number
- Exp( ). Raises a number to a specific exponential value
- Log( ). Returns the natural logarithm of a number
- Sin( ). Returns the sine of a number
- Sqr( ). Returns the square root of a number
- Tan( ). Returns the tangent of a number

When executed, the code in Listing 8.9 presents the output shown in Figure 8.2.

Listing 8.9 MathFunctions.asp

```
<head>
<title>Example of Mathematical Functions in VBScript</title>
</head>
<body>
<b>For this example, let's work with the number 31</b>
<hr>
<ul>
  <li>The arctangent value is: <%=Atn(31)%></li>
  <li>The cosine value is: <%=Cos(31)%></li>
  <li>The exponential value is: <%=Exp(31)%></li>
  <li>The natural logarithm value is <%=Log(31)%></li>
  <li>The square root value is: <%=Sqr(31)%></li>
  <li>The sine value is: <%=Sin(31)%></li>
  <li>The tangent value is: <%=Tan(31)%></li>
</ul>
</body>
</html>
```

I won't say more about these functions, other than to remind you that if you have a need for them and you understand them, you can use these to perform powerful number crunching. Enjoy!

The Is Functions

The Is functions, as I like to call them, are quite useful in testing whether a value meets specific criteria. You saw an example of one of these, IsArray(), earlier.

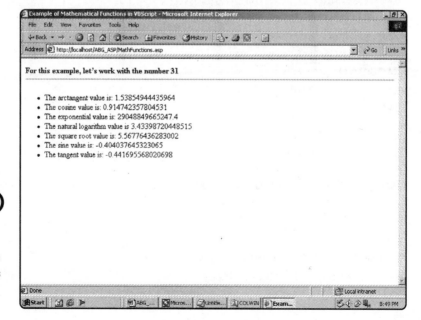

FIGURE 8.2

An example of the trigonometric functions available within VBScript, as performed on the number 31.

In addition to this function, you should be aware of several others:

- `IsDate()`. Determines whether an expression can be converted into a date format
- `IsEmpty()`. Determines whether a variable has been initialized or set to an initial value
- `IsNull()`. Measures whether the expression in question is null
- `IsNumeric()`. Tests an expression to see whether it is a number

When do you use the `Is` functions? These functions are particularly useful when you want to test whether a given expression meets specific criteria. In plain English, you are asking yourself, *Is* the expression I'm looking at a number? *Is* the expression I'm looking at `null` in value?

One very useful application of these functions is to test whether submitted form data meets your criteria. Listing 8.10 is a simple form that asks users to enter the date they were born and their age. Listing 8.11 is a typical form-processing page that uses two of these functions to ensure that the data submitted by the user meets specified criteria. Figure 8.3 shows the form that users are asked to complete.

Listing 8.10 IsFunctionForm.asp

```
<html>

<head>
<title>Working with "Is" Functions in VBScript</title>
</head>
<body>
<p align="center"><font face="Bookman Old Style" color="#008000"><b>Working
with the &quot;Is&quot; Functions</b></font></p>
<p align="center"><hr>
<form method="POST" action="IsFunctionProcess.asp"
<p align="left">Enter the date of your birth, in the format shown:
<input type="text" name="DOB" size="20" value="mm/dd/yy"></p>
<p align="left">Enter your age in years: <input type="text" name="Age"
size="10"></p>
<p align="center"><input type="submit" value="Verify your data!"
name="B1"></p>
</form>
</body>
</html>
```

Listing 8.11 IsFunctionProcess.asp

```
<html>

<head>
<title>Working with "Is" Functions in VBScript</title>
</head>
<body>
```

```
<%
DOB=Request.Form("DOB")
CheckDOB=IsDate(DOB)
IF CheckDOB="False" THEN
%>
<b>Submission error!</b>
<hr>
You must enter your DOB in the proper format.  Click the Back button on your
browser to re-enter this information.
<hr>
<%
END IF
Age=Request.Form("Age")
CheckAge=IsNumeric(Age)
IF CheckAge="False" THEN
%>
<b>Submission error!</b>
<hr>
You must enter your age in the proper format.  Click the Back button on your
browser to re-enter this information.
<hr>
<%
END IF
%>
</body>
</html>
```

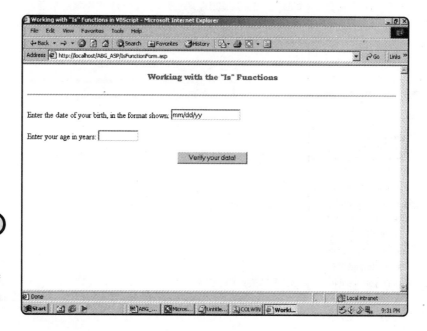

FIGURE 8.3

A simple form asking visitors to enter their date of birth and age in specific formats.

When you load this page into your Web browser, the first time you submit your data, enter your name in the date of birth field, but enter your age in numeric value. When you click the Verify your data! button, your screen looks like Figure 8.4.

To illustrate the IsNumeric() function, go back to the form, but this time enter your date of birth in the proper format, and then enter your name in the age field. When you submit your data, your screen looks like Figure 8.5.

The code listings are simple, but you can see how the various Is functions can be used to verify whether certain data is of the proper format. Don't forget to implement these powerful functions in your code when you have to do rudimentary data checking. This method of safeguarding your data can be very important. Imagine that you are trying to build a comprehensive database of user information and you want to make sure that you capture information (street address, state, ZIP) in the proper format. In other words, you don't want users to enter their age in the state field of your form, their date of birth in the street address field, and so on. By using the Is functions as described here, you can check the data before it is submitted to your database. If it can't be converted (that is, checked) into specific formats, you ask users to resubmit the data (refer to Figures 8.4 and 8.5).

TRICK

Many HTML editing tools, such as Microsoft FrontPage, have built-in form field validation features. However, don't forget to use the built-in validation features of VBScript—the Is functions.

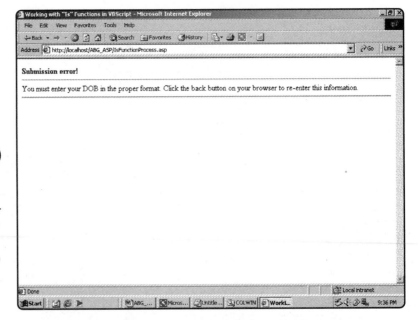

FIGURE 8.4

The IsDate() function in Listing 8.11 checks whether the value you enter into the DOB field can be converted to a date format. If it can't, you see this error message.

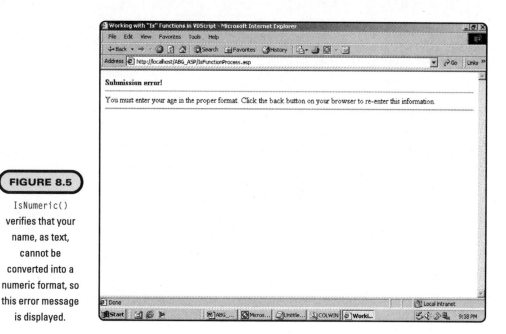

FIGURE 8.5

IsNumeric()
verifies that your
name, as text,
cannot be
converted into a
numeric format, so
this error message
is displayed.

Time and Date Functions

Not surprisingly, VBScript has several functions that make working with and manipulating date and time values much easier:

- `Date()`. Returns the date as it is being kept on the particular system where IIS is running
- `Hour()`. Returns the hour, as specified
- `Minute()`. Returns the minute as specified
- `Month()`. Returns the month, as specified
- `Now()`. Returns the current date and time, as specified on the server where IIS is running
- `Second()`. Returns the second of the specified minute
- `Time()`. Returns the current time, as specified on the server where IIS is running

Of all the functions, these date and time functions are probably the most self-explanatory. Nevertheless, take a look at a Web page that shows them all in action, in Listing 8.12.

Listing 8.12 DateTimeFunctions.asp

```
<html>
<head>
<title>Working with VBScript Date/Time Functions</title>
</head>
```

```
<body>
<p align="center"><font face="Bookman Old Style" color="#008000">
<b>Working with Date/Time Functions</b></font></p>
<hr>
<ul>
  <li>The date is: <%=DATE%></li>
  <li>The hour right now is: <%=Hour(NOW)%></li>
  <li>The minute right now is: <%=Minute(NOW)%></li>
  <li>The time right now is: <%=NOW%></li>
  <li>The second of the minute right now is: <%=Second(NOW)%></li>
  <li>The time on the Web server computer is:  <%=Time%></li>
</ul>
</body>
</html>
```

Figure 8.6 shows how these functions return specific values.

The functions described here are just a few of the date and time functions available within VBScript.

Programming the ASP War! Game

When you were a kid, before you knew how to play poker, you probably laid down a few exciting games of War. Now, as I remember playing it, the game consists of dealing half the deck to yourself and the other half to your buddy. Then, you each turn over one card at a time, with the highest card winning the hand. When there are no cards left to play, the person who wins the most hands wins the war.

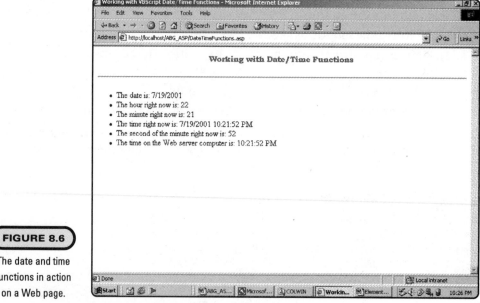

FIGURE 8.6

The date and time functions in action on a Web page.

Admittedly, this isn't the most exciting game, but with help from ASP, you can turn a simple children's game into something more entertaining. Before you examine the code, take a look at the rules for playing ASP War!:

- To begin the game, you are asked to enter your name and the initial number of armies with which you want to battle. Note that you start the game with 200 armies.
- Your computer is the opponent. The computer starts the game with 100 armies.
- There are 10 battles (or rounds) per game. For each round, you have to gamble at least half your available armies.
- The winner of each battle is determined by adding up the value of all the cards displayed. In many card games, face cards are assigned a value of 10, with all other cards being awarded their face value. However, in ASP War!, the face cards (including the Ace) are assigned the following point values:
  - 10 card—10 points
  - Jack card—11 points
  - Queen card—12 points
  - King card—13 points
  - Ace card—14 points
- At the end of 10 rounds, the total points for the player and for the computer are added. The highest point total wins the war!

Let me take you through a game so that you can see how the rules are applied:

1. To begin the game, load the page *ASPWar_Home.asp* into your Web browser (see Figure 8.7).
2. When you click the Begin the War! button, the game begins. Three cards are drawn for you and for the computer. The total of the three cards is computed, with the highest total winning that battle (see Figure 8.8).

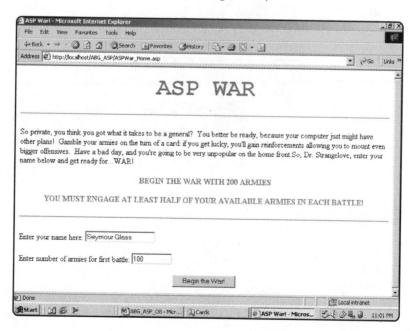

FIGURE 8.7

Enter your name and the number of armies you want to gamble on the initial battle.

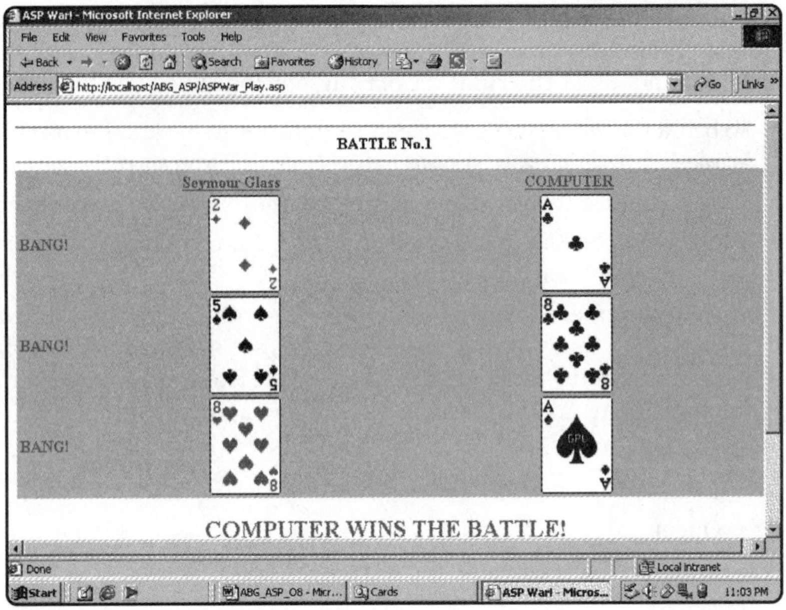

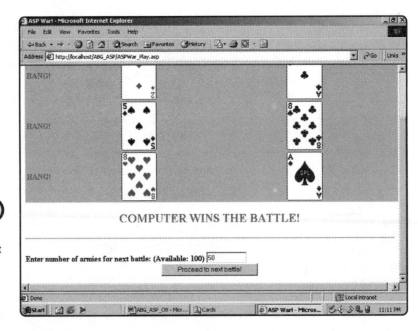

FIGURE 8.8

The computer wins the battle. With two Aces and an 8, the computer's total score is 36 (each Ace is worth 14 points, and the 8 card equals 36).

3. If you scroll down the page, underneath the COMPUTER WINS THE BATTLE! message, you will see a prompt to enter the number of armies you want to gamble in the next battle (see Figure 8.9). Note how the total of your available armies is automatically computed, based on the results of the current round. In this example, the player gambled 100 of his 200 armies. Because the computer won the battle, he now has only 100 armies left (200 - 100 = 100). The computer, whenever it wins, adds to its total the number of armies the player gambled.

FIGURE 8.9

Enter the number of armies you want to gamble for the next round. Click Proceed to next battle!

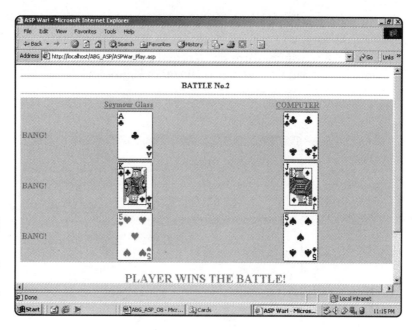

4. As the game continues, note how the current round is tracked (in Figure 8.10, the game is in round 2). Also, in this figure, the player has won the battle with a total score of 32 (Ace = 14, King = 13, and a 5).

5. Scrolling to the bottom of this screen (refer to Figure 8.10), the player has a total of 150 armies, but this time he forgets the rule that he must gamble at least half his armies and enters only 50. When he clicks the submit button, he is presented with an error message, shown in Figure 8.11.

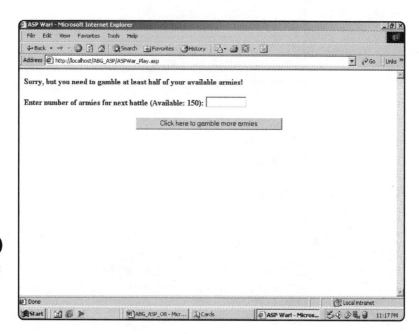

6. The game is also smart enough to know whether you are trying to gamble more armies than you have available. If you do, you see the message shown in Figure 8.12.

7. The game continues through 10 rounds. The highest score at the end of the tenth round wins the game, as shown in Figure 8.13.

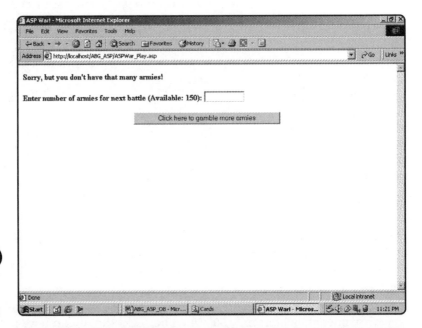

FIGURE 8.12

Don't try to gamble more armies than you have available!

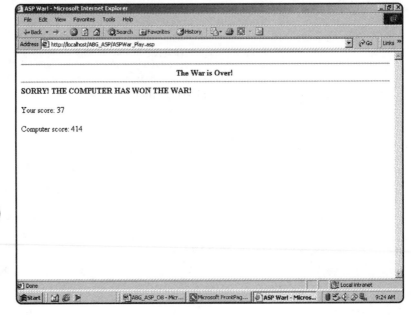

FIGURE 8.13

The war is over! Can you fight the evil computer and bring peace to Silicon Valley?

Analyzing the Code

The game consists of two ASP pages:

- *ASPWar_Home.asp*. This displays the opening text and asks you to enter your name and the initial number of armies you want to fight with.

- *ASPWar_Play.asp*. This is where all the action of the game occurs, including the display of the cards, determining who wins each round, the tracking of the round and score, and the final determination of who wins the war (the game).

- The *War.mdb* database. This is used to track the randomly selected cards from hand to hand so that the player and the computer are not dealt the same card(s).

Listing 8.13 is the *ASPWar_Home.asp* page.

Listing 8.13 ASPWar_Home.asp

```
<html>
<head>
<title>ASP War!</title>
</head>
<body>
<p align="center"><font face="Courier New" size="7" color="#FF0000">
<b>ASP WAR</b></font></p>
<hr>
<p align="left"><font size="3">So private, you think you got what it takes to
be a general?  You better be ready, because your computer just might have
other plans!  Gamble your armies on the turn of a card: if you get lucky,
you'll gain reinforcements allowing you to mount even bigger offensives. 
Have a bad day, and you're going to be very unpopular on the home front. So,
Dr. Strangelove, enter your name below and get ready for...WAR!</font></p>
<p align="center"><b><font size="3" color="#008000">BEGIN THE WAR WITH 200
ARMIES</font></b></p>
<p align="center"><b><font size="3" color="#008000">YOU MUST ENGAGE AT LEAST
HALF OF YOUR AVAILABLE ARMIES IN EACH BATTLE!</font></b></p>
<hr>

<form method="POST" action="ASPWar_Play.asp">
  <p align="left">Enter your name here: <input type="text" name="Player"
size="20"></p>
  <p align="left">Enter number of armies for first battle: <input type="text"
name="Armies" size="10"></p>
  <p align="center"><input type="submit" value="Begin the War!" name="B1"></p>
<input type="hidden" name="TotalArmies" value="200">
<input type="hidden" name="CTotalArmies" value="100">
<input type="hidden" name="Round" value="1">
</form>
</body>
</html>
```

This is a very simple form, but you should take note of the specific hidden form fields set and passed along with the initial number of armies to be used (form element Armies), as well as the player's name (form element Player). Specifically, three hidden form fields are initially set on this page:

- TotalArmies. Tracks the total number of armies you gain or lose throughout the course of the game. As you progress through each round, TotalArmies tracks the total number of armies you have available to fight with. To begin the game, you have 200 armies at your disposal.

- CTotalArmies. Functions in exactly the same way as the TotalArmies variable but tracks the armies available to the computer. Note that the initial value of this variable is set to 100.

- Round. Tracks the current round of the game. After the tenth round, the TotalArmies and CTotalArmies variables are compared, with the highest one indicating who wins the game.

TRICK Why make the TotalArmies, CTotalArmies, and Round variables hidden? They are used to track specific game components, so they can remain behind the scenes because they require no direct manipulation by the user.

Listing 8.14 is the *ASPWar_Play.asp* page, where all the game action takes place. Although at first glance this might seem complicated, it's quite straightforward and easy to understand.

Listing 8.14 ASPWar_Play.asp

```
<html>
<head>
<title>ASP War!</title>
</head>
<body>

<%
        ArmyCheck=Request.Form("TotalArmies")
        ArmyCheck=CInt(ArmyCheck)
        ArmyCheckStatic=ArmyCheck
        ArmyCheck=ArmyCheck / 2
        ArmyBet=Request.Form("Armies")
        ArmyBet=CInt(ArmyBet)

        'Check to see if game is over
        'Only 10 rounds are played
        IF Request.Form("Round")=11 THEN
%>
<hr>
<b><center>The War Is Over!</center></b>
<hr>
```

```
<%
        'Check to see who won the game

        IF Request.Form("TotalPoints") > Request.Form("CTotalPoints") THEN
        %>
        <b>YOU WIN THE BATTLE!</B><p>
        Your score: <%=Request.Form("TotalArmies")%><p>
        Computer score: <%=Request.Form("CTotalArmies")%>
        <%
        ELSE
        %>
        <b>SORRY!  THE COMPUTER HAS WON THE BATTLE!</b><p>
        Your score: <%=Request.Form("TotalArmies")%><p>
        Computer score: <%=Request.Form("CTotalArmies")%>
        <%END IF%>


<%
        'Check to see number of armies.  Remember, the player must
        'gamble at least half his or her available armies

        'Check to see if player has gambled more armies
        'than she or he has available

        ELSEIF ArmyBet > ArmyCheckStatic THEN
        'Player needs to reduce number of gambled armies
%>

<b>Sorry, but you don't have that many armies!</b><p>
<form method="POST" action="ASPWar_Play.asp">
<b>Enter number of armies for next battle (Available: <%=Request.Form
("TotalArmies")%>): <input type="text" name="Armies" size="10"></b>
<p>
<center><input type="submit" value="Click here to gamble more armies"></center>
<input type="hidden" name="player" value="<%=Request.Form("Player")%>">
<input type="hidden" name="TotalArmies" value="<%=Request.Form
("TotalArmies")%>">
<input type="hidden" name="round" value="<%=Request.Form("Round")%>">
<input type="hidden" name="CTotalArmies" value="<%=Request.Form
("CTotalArmies")%>">
</p>
</form>
<p>
<%
        ELSEIF ArmyCheck > ArmyBet THEN
        'Player needs to gamble more armies.
```

```
%>
<b>Sorry, but you need to gamble at least half of your available armies!</b><p>
<form method="POST" action="ASPWar_Play.asp">
<b>Enter number of armies for next battle (Available: <%=Request.Form
("TotalArmies")%>): <input type="text" name="Armies" size="10"></b>
<p>
<center><input type="submit" value="Click here to gamble more armies"></center>
<input type="hidden" name="player" value="<%=Request.Form("Player")%>">
<input type="hidden" name="TotalArmies" value="<%=Request.Form
("TotalArmies")%>">
<input type="hidden" name="round" value="<%=Request.Form("Round")%>">
<input type="hidden" name="CTotalArmies" value="<%=Request.Form
("CTotalArmies")%>">
</p>
</form>
<p>
<%
'If player has gambled at least half of his or her available armies,
'then the game may continue
ELSE
'Define Arrays
Dim PlayerCards(3)
Dim ComputerCards(3)
Dim ComputerScore(3)
Dim PlayerScore(3)

'Set player name
Player=Request.Form("Player")
%>
<hr>
<b><center>BATTLE No.<%=Request.Form("Round")%></center></b>
<hr>
<table border="0" width="100%" bgcolor="#C0C0C0">
  <tr>
    <td width="50%" colspan="2">
      <p align="center"><b><font color="#008000">    
                
      </font><font color="#008000"><u> <%=Request.Form("Player")%></u>
      </font></b></td>
    <td width="50%" colspan="2">
      <p align="left"><b><font color="#008000">     
                  
                  
          
      <u>COMPUTER</u>
```

```
        </font></b></td>
    </tr>
<%
'Randomly select the cards from the database, for this battle
'We will need six cards, so the loop will repeat six times
'As each card is randomly selected, the Selected column is marked in the
'database, and the card name is placed into one of the two arrays
'for retrieval during the battle!

'Determine Player Cards
For a=1 to 3
CheckVar=0
'Check to see if this card has already been selected from the database
DO UNTIL CheckVar=1
CheckVar=0
        RANDOMIZE
        RndCheck=INT((52-1+1) * RND + 1)


set CardCheck=Server.CreateObject("ADODB.Recordset")
sqlstmt="SELECT * FROM Cards WHERE ID="& RndCheck
CardCheck.Open sqlstmt, "DSN=War", 3, 3, 1


IF CardCheck("Selected")=0 THEN
CheckVar=1
PlayerCards(a)=CardCheck("CardName")
PlayerScore(a)=CardCheck("CardValue")
'Update Database
set CardUpdate=Server.CreateObject("ADODB.Recordset")
sqlstmt="UPDATE Cards SET Selected=1 WHERE ID="&RndCheck
CardUpdate.Open sqlstmt, "DSN=War", 3, 3, 1


END IF
LOOP
Next


'Determine Computer Cards
For a=1 to 3
CheckVar=0
'Check to see if this card has already been selected from the database
DO UNTIL CheckVar=1
CheckVar=0
        RANDOMIZE
        RndCheck=INT((52-1+1) * RND + 1)


set CardCheck=Server.CreateObject("ADODB.Recordset")
```

```
sqlstmt="SELECT * FROM Cards WHERE ID="& RndCheck
CardCheck.Open sqlstmt, "DSN=War", 3, 3, 1

IF CardCheck("Selected")=0 THEN
CheckVar=1
ComputerCards(a)=CardCheck("CardName")
ComputerScore(a)=CardCheck("CardValue")
'Update Database
set CardUpdate=Server.CreateObject("ADODB.Recordset")
sqlstmt="UPDATE Cards SET Selected=1 WHERE ID="&RndCheck
CardUpdate.Open sqlstmt, "DSN=War", 3, 3, 1

END IF
LOOP
Next
'Now, begin the battle!
%>

  <tr>
    <td width="11%"><font color="#FF0000"><b>BANG!</b></font></td>
    <td width="39%">
      <p align="center"><img border="0" src="Cards/<%=PlayerCards(1)%>.gif"
      width="73" height="97"></td>
    <td width="41%">
      <p align="center"><img border="0" src="Cards/<%=ComputerCards(1)%>.gif"
width="73" height="97"></td>
  </tr>
  <tr>
    <td width="11%"><font color="#FF0000"><b>BANG!</b></font></td>
    <td width="39%">
      <p align="center"><img border="0" src="Cards/<%=PlayerCards(2)%>.gif"
      width="73" height="97"></td>
    <td width="41%">
      <p align="center"><img border="0" src="Cards/<%=ComputerCards(2)%>.gif"
      width="73" height="97"></td>
  </tr>
  <tr>
    <td width="11%"><font color="#FF0000"><b>BANG!</b></font></td>
    <td width="39%">
      <p align="center"><img border="0" src="Cards/<%=PlayerCards(3)%>.gif"
      width="73" height="97"></td>
    <td width="41%">
      <p align="center"><img border="0" src="Cards/<%=ComputerCards(3)%>.gif"
      width="73" height="97"></td>
  </tr>
```

```
</table>
<%
'Determine who won this battle
PScore=PlayerScore(1)+PlayerScore(2)+PlayerScore(3)
CScore=ComputerScore(1)+ComputerScore(2)+ComputerScore(3)

IF PScore > CScore THEN
'Set Armies
A=Request.Form("TotalArmies")
B=Request.Form("Armies")
A=CInt(A)
B=CInt(B)
TotalArmies=A+B
CTotalArmies=Request.Form("CTotalArmies")
%>
<p align="center"><b><font color="#FF0000" size="5">PLAYER WINS THE
BATTLE!</font></b></p>
<%END IF%>
<%
IF CScore > PScore THEN
A=Request.Form("TotalArmies")
B=Request.Form("Armies")
TotalArmies=A-b
'When the computer wins, they get armies added to their total
C=Request.Form("CTotalArmies")
C=CInt(C)
CTotalArmies=C+B
%>
<p align="center"><b><font color="#FF0000" size="5">COMPUTER WINS THE
BATTLE!</font></b></p>
<%END IF%>
<%IF PScore=CScore THEN
TotalArmies=Request.Form("TotalArmies")
CTotalArmies=Request.Form("CTotalArmies")
%>
<p align="center"><b><font color="#FF0000" size="5">STALEMATE!</font></b></p>
<%
END IF

%>
<%
'Reset the database
set CardReset=Server.CreateObject("ADODB.Recordset")
sqlstmt="UPDATE Cards SET Selected=0"
CardReset.Open sqlstmt, "DSN=War", 3, 3, 1
```

```
%>
<hr>
<form method="post" action="ASPWar_Play.asp">
<%
'Set values to pass
CurrentRound=Request.Form("Round")+1
Player=Request.Form("Player")
%>
<input type="hidden" name="player" value="<%=Player%>">
<input type="hidden" name="TotalArmies" value="<%=TotalArmies%>">
<input type="hidden" name="round" value="<%=CurrentRound%>">
<input type="hidden" name="CTotalArmies" value="<%=CTotalArmies%>">
<b>Enter number of armies for next battle: (Available: <%=TotalArmies%>) </b>
<input type="text" size="10" name="Armies">  <center><input type="submit"
value="Proceed to next battle!"></center>
</form>
<%
END IF
%>
</body>
</html>
```

How does all of this work? Let's go through the code and see what's happening within this page:

1. The opening lines of code request the total armies and number of armies that have been gambled for the particular round. The ArmyCheck variable is used to determine whether at least half the available armies have been gambled (remember, this is a central rule of the game).

2. The next section, focusing on the line IF Request.Form("Round")=11, checks whether the game is over (the round variable increases by 1 as each round is played). If this variable is equal to 11, this indicates that 10 rounds have been played and the game is over (so the IF...THEN statement evaluates to true in this case). The code then checks to see who won the war, by comparing the TotalArmies (player armies) with the CTotalArmies (computer armies) variables. Whichever is highest wins the game, and the appropriate message is displayed (either YOU WIN THE WAR or SORRY! THE COMPUTER HAS WON THE WAR!).

3. If the round variable is not equal to 1, this indicates that the game is still in progress. The first action that must occur is to determine whether the player has gambled at least half his armies and to check whether he has tried to gamble more armies than he possesses. The use of the ELSEIF statement facilitates this: If either of the preceding conditions are true, the appropriate code is displayed (Sorry, but you don't have that many armies! or Sorry, but you need to gamble at least half of your available armies). The code is stopped at this point, and a form is displayed, asking the user to gamble more or fewer of his armies.

TRICK

Note that in both these sections, the form action is set to `"ASPWar_Play.asp"`. **In other words, the form submits back to the same page. This is a useful trick for keeping your ASP applications smaller in size by limiting the number of Web pages you need to build.**

4. Assuming that round 10 has not passed and the player has gambled at least half his armies (without trying to gamble more armies than he already has), the code proceeds. The first action to occur is that the four arrays are initially set (`PlayerCards`, `ComputerCards`, `ComputerScore`, and `PlayerScore`). These arrays are used to display the cards on screen and to tally the total of these cards so that a winner for each round can be determined.

5. A typical HTML table is begun (to keep the card display neat, you place the cards into specific cells within the table). The round is displayed at the top of the table (via the line `BATTLE no. <%=Request.Form("Round")%>`).

6. The specific cards for each round are randomly selected. Notice the use of the `CheckVar` variable to determine whether the card has already been selected. This works exactly the same as the Memory Game you developed in Chapter 6. A random number is generated (in this case, a number between 1 and 52 to correspond to the number of cards in the deck). This number is then used in a SQL query to the database. This query continues to be executed (via the `DO UNTIL` loop) until a card is found that has not been selected. When such a card is found, its value within the database is set to `selected`, and the `DO UNTIL` loop ends. The card name is inserted into the `PlayerCard` array (by the line `PlayerCards(a)=CardCheck("CardName")`), and the card's specific value is inserted into the array `PlayerScore` (by the line `PlayerCards(a)=CardCheck("CardValue")`).

7. This process is repeated for the computer cards so that, for each round, all four arrays (`PlayerCards`, `ComputerCards`, `ComputerScore`, and `PlayerScore`) are set with specific values.

8. The cards are displayed on the screen inside the table. Notice how the various card image files are referenced:

```
<img border="0" src="Cards/<%=PlayerCards(1)%>.gif"
```

The name of the card is dynamically generated by calling a specific element of either the `PlayerCard` or `ComputerCard` array and then adding the *.gif* extension to the end.

9. After all the cards are displayed, the code determines who won this particular round. The player score and computer score are computed (by adding together the respective elements of both the `PlayerScore` and `ComputerScore` arrays), with each of these values being set to two variables: `PScore` and `CScore`. Then, these two variables are compared. The highest score indicates the winner of this particular round, and the appropriate message is displayed (PLAYER WINS THE BATTLE!, COMPUTER WINS THE BATTLE!, or STALEMATE!).

10. Finally, the database is reset. Specifically, the Selected field for each record is set back to 0 (this is done so that, when the cards for the next round are determined, all the cards are initially unselected). A form is presented to the player, asking him to enter the number of armies he wants to gamble for the next round. Note that within this line of code, the `TotalArmies` variable value is displayed so that players know how many armies are available to them.

The card images are freeware and were obtained from the Web. However, in an effort to give proper credit to the creator of these cards and to encourage the free and honest distribution of others' work, please be sure to read the Card_Graphic_Agreement file included on the enclosed CD-ROM.

Summary

This chapter presents you with more useful VBScript functions and gives examples of how to integrate them within your ASP Web pages. Using arrays, manipulating and formatting time and dates, determining whether variables meet specific criteria (the Is functions) and working with trigonometric functions, you should take advantage of all the functions within VBScript to make your coding more powerful and, ultimately, easier to understand. Finally, by developing the ASP War! game, you again saw how various VBScript functions and statements can come together to produce nifty results (especially when combined with straightforward HTML). You will learn more about formatting your VBScript output with HTML in Chapter 9.

EXERCISES

Try these exercises to further your understanding of how to work with VBScript functions:

1. Develop a form that asks for a user's name, street address, city, state, and ZIP. When the form is processed, place all this information into a multidimensional array named UserInfo( ), and then, reading from this array, display the information back on the screen. Do not use request.form to display the information. Instead, insert the form data into the UserInfo( ) array. Then display the information by reading from this array.

2. Develop a form that asks for information in a specific format (text, date, numbers, and the like). When the form is processed, use the Is functions to determine whether the information entered meets the specific format you set.

3. Develop an ASP Trigonometry Calculator. Format a typical HTML table, and within each cell, place a submit button that is titled *Sin, Cos, Tan*, and so on (list all the trigonometric functions discussed in this chapter). Also, in one of the cells, insert a text box so that the user can insert a number. Then, depending on the number entered and the specific button selected, the value will be displayed on screen.

4. Customize the ASP War! game so that, on the *ASPWar_Home.asp* page, it also asks users how many rounds they would like to play, instead of forcing them to play the default 10 rounds.

5. Customize the ASP War! game (and database) so that, after the game is over, the player has the option to save his scores (within the database) for future reference.

6. Troubleshoot (that is, add functionality to account for possible errors) the following possibilities: upon the first turn, user bets all his armies and loses (what screen/options should appear to him)? Also, add a feature into the code so that the system checks to make sure he entered a username.

CHAPTER 9

Formatting Processed Output

I n this chapter, you will

- Learn how to format tables, lists, and hyperlinks and to perform general page formatting as a result of your processed VBScript.

- Learn how to integrate query results dynamically from a database into your Web pages.

- Learn how to make the ASP MadLibs game presented in Chapter 3, "Working with ASP Objects," more visually appealing and more functional.

One look at the title of this chapter and you might think that it's referring to one of those not-so-tasty food substitutes you find in a box of imitation macaroni and cheese. This is not the case, however. Formatting processed output refers to methods and mechanisms for making the VBScript you execute within your ASP Web pages come to life in the best way possible. Remember, one of the most appealing attributes of ASP is that your VBScript executes on the server, so only regular HTML is sent to the user's Web browser for display. However, in comparison to static HTML, the dynamic Web pages you create with ASP can produce HTML that is a result of users' providing information via a form, the integration of information stored in a database with the Web page, the actual processing of your VBScript code on the server, and so on. In short, your Web pages come alive with ASP. Learning how to format the executed code and its resulting output ensures that your pages—and the functionality contained within them—always look their best.

Think of this chapter as a workshop lesson on how to improve your existing skill set in working with VBScript, ASP, and database design.

HTML Formatting—Beyond the Basics

By using typical HTML formatting, you can neatly arrange your text and graphics on a Web page. Consider the typical HTML code for a table in Listing 9.1.

Listing 9.1 Table.asp

```
<html>
<head>
<title>Simple HTML Formatting</title>
</head>
<body>
<table border="1" width="100%">
  <tr>
    <td width="100%" colspan="2">
      <p align="center"><font color="#008000" size="6" face="Bookman
Old Style"><b>Welcome
      to Active Server Pages</b></font></td>
  </tr>
  <tr>
    <td width="50%"> </td>
    <td width="50%"> </td>
  </tr>
  <tr>
    <td width="50%"> </td>
    <td width="50%"> </td>
  </tr>
  <tr>
    <td width="50%"> </td>
    <td width="50%"> </td>
  </tr>
  <tr>
```

```
    <td width="50%"> </td>
    <td width="50%"> </td>
  </tr>
  <tr>
    <td width="50%"> </td>
    <td width="50%"> </td>
  </tr>
  <tr>
    <td width="50%"> </td>
    <td width="50%"> </td>
  </tr>
  <tr>
    <td width="50%"> </td>
    <td width="50%"> </td>
  </tr>
  <tr>
    <td width="50%"> </td>
    <td width="50%"> </td>
  </tr>
  <tr>
    <td width="50%"> </td>
    <td width="50%"> </td>
  </tr>
</table>
</body>
</html>
```

When this page is loaded within a Web browser, it looks like Figure 9.1.

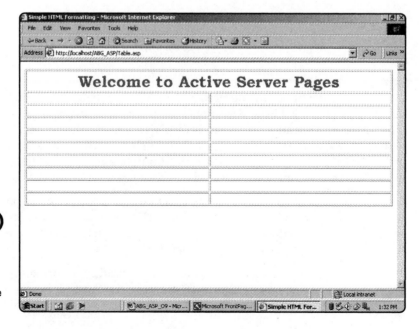

FIGURE 9.1

A simple HTML table. Note the amount of code required to produce this simple page.

If you didn't know anything about VBScript or ASP, you would be relegated to typing in all the preceding code to produce the table in Figure 9.1. Fortunately, you decided to learn ASP and are becoming quite proficient at it, so you have other options available! Take a look at the code in Listing 9.2, which produces the same table shown in Figure 9.1 but uses VBScript to do the job.

Listing 9.2 Table2.asp

```
<html>
<head>
<title>Simple HTML Formatting</title>
</head>
<body>
<table border="1" width="100%">
  <tr>
    <td width="100%" colspan="2">
      <p align="center"><font color="#008000" size="6" face="Bookman Old
      Style"><b>Welcome
      to Active Server Pages</b></font></td>
  </tr>
<%
For i=1 to 10
%>
  <tr>
    <td width="50%"> </td>
    <td width="50%"> </td>
  </tr>
<%
Next
%>
</table>
</body>
</html>
```

Undoubtedly, you notice the difference in code length between Listings 9.1 and 9.2; the latter is considerably shorter. Also, note how much easier Listing 9.2 is to read and understand. After the opening `<table>` tag is displayed and the initial table cell is formatted with the `Welcome to Active Server Pages` text, a simple `For...Next` loop is inserted. This loop is programmed to run 10 times; each time through, a new row of the table is inserted. After the loop is complete, the closing `</table>` tag is inserted, and the page ends.

Because this example is simple, you should not underestimate the power of VBScript to reduce the size and complexity of your HTML formatting drastically. Tables are a good example, especially when used to read information from a database (as you learned to do in Chapter 5, "Database Access with ADO").

To reinforce that point, here is another look at reading information into your Web pages via an Access database. Listing 9.3 draws on the Music database you worked with in Chapter 5.

Listing 9.3 Database.asp

```
<html>
<head>
<title>Formatting Database Information</title>
</head>
<body>
<table border="1" width="100%">
  <tr>
    <td width="100%" colspan="2">
    <p align="center"><font color="#008000" size="6" face="Bookman Old
    Style"><b>A sample of our music catalog</b></font></td>
  </tr>
<%
Set Catalog=Server.CreateObject("ADODB.Recordset")
Catalog.open "SELECT * FROM Catalog", "DSN=Music"
Do WHILE NOT Catalog("ID")=11
%>
  <tr>
    <td width="50%"> <%=Catalog("Artist")%></td>
    <td width="50%"> <%=Catalog("Title")%></td>
  </tr>
<%
Catalog.MoveNext
Loop
Catalog.Close
Set Catalog=Nothing
%>
</table>
</body>
</html>
```

When this code is loaded into a Web browser, it looks like Figure 9.2.

Think for a moment about the drawbacks of *not* using a database to present this kind of information. You have to deal with the following issues:

- You have to enter each line of the table manually. Aside from the time involved, your code will be twice as long (like Listing 9.1).
- Whenever the information within your Web page changes, you have to update the Web page (and any related formatting) to display the information.

By keeping the information within a database, you only make the change there and let the SQL query in the Web page do all the work. You can take the information you retrieve from the SQL query and use it within other pages to which this page links (as you will soon see).

The point here is that you should always take advantage of the time-saving, code-minimizing capabilities of VBScript and ASP. Now you will see how VBScript and ASP bring spice to your HTML.

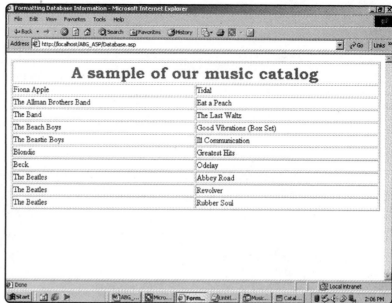

FIGURE 9.2

By integrating information stored within a database into your Web pages, you add a whole new level of functionality and power.

Creating Dynamic Form Elements

In Chapter 6, "Using Forms," you learned how to use ASP to gather and process information and, in conjunction with ADO, to integrate this information with a database. You can also use VBScript to create the form and its corresponding form elements dynamically.

To illustrate this, Listing 9.4 is a typical HTML form that uses a drop-down menu element.

Listing 9.4 Hard Coded Form Elements

```
<html>
<head>
<title>Dynamic Form Elements</title>
</head>
<body>
<p>Please select one of the titles listed below, and then click the
Submit button:</p>
<form method="POST" action="TitleChoice.asp">
  <p><select size="1" name="Choice">
    <option value="37">Dixie Chicken</option>
    <option value="38">Astral Weeks</option>
    <option value="39">In my Tribe</option>
    <option value="40">Scarecrow</option>
    <option value="41">Blue</option>
  </select><input type="submit" value="Submit" name="B1"></p>
</form>
```

```
</body>
</html>
```

When loaded into a Web browser, this code produces the results shown in Figure 9.3.

In Listing 9.4, notice how all the items in the drop-down menu have a numeric value assigned to them (37–41). This number corresponds to each record's specific ID, as contained in the Catalog table of the *Music.mdb* database. Figure 9.4 shows this table.

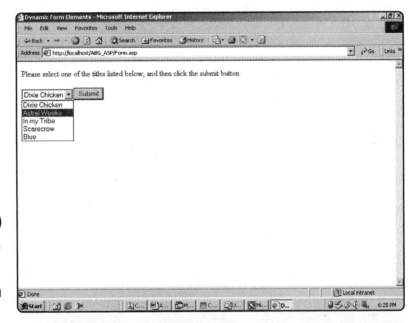

FIGURE 9.3

A typical drop-down menu form element populated with five titles, each assigned a specific value.

FIGURE 9.4

The Catalog table of the *Music.mdb* database. Note the ID field for each highlighted entry.

Although it is possible to list each of these items statically within the HTML itself (in other words, to have this specific information contained directly within the HMTL), it is more practical and secure and, generally, better programming to read this information from a database. That way, if you want to update or change it later, all you have to worry about is changing the source of the information. All the Web pages that read or manipulate this information can stay intact.

Listing 9.5 is an example of how this information can be read directly from the database, with each of the items in the drop-down menu dynamically populated, based on that information.

Listing 9.5 Form.asp

```
<html>
<head>
<title>Dynamic Form Elements</title>
</head>
<body>
<%
Set Catalog=Server.CreateObject("ADODB.Recordset")
Catalog.open "SELECT * FROM Catalog WHERE ID > 36 AND ID < 42", "DSN=Music"
%>
<p>Please select one of the titles listed below, and then click the
Submit button:</p>
<form method="POST" action="TitleChoice.asp">
<p><select size="1" name="Choice">
<%
DO WHILE not Catalog.EOF
%>
<option value="<%=Catalog("ID")%>"><%=Catalog("Title")%></option>
<%
Catalog.MoveNext
Loop
Catalog.Close
Set Catalog=Nothing
%>
</select><input type="submit" value="Submit" name="B1"></p>
</form>
</body>
</html>
```

When this code executes, the same result shown in Figure 9.3 is displayed in the Web browser: a drop-down menu presenting five options. However, note that in Listing 9.5, the drop-down menu and each of the five selections are dynamically read and defined in the following line:

```
<option value="<%=Catalog("ID")%>"><%=Catalog("Title")%></option>
```

Using ADO techniques you learned in Chapter 5, the ID and Title values are read from the Catalog query. Because you also are using a DO...WHILE loop (to loop through each of

FIGURE 9.5

Although the HTML sent to the browser appears the same, integrating the page with a database enables you to define and generate these form elements dynamically, as well as other material on your page.

```
Form[1] - Notepad
File  Edit  Format  Help
<html>
<head>
<title>Dynamic Form Elements</title>
</head>
<body>

<p>Please select one of the titles listed below, and then click the
submit button:</p>
<form method="POST" action="TitleChoice.asp">
<p><select size="1" name="Choice">

<option value="37">Dixie Chicken</option>

<option value="38">Astral Weeks</option>

<option value="39">In My Tribe</option>

<option value="40">Scarecrow</option>

<option value="41">Blue</option>

    </select><input type="submit" value="submit" name="B1"></p>
</form>
</body>
</html>
```

the records returned from the SQL query), the five options are built on-the-fly, thus eliminating the need to hard-code (that is, include within the page itself) these values. If you look at the source code for this page after it loads within your Web browser, you can see that both the ID and Title values for each of the five records have been defined (see Figure 9.5).

Creating Dynamic Hyperlinks and QueryStrings

Aside from dynamically generating form elements via data queried from a database, it is also beneficial to use this on-the-fly HTML creation with hyperlinks and QueryStrings. In this section, I'll show you how to do just that.

TRICK

All the techniques described in this chapter are particularly useful when you are providing customized responses to user requests on your Web pages. For example, imagine that you own a small business and develop a Web site to market and sell your goods or services. Rather than present every user with your entire inventory, you offer a form where users can search through your catalog, based on specific criteria. Then you use this information to query your database and return only the items in which they are interested. This type of customized Web design is central to presenting the most functional and easiest-to-use Web site and also enables you to make efficient use of your databases (where most of your information is likely stored).

Creating dynamic hyperlinks and QueryStrings works very much like the other dynamic content creation so far in this chapter. It's a matter of integrating the VBScript that generates the dynamic content directly within your standard HTML. Whether this be within the tags for a table, form, or hyperlink, you should take advantage of this powerful technique to make your code simpler to understand and manage.

Take a look at Listing 9.6 for an example of how you can dynamically create hyperlinks based (again) on a database query.

Listing 9.6 Hyperlink.asp

```
<html>
<head>
<title>Dynamically created hyperlinks and querystrings</title>
</head>
<body>
<%
Set Catalog=Server.CreateObject("ADODB.Recordset")
Catalog.open "SELECT * FROM Catalog WHERE ID=72", "DSN=Music"
LinkName=Catalog("Title")&".html"
%>
<a href="<%=LinkName%>">Click here to view more information about
<%=Catalog("Title")%> by <%=Catalog("Artist")%></a>
</body>
</html>
```

When this code is executed within a Web browser, it looks like Figure 9.6.

In Figure 9.6, within the status bar, note that the URL for this hyperlink is the name of the particular CD (in this case, *Songs in the Key of Life*) followed by the *.html* extension. This hyperlink was defined within the following line:

```
LinkName=Catalog("Title")&".html"
```

The variable LinkName is defined and given the value of the Title field as returned from the Catalog query, plus the *.html* extension. Again, this type of dynamic creation of

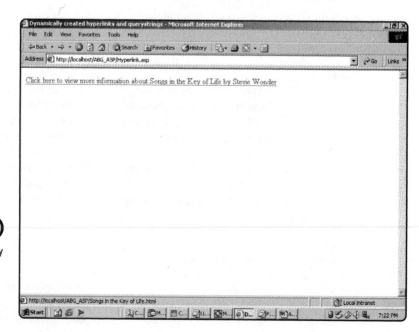

FIGURE 9.6

You can dynamically create hyperlinks just as you can other database-driven information.

information is far more efficient and practical and (ultimately) easier to manipulate than static or hard-coded information.

You can do similar things with QueryStrings as well. Consider the simple form in Listing 9.7, which asks users to enter their last name so that their records can be obtained from a database.

TRAP

Be cautious when assigning values to QueryStrings because some browsers can't handle the spaces that are often present in many values. For example, if you had the following QueryString URL:

```
http://www.someplace.com/Name=Susan Jones
```

the space between Susan and Jones might cause problems when some browsers attempt to read this value.

You also should be cautious in transferring potentially sensitive information via a QueryString. Consider the following example:

```
http://www.someplace.com/Name=Jones?Password=hjdk12
```

This is an exaggerated example, but you can see how this method of passing information can, in some cases, be an insecure method.

Listing 9.7 Working with QueryStrings

```
<html>
<head>
<title>Dynamic Querystring Creation</title>
</head>
<body>
<form method="POST" action="InfoRetrieve.asp">
  <p>Please enter your last name so that we can retrieve your information from
  our database:<input type="text" name="Name" size="20"></p>
  <p><input type="submit" value="Submit" name="B2"></p>
</form>
</body>
</html>
```

This code, when executed, looks like Figure 9.7.

Imagine that on the *InfoRetrieve.asp* page (the page to which this form points—check the action attribute of the form element in Listing 9.7), the information entered by the user is used to search the database. From that search, the following information is returned:

- The individual's first name (Robert)
- The individual's age (41)
- The individual's employer (ABC Company)

Now imagine that you want to pass on these three pieces of information to another page. Say, for example, that this page is named *InfoRetrieve2.asp*. On this page, additional information from the individual's file will be pulled, based on these three pieces

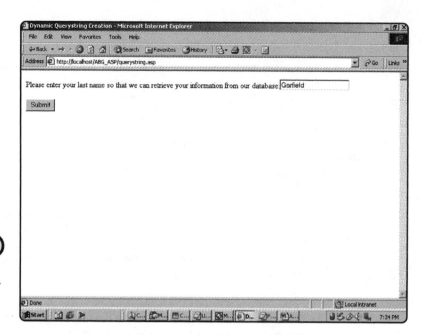

FIGURE 9.7

A simple form
prompting the user
to enter his or her
last name.

of information . You can add these three pieces of information to the URL of the page used to call the *InfoRetrieve2.asp* page, by dynamically assigning the QueryString values, as shown in Listing 9.8.

For this example, I'm pretending that a SQL query has been made to a fictional database that stores the information being placed into the QueryString. For illustration purposes, I have not written this query. In a typical page, though, this action would occur.

Listing 9.8 QueryString.asp

```
<html>
<head>
<title>Dynamic Querystring Creation</title>
</head>
<body>
<%
FirstName="Robert"
LastName="Garfield"
Age="41"
Employer="ABC"
%>
Thank you for the information.  Based on what you have provided, we
can continue to retrieve the rest of your file.
<hr>
<form method="post" action="InfoRetrieve2.asp?FirstName=<%=FirstName%>
&LastName=<%=LastName%>&Age=<%=Age%>&Employer=<%=Employer%>">
```

```
<input type="submit" value="Click here to continue to retrieve your file">
</form>
</body>
</html>
```

When the source code for this page is viewed within a Web browser, it looks like Figure 9.8.

As you can see in Figure 9.8, the first name, last name, age, and company values are tacked on to the URL of the form-processing page. Once there, these values can be retrieved from the QueryString and used for whatever data manipulation purposes are necessary in that page.

TRICK

Remember from previous discussions that you can retrieve QueryString values using the `Request.Querystring` **method. For example, if the URL had a value of** `somepage.asp?FirstName=John&LastName=Gosney`, **you could retrieve the values** John **and** Gosney **by using the following code:**

```
FirstName=Request.Querystring("FirstName")
LastName=Request.Querystring("LastName")
```

TRAP

You should avoid relying too heavily on the use of the QueryString because you can potentially expose sensitive information to visitors of your Web site. For example, consider the following URL and QueryString:

```
somepage.asp?Salary=38000&Probation=Yes
```

Depending on the sensitivity of the information (in this case, salary level and whether the individual has been on probation), you might not want to make it readily visible. This is the major drawback of QueryStrings because they are not a particularly good method of keeping private information, well, private! Therefore, use with caution.

FIGURE 9.8

You can dynamically assign QueryString values so that information can be easily passed from one page to another.

ASP Programming for the Absolute Beginner

Another Look—ASP MadLibs

Now that you are aware of ways to generate and manipulate information dynamically within your ASP pages, you will review the game you created in Chapter 3, "Working with ASP Objects"—ASP MadLibs. You will see how it can be updated and revised to take advantage of techniques presented in this chapter.

As you recall, the game consists of two pages: *MadLibHome.asp* and *MadLibProcess.asp*. Figures 9.9 and 9.10, respectively, illustrate these two pages.

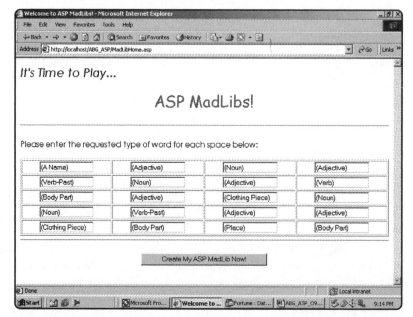

FIGURE 9.9

The opening page of the ASP MadLibs game asking you to provide the required words.

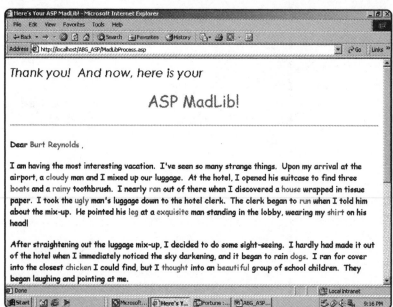

FIGURE 9.10

The MadLib is completed, based on the information you provided.

So that you can review the code, Listing 9.9 presents the *MadLibHome.asp* page.

Listing 9.9 MadLibHome.asp

```
<html>
<head>
<title>Welcome to ASP MadLibs!</title>
</head>
<body>

<p><font face="Century Gothic" size="5"><i>It's Time to Play...</i></font></p>
<p align="center"><font face="Comic Sans MS" color="#FF0000" size="6">ASP
MadLibs!</font></p>
<hr>

<p align="left"><font face="Century Gothic">Please enter the requested type of
word for each space below:</font></p>
<form method="POST" action="MadLibProcess.asp">
<p>
<table border="1" width="100%" height="139">
  <tr>
    <td width="25%" align="center" height="23"><input type="text"
    name="Word1" size="15" value="(A Name)"></td>
    <td width="25%" align="center" height="23"><input type="text"
    name="Word2" size="15" value="(Adjective)"></td>
    <td width="25%" align="center" height="23"><input type="text"
    name="Word3" size="15" value="(Noun)"></td>
    <td width="25%" align="center" height="23"><input type="text"
    name="Word4" size="15" value="(Adjective)"></td>
  </tr>
  <tr>
    <td width="25%" align="center" height="23"><input type="text"
    name="Word5" size="15" value="(Verb-Past)"></td>
    <td width="25%" align="center" height="23"><input type="text"
    name="Word6" size="15" value="(Noun)"></td>
    <td width="25%" align="center" height="23"><input type="text"
    name="Word7" size="15" value="(Adjective)"></td>
    <td width="25%" align="center" height="23"><input type="text"
    name="Word8" size="15" value="(Verb)"></td>
  </tr>
  <tr>
    <td width="25%" align="center" height="23"><input type="text"
    name="Word9" size="15" value="(Body Part)"></td>
    <td width="25%" align="center" height="23"><input type="text"
    name="Word10" size="15" value="(Adjective)"></td>
    <td width="25%" align="center" height="23"><input type="text"
    name="Word11" size="15" value="(Clothing Piece)"></td>
```

```
          <td width="25%" align="center" height="23"><input type="text"
          name="Word12" size="15" value="(Noun)"></td>
      </tr>
      <tr>
          <td width="25%" align="center" height="23"><input type="text"
          name="Word13" size="15" value="(Noun)"></td>
          <td width="25%" align="center" height="23"><input type="text"
          name="Word14" size="15" value="(Verb-Past)"></td>
          <td width="25%" align="center" height="23"><input type="text"
          name="Word15" size="15" value="(Adjective)"></td>
          <td width="25%" align="center" height="23"><input type="text"
          name="Word16" size="15" value="(Adjective)"></td>
      </tr>
      <tr>
          <td width="25%" align="center" height="17"><input type="text"
          name="Word17" size="15" value="(Clothing Piece)"></td>
          <td width="25%" align="center" height="17"><input type="text"
          name="Word18" size="15" value="(Body Part)"></td>
          <td width="25%" align="center" height="17"><input type="text"
          name="Word19" size="15" value="(Place)"></td>
          <td width="25%" align="center" height="17"><input type="text"
          name="Word20" size="15" value="(Body Part)"></td>
      </tr>
</table>
<hr>

<p align="center"><input type="submit" value="Create My ASP MadLib Now!"
name="B1"></p>

</form>
</body>

</html>
```

Also, Listing 9.10 presents the *MadLibProcess.asp* page code.

Listing 9.10 MadLibProcess.asp

```
<html>

<head>
<title>Here's Your ASP MadLib!</title>
</head>

<body>

<p><font face="Century Gothic" size="5"><i>Thank you!  And now, here is
```

```
your </i></font></p>
<p align="center"><font face="Comic Sans MS" color="#FF0000" size="6">ASP
MadLib!</font></p>
<hr>
<p align="left"><font face="Comic Sans MS" size="3">Dear <font
color="#FF0000"><%=Request.Form("Word1")%> ,</font></p>
<p align="left"><font face="Comic Sans MS" size="3">I am having the most
interesting vacation.  I've seen so many strange things. 
Upon my arrival at the airport, a <font color="#FF0000">
<%=Request.Form("Word2")%></font>
man and I
mixed up our luggage.  At the hotel, I opened his suitcase to find
three <font color="#FF0000"><%=Request.Form("Word3")%>s</font>
and a <font color="#FF0000"><%=Request.Form("Word4")%></font>
toothbrush.  I nearly
<font color="#FF0000"><%=Request.Form("Word5")%></font> out of there when
I discovered a
<font color="#FF0000"><%=Request.Form("Word6")%></font> wrapped in
tissue paper.  I took the
<font color="#FF0000"><%=Request.Form("Word7")%></font> man's luggage down
to the hotel clerk.  The clerk began to
<font color="#FF0000"><%=Request.Form("Word8")%></font> when I told him
about the mix-up.  He pointed his
<font color="#FF0000"><%=Request.Form("Word9")%></font> at a <font
color="#FF0000"><%=Request.Form("Word10")%></font>
man standing in the
lobby, wearing my <font color="#FF0000"><%=Request.Form("Word11")%></font>
on his head!</font></p>
<p align="left"><font face="Comic Sans MS" size="3">After straightening out the
luggage mix-up, I decided to do some sight-seeing.  I hardly had made it
out of the hotel when I immediately noticed the sky darkening, and it began to
rain <font color="#FF0000"><%=Request.Form("Word12")%>s</font>. 
I ran for cover into the closest <font color="#FF0000">
<%=Request.Form("Word13")%></font>
I could
find, but I <font color="#FF0000"><%=Request.Form("Word14")%></font> into an
<font color="#FF0000"><%=Request.Form("Word15")%></font>
group of school children.  They began laughing and pointing at me. 
</font></p>
<p align="left"><font face="Comic Sans MS" size="3">I checked my reflection in
a storefront window, only to discover I had the <font color="#FF0000">
<%=Request.Form("Word16")%></font>
man's <font color="#FF0000"><%=Request.Form("Word17")%></font> hanging from
my <font color="#FF0000"><%=Request.Form("Word18")%></font>! 
Wow!  I've only been
```

```
<font color="#FF0000"><%=Request.Form("Word19")%></font> for three hours
and I'm ready for a vacation from my vacation!  I figure it can't get
much worse. 
Oh, no!  It seems the stamp I wanted to use to mail this letter is stuck
to my <font color="#FF0000"><%=Request.Form("Word20")%></font>!</font></p>
<HR>

<p align="left"><font face="Comic Sans MS" size="3">Would you like to save this
ASP MadLib to a text file?</font></p>
<form method="POST" action="MadLibSave.asp">
   <p align="left">Please enter a name for this file: <input type="text"
name="MadLibName" size="20"></p>
   <p align="center"><input type="submit" value="Save this ASP MadLib!"
name="B1"></p>
   <input type="hidden" name="Word1" value="<%=Request.Form("Word1")%>">
<input type="hidden" name="Word10" value="<%=Request.Form("Word10")%>">
<input type="hidden" name="Word11" value="<%=Request.Form("Word11")%>">
<input type="hidden" name="Word12" value="<%=Request.Form("Word12")%>">
<input type="hidden" name="Word13" value="<%=Request.Form("Word13")%>">
<input type="hidden" name="Word14" value="<%=Request.Form("Word14")%>">
<input type="hidden" name="Word15" value="<%=Request.Form("Word15")%>">
<input type="hidden" name="Word16" value="<%=Request.Form("Word16")%>">
<input type="hidden" name="Word17" value="<%=Request.Form("Word17")%>">
<input type="hidden" name="Word18" value="<%=Request.Form("Word18")%>">
<input type="hidden" name="Word19" value="<%=Request.Form("Word19")%>">
<input type="hidden" name="Word2" value="<%=Request.Form("Word2")%>">
<input type="hidden" name="Word20" value="<%=Request.Form("Word20")%>">
<input type="hidden" name="Word3" value="<%=Request.Form("Word3")%>">
<input type="hidden" name="Word4" value="<%=Request.Form("Word4")%>">
<input type="hidden" name="Word5" value="<%=Request.Form("Word5")%>">
<input type="hidden" name="Word6" value="<%=Request.Form("Word6")%>">
<input type="hidden" name="Word7" value="<%=Request.Form("Word7")%>">
<input type="hidden" name="Word8" value="<%=Request.Form("Word8")%>">
<input type="hidden" name="Word9" value="<%=Request.Form("Word9")%>">
</form>
<hr>
<p align="left"><font face="Comic Sans MS" size="3">
<a href="http://localhost/ABG_ASP/MadLibHome.asp">No
thanks, I want to generate another ASP MadLib!</a></font></p>

</body>
</html>
```

This game and the two pages that compose it are particularly good examples of how to apply the techniques in this chapter because both pages are very heavy with static or hard-coded text. If the game programmer (you!) wanted to make changes to these pages, he would have to work directly within the Web page code itself rather than simply open a database and make the change there.

You can remedy this situation and make the game code easier to understand and more efficient.

Improving ASP MadLibs!: Integrating with a Database

If you look closely at Listing 9.9, you can see that the HTML to compose the table has been hard-coded into the page. Recall from the section "HTML Formatting—Beyond the Basics" that I explained how you can drastically cut down the amount of code required to build a typical HTML table, by using simple For...Next loops.

You can do the same thing with the *MadLibHome.asp* page and its table. However, you must first create an Access database to integrate with this game. Even though you are probably familiar with the process of creating an ODBC connection for use within your ASP page, here is the process again. (For a general overview of Microsoft Access basics, see Appendix C, "Access Essentials.")

1. Create the database by opening Microsoft Access and selecting File, New. When the New dialog box appears, select Database and click OK.

2. In the File New Database dialog, name the database **MadLib**, and save it in your ABG_ASP directory in the Inetpub folder.

3. You can now begin creating tables within the database. From the Insert menu, select Table.

4. Within the New Table dialog box, select Design View and click OK.

5. Enter the table field names so that your table looks like Figure 9.11.

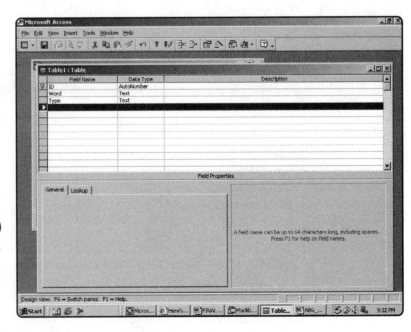

FIGURE 9.11

Make sure that your fields are named and configured exactly as you see them here.

6. Close the table. You are asked to give it a name. Name it **WordInfo**, as shown in Figure 9.12.

7. Open the table in datasheet view, and enter each of the 20 words. For the Word field, enter the number of the word (Word1, Word2, Word 3) and for the Type field, enter the element of speech that each of the individual words is calling for (refer to Figure 9.9 to determine the element of speech each word should be). Figure 9.13 illustrates how your table should appear.

8. Now you are ready to establish the ODBC connection to this database. Depending on your version of Windows, navigate to the ODBC Data Source Administrator dialog box. Click the System DSN tab, and click Add.

9. In the Create New Data Source dialog box, select the Microsoft Access Driver option, and click Finish (see Figure 9.14).

FIGURE 9.12

Save the table using the name **WordInfo**.

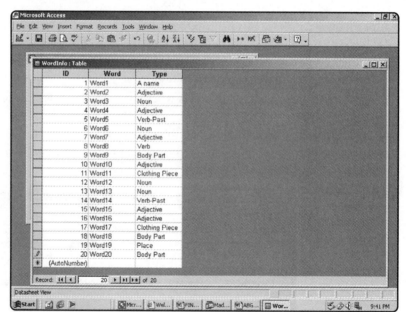

FIGURE 9.13

Entering this information in the database makes your code shorter and easier to change at a later date.

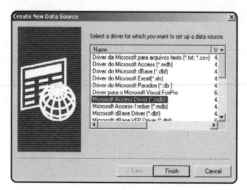

FIGURE 9.14

Preparing to create the ODBC connection for the *MadLib.mdb* database.

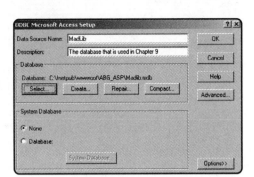

FIGURE 9.15

Configuring the
MadLib.mdb
database so that it
can be accessed
via ODBC.

10. In the ODBC Microsoft Access database, configure it so that it looks like
Figure 9.15.

11. Click OK. Your connection is now added to the System DSN tab.

Improving ASP MadLibs!: Dynamic Page Formatting

Now that the database is created, you can do some things to improve the code on the
MadLibHome.asp page. In the revised code in Listing 9.11, see whether you can spot the
changes (many of which are discussed in this chapter).

Listing 9.11 MadLibHome_REV.asp

```
<html>
<head>
<title>Welcome to ASP MadLibs!</title>
</head>
<body>
<p><font face="Century Gothic" size="5"><i>It's Time to Play...</i></font></p>
<p align="center"><font face="Comic Sans MS" color="#FF0000" size="6">ASP
MadLibs!</font></p>
<hr>
<p align="left"><font face="Century Gothic">Please enter the requested type of
word for each space below:</font></p>
<form method="POST" action="MadLibProcess_REV.asp">
<p>
<table border="1" width="100%" height="139">
<tr>
<%
i=0
Set TableFormat=Server.CreateObject("ADODB.Recordset")
sqlstmt="SELECT * FROM WordInfo"
TableFormat.Open sqlstmt, "DSN=MadLib", 3, 3, 1
DO WHILE NOT TableFormat.EOF
i=i+1
%>
```

```
<td width="25%" align="center" height="23"><input type="text" name=
"<%=TableFormat("Word")%>" size="15" value="(<%=TableFormat("Type")%>)"></td>
<%
IF i=5 then
i=0
%>
</tr>
<tr>
<%
END IF
TableFormat.MoveNext
Loop
TableFormat.Close
Set TableFormat=Nothing
%>
</table>
<hr>
<p align="center"><input type="submit" value="Create My ASP MadLib Now!"
name="B1"></p>
</form>
</body>
</html>
```

Quite a bit shorter, isn't it? However, when this new page is loaded into a Web browser, it appears exactly the same as the original *MadLibHome.asp* page (refer to Figure 9.9). To ensure that you understand how this code has been shortened and improved, take a moment to review the following:

- First, the introductory welcome message is displayed, and the opening <table> tag is inserted.

- Next, a connection is established to the MadLib database, and a SQL query is run to return all the records from the WordInfo table.

- To run through the entire recordset so that each particular record is viewed, you use a DO WHILE loop.

- If you look at how the table is formatted and displayed on screen, there are only four fields per row. To format the table dynamically (that is, so that a new row is inserted after four cells have been placed), you use a simple variable (i) that increases by 1 each time through the loop. When this variable reaches 5, the closing row tag (</tr>) is inserted, and this variable is reset to 0.

- For each column (<td>) of the table, the default value that should appear in each text box, as well as the name of each text box, is derived from the information stored within the WordInfo table of the database:

```
<td width="25%" align="center" height="23"><input type="text" name=
"<%=TableFormat("Word")%>" size="15" value="(<%=TableFormat("Type")%>)"></td>
```

In the section "Creating Dynamic Form Elements," you saw how you can dynamically name and assign form elements. The preceding code is a prime example of how this is done. Both the form element name and value are set dynamically, based on information contained within the database. Note how this technique drastically cuts down on the length of this code.

- Finally, the connections to the database are closed, and a Submit button is inserted so that the information the player enters can be passed on to the *MadLibProcess_REV.asp* page.

Now that you have improved the *MadLibHome.asp* page, see what you can do to the *MadLibProcess.asp* page. Take a look at the revised code in Listing 9.12.

Listing 9.12 MadLibProcess_REV.asp

```
<html>
<head>
<title>Here's Your ASP MadLib!</title>
</head>
<body>
<p><font face="Century Gothic" size="5"><i>Thank you!  And now, here is
your </i></font></p>
<p align="center"><font face="Comic Sans MS" color="#FF0000" size="6">
ASP MadLib!</font></p>
<hr>
<p align="left"><font face="Comic Sans MS" size="3">Dear <font color="#FF0000">
<%=Request.Form("Word1")%> ,</font></p>
<p align="left"><font face="Comic Sans MS" size="3">I am having the most
interesting vacation.  I've seen so many strange things.  Upon my
arrival at the airport, a <font color="#FF0000"><%=Request.Form("Word2")%>
</font>
man and I mixed up our luggage.  At the hotel, I opened his suitcase
to find three <font color="#FF0000"><%=Request.Form("Word3")%>s</font>
and a <font color="#FF0000"><%=Request.Form("Word4")%></font>
toothbrush.  I nearly
<font color="#FF0000"><%=Request.Form("Word5")%></font> out of there when
I discovered a
<font color="#FF0000"><%=Request.Form("Word6")%></font> wrapped in
tissue paper.  I took the
<font color="#FF0000"><%=Request.Form("Word7")%></font> man's luggage down
to the hotel clerk.  The clerk began to
<font color="#FF0000"><%=Request.Form("Word8")%></font> when I told him
about the mix-up.  He pointed his
<font color="#FF0000"><%=Request.Form("Word9")%></font> at a
<font color="#FF0000"><%=Request.Form("Word10")%></font>
man standing in the
lobby, wearing my <font color="#FF0000"><%=Request.Form("Word11")%></font>
on his head!</font></p>
<p align="left"><font face="Comic Sans MS" size="3">After straightening out the
luggage mix-up, I decided to do some sight-seeing.  I hardly had made it
```

out of the hotel when I immediately noticed the sky darkening, and it began to
rain <font color="#FF0000"><%=Request.Form("Word12")%>s</font>.
I ran for cover into the closest <font color=
"#FF0000"><%=Request.Form("Word13")%></font>
I could
find, but I <font color="#FF0000"><%=Request.Form("Word14")%></font> into an
<font color="#FF0000"><%=Request.Form("Word15")%></font>
group of school children. They began laughing and pointing at me.
</font></p>
<p align="left"><font face="Comic Sans MS" size="3">I checked my reflection
in a storefront window, only to discover I had the <font color=
"#FF0000"><%=Request.Form("Word16")%></font>
man's <font color="#FF0000"><%=Request.Form("Word17")%></font> hanging from
my <font color="#FF0000"><%=Request.Form("Word18")%></font>! Wow!
I've only been
<font color="#FF0000"><%=Request.Form("Word19")%></font> for three hours
and I'm ready for a vacation from my vacation! I figure it can't get
much worse.
Oh, no! It seems the stamp I wanted to use to mail this letter is stuck
to my <font color="#FF0000"><%=Request.Form("Word20")%></font>!</font></p>
<HR>

<p align="left"><font face="Comic Sans MS" size="3">Would you like to save this
ASP MadLib to a text file?</font></p>
<form method="POST" action="MadLibSave.asp">
  <p align="left">Please enter a name for this file: <input type="text"
name="MadLibName" size="20"></p>
  <p align="center"><input type="submit" value="Save this ASP MadLib!"
name="B1"></p>
<%
For i=1 to 20
Word="Word"&i
Word=Evaluate(Word)
%>
<input type="hidden" name="Word<%=i%>" value="<%=Word%>">
<%
Next
%>
</form>
<hr>
<p align="left"><font face="Comic Sans MS" size="3">
<a href="http://localhost/ABG_ASP/MadLibHome.asp">No
thanks, I want to generate another ASP MadLib!</a></font></p>
</body>
</html>

Although fewer changes have been made to this page, note the end of the code where, using a `For...Next` loop and the `Evaluate` function, you significantly reduce the amount of static code used to define and assign the 20 hidden form fields.

TRICK You could place the entire ASP MadLib story template into a database and then have it read directly from there. See exercise 3 at the end of this chapter for more on this possibility.

Summary

In this chapter, I showed you various techniques for integrating basic HTML with your VBScript to produce efficient, easy-to-understand code. By looking at forms and form elements, hyperlinks and QueryStrings, table formatting and integration with Access databases, taking advantage of the various functions available within VBScript (especially the looping capabilities, combining them with the power to step through a returned SQL query recordset), you can add an entire new dimension to your ASP pages. When working on your pages and designing your databases, always be on the lookout for how you can make your coding more efficient. Your code will be more functional and easier for both you and others to understand.

EXERCISES

Try these exercises to improve your understanding of the techniques described in this chapter.

1. Dynamically create three tables within an ASP Web page so that you have only one hard-coded set of opening and closing `<tr>` and `<td>` tags. Using loops and other techniques you've learned, build the table with as little code as possible.

2. Design a simple database, and then query it using the ADO techniques you have mastered. Then, pass the information you query from the database to another page via a QueryString. Have the page that processes the information read and manipulate the information stored in the QueryString.

3. Looking again at the ASP MadLibs game, place the entire story template into a new table in the *MadLib.mdb* database. As the game is executed, read and integrate the information from the story template database into the game itself (in other words, program the game so that none of the story template is hard-coded into the *MadLibProcess_REV.asp* page).

4. Go back and look at another game you've programmed in this book to see whether you can apply techniques from this chapter to minimize the game code and make it more efficient.

5. Finally, after you do exercise 4, compare it to the original code. What are the major changes you made? Can you remember to think about these more efficient methods of programming before you write even one line of code? Doing so will save you a tremendous amount of time in the long run and also remind you to plan and sketch out your Web pages (and corresponding databases) before you start to program or develop them.

ASP and HTML Scripting with FrontPage 2000

I n this chapter, you will

- Become familiar with the general interface of FrontPage 2000, through an introduction to its primary features and functions.

- Utilize FrontPage with your Web server so that you can use it as part of a complete Web development environment.

- Learn to appreciate how, by taking advantage of its numerous wizards and other automated features, FrontPage can significantly cut the time you spend on mundane or routine tasks involved with ASP programming.

- Review the ADO/SQL examples you worked through in Chapter 5, "Database Access with ADO," via the FrontPage 2000 Database Results Wizard.

As you know, Active Server Pages is a Microsoft convention. That said, it should come as no surprise that other Microsoft products extensively incorporate ASP functionality. One of those products is FrontPage 2000, the very popular HTML editing application that, because of its functionality and ease of use, is popular with both beginning and advanced Web developers. Although I want you to avoid using an application like FrontPage for this book (to get a more effective, hands-on tutorial of ASP programming), you should be aware of the tremendous time-saving attributes of programming with an HTML editor such as this. When you are comfortable with the foundations of programming, by hand-coding everything yourself, you can move to an HTML editor to help with much of the grunt work or otherwise routine tasks of Web development.

Building a FrontPage Web

A *FrontPage Web* is a folder for storing all your Web pages and related elements. However, in addition to the usual Windows folders, you can apply other properties to a FrontPage Web as you allow the contents of the Web to be accessed (via a Web server, such as the Personal Web Server or Internet Information Server) using a browser.

You should think of building a Web as step Numero Uno because you can, from the start, keep everything organized. Now you will start a deeper exploration of FrontPage by building a Web.

Naming a FrontPage Web

If FrontPage isn't running on your machine, start it now.

When the application starts, follow these steps to create your first FrontPage Web:

1. From the File menu, select New, Web (see Figure 10.1).
2. You are now presented with the New dialog box (see Figure 10.2). For now, select One Page Web, but don't click OK just yet.
3. Take a look in Figure 10.2 at the drop-down menu under Specify the Location of the New Web in the Options section. Depending on your machine (and on whether you are connected to a network or have used a previous version of FrontPage on your machine before upgrading to FrontPage 2000), the options presented here can differ. However, you want to create your Web in the home directory of either the Personal Web Server (PWS) or Internet Information Server (IIS), whichever you have running on your computer.

FIGURE 10.1

Beginning the new FrontPage Web creation process.

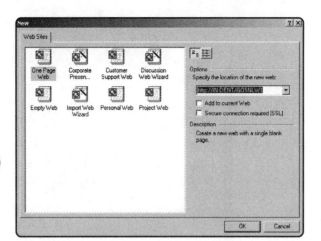

FIGURE 10.2

Selecting One Page
Web. Take note of
the location of the
new Web.

4. What's the home directory of your server? You can find the address of your home page via the Personal Web Manager opening dialog box (see Figure 10.3).

5. After you select your home page URL from the drop-down menu, click the drop-down menu field, and add the following to the home URL:

/ABG_FP

The New dialog box should now look like Figure 10.4.

6. Click OK. You should see the Create New Web dialog as your new Web is created, in the location you specified.

7. Congratulations! You've just created your first FrontPage Web. You should now be looking at the FrontPage editor in Page view, with the Folder List pane displaying your new Web (see Figure 10.5).

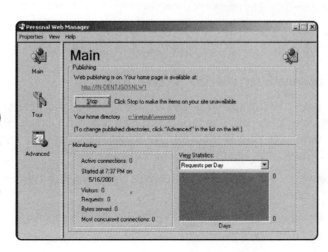

FIGURE 10.3

You can see the URL
of the PWS home
page, as well as
your home directory,
from the Personal
Web Manager
home page.

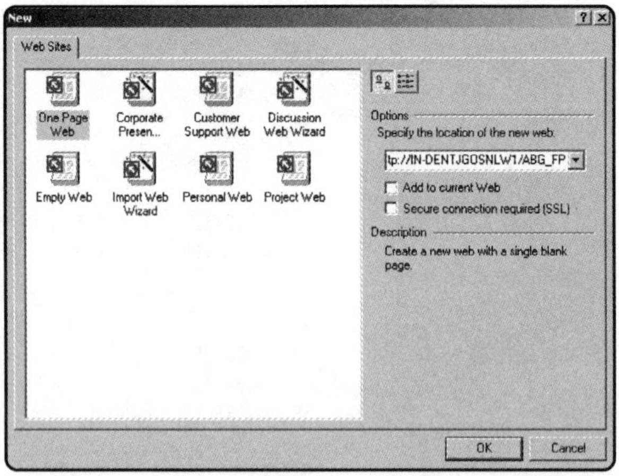

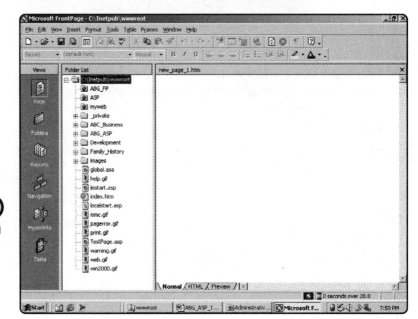

FIGURE 10.4

Specifying the exact location of your new FrontPage Web.

FIGURE 10.5

Your newly created FrontPage Web. If you don't see the folders, select Folders from the View menu.

Adding New Pages to Your Web

Now that you have a brand-spanking-new FrontPage Web, you need to add some Web pages. Adding a new Web page to a FrontPage Web is done in exactly the same fashion as creating a new page that is placed in another folder on your computer (or on a floppy disk, ZIP drive, and so on) rather than inside a Web.

When your new Web was created, a blank Web page was also created. Save this page into your Web, giving it a name in the process:

1. From the File menu, select Save As. This opens the Save As dialog box (see Figure 10.6).

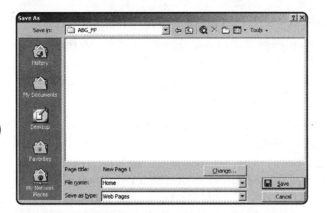

FIGURE 10.6

Setting the parameters for saving a page into your Web.

2. In the File Name field, type **Home**. Also, take a moment to notice in which directory you are saving this page; the Save In drop-down menu should be displaying your newly created Web.

3. For now, leave the Save as Type field set to the default Web Pages option.

4. Click Save. Your page is saved into your Web directory (in this case, ABG_FP) with the name you specified (in this example, *Home*).

TRICK

You will notice that the default extension that FrontPage adds to all Web pages (when you try to save them) is *.htm*. Obviously, you know by this point that you need to store your Active Server Pages with the *.asp* extension. However, for straight HTML pages, you can also save them with the usual *.html* extension (in other words, there is no functional difference between *.htm* and *.html*). The main point here is to pay close attention to what you are naming your pages, not just in regard to the extension but the actual name, too (the more descriptive the name, the better: just try—for simplicity's sake—to keep the names of your pages as small as possible).

NETSCAPE NAVIGATOR OR INTERNET EXPLORER?

In case you haven't noticed, FrontPage 2000 is a Microsoft product. You need to be aware that although the application is extremely powerful and easy to use, the Web pages you develop within FrontPage are intended (well, intended by Microsoft, anyway) to be displayed using Microsoft's Web browser, Internet Explorer.

Now, this doesn't mean that Netscape Navigator won't display pages created in FrontPage. In fact, nothing could be further from the truth. However, as you move through the functions and features of FrontPage, you need to know that some of the nifty effects you can add to your Web pages (from within FrontPage, that is) will display only if your visitors are using Internet Explorer as their browser.

Fortunately, most of these features are simply window dressing. In other words, you don't have to be concerned that you will lose major functionality if Netscape Navigator is your customers' browser of choice. For example, you can still database-enable your Webs without worrying about this browser conundrum.

FrontPage 2000 Basics

To understand FrontPage 2000 best, take a moment to review its general interface, illustrated in Figure 10.7.

When FrontPage opens, you are immediately placed in Page view. What are the different views, and what do they mean?

Take another look at Figure 10.7, along the left side of the screen. The icons running horizontally (Page, Folders, Reports) represent the different views you can work in within FrontPage:

- **Page view.** This is the default view in which FrontPage places you upon first launching the program. Like a blank Word document, Page view represents a blank Web page. You can think of the large white space as your Web canvas because you can place Web elements (form elements, text, and so on) right into this space.

  There are three specific view tabs within Page view: Normal, HTML, and Preview. Just take note of them now, because I discuss these in more detail when you create your first Web page.

- **Folders view.** As you create Webs in FrontPage, you organize the Web pages that make up the site into folders. The Folders view allows you to get a snapshot of this organization, including the (file) size of your Web pages, the date they were last modified, and so on.

- **Reports view.** This gives a more specific analysis of your Web site's content, from an administrative viewpoint. For example, from within Reports view, you can take note of Web pages that don't have any hyperlinks to them, pages that are slow(er) to load in a Web browser, and other related functions.

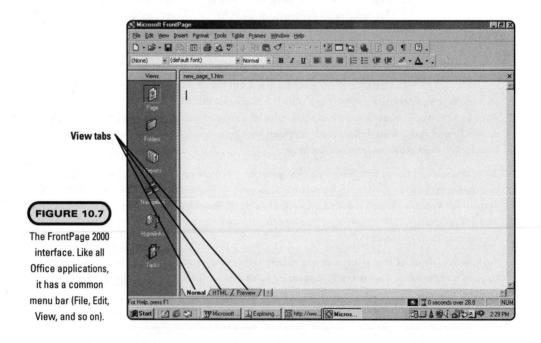

View tabs

FIGURE 10.7

The FrontPage 2000 interface. Like all Office applications, it has a common menu bar (File, Edit, View, and so on).

- **Navigation view.** This view allows you to add navigation elements quickly to the various Web pages within your site.

- **Hyperlinks view.** Just as you wouldn't think of taking a cross-country trip without a good map or atlas, you shouldn't have to design your Web site without a way of seeing, at a glance, its overall structure. In this view, you can see all the hyperlinks between your pages. This picture of your Web site is presented graphically, which makes it easy to see which pages link to other pages.

- **Tasks view.** Usually, building a Web site is a team effort because several individuals with different areas of expertise are called on to design one or more features or areas of the Web site. FrontPage is equipped with this functionality to assign and track tasks to specific individuals, to facilitate a team effort approach in building a Web site. The Tasks view displays this type of information, including to whom a specific task was assigned, its priority, and when it is due to be completed. Because you are flying solo here in your Web development endeavors, I won't discuss Tasks view in much detail.

Feeling confused about all these views? Don't let the view conundrum concern you. The vast majority of the time, you will be working exclusively in Page view. As a matter of fact, think of the other views as administrative views (which in reality they are), placed within FrontPage to help you quickly view your site's organizational structure.

Creating Your First Web Page

Because you have FrontPage open, you might as well create your first Web page, right?

For this exercise, you are going to construct a basic home page for a fictitious company. Don't worry if, after completing this section, your work doesn't quite, ah, make the grade. The point of this session is to get you comfortable working within the FrontPage environment, as well as with the toolsets available to you for Web page creation.

Placing and Formatting Text

If you have FrontPage running now on your computer (if you don't, start the application so that you can follow along with the discussion), you will note that the formatting toolbar is very similar to what you see in other Office applications (see Figure 10.8).

 TRICK Can't see the formatting toolbar? It might be hidden. From the FrontPage menu, click View, and select the Toolbars option. On the list of toolbars that appears, make sure that Formatting is selected.

To familiarize yourself with formatting text in FrontPage, here is a simple formatting exercise:

1. The first text you want to appear on the page is the name of your company. You want to center the name of your company, so click the center icon on the formatting toolbar. Notice how the cursor moves to the center of the page.

2. Change the font and font size. From the font menu, select a style that appeals to you. For the font size, select 14 point.

Font
Style
Font size
Formatting toolbar
Text alignment
Numbering
Bullets
Text indent
Highlight color
Font color

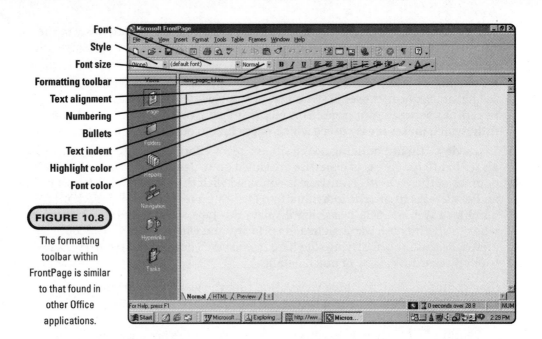

FIGURE 10.8

The formatting toolbar within FrontPage is similar to that found in other Office applications.

3. To give your company name more emphasis, bold the text you are about to type by clicking the bold icon. Also, select a color for the text by clicking the font color icon.

4. Type the name of your company (see Figure 10.9). Take some time to experiment with different font styles, sizes, and colors.

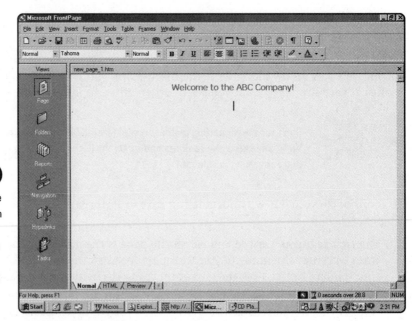

FIGURE 10.9

An example of some simple formatting. In this example, I've chosen the Tahoma font style, 14 point, bold, centered, and with a font color of green.

Got the idea with formatting text? If you've done any work within Microsoft Word (or any other word processing application), formatting text is probably second nature. FrontPage is no different.

Inserting Graphics

The most visually appealing Web sites are the ones that make good use of graphics.

However, you must temper your desire to go wild with graphic placement, keeping the following important tips in mind:

- Most importantly, graphics (as compared to text) can take a longer time to download. You've probably surfed the Web and come across a site that seemed to take forever to download to your browser because of an excessive use of graphics. Keep this in mind when using graphics on your site: If a site takes a long time to load, visitors will move on. Don't let this happen to your Web site because you've placed too many graphics in your pages.

- Be savvy when choosing graphics because they can give your site a very professional or, if chosen poorly, a very sloppy look. When choosing graphics, keep in mind the general tone you are attempting to set with your Web site. If, for example, you are creating a Web site for a daycare center, it would be perfectly appropriate to have graphics of cartoon children, animals, and so on, on your site. However, these types of graphics would be inappropriate (and give the wrong impression) if the business is not a daycare. Choose wisely.

- Finally (and perhaps most importantly, especially if you are not an artist), don't frustrate yourself—and waste valuable time—by trying to design your own graphics. Literally millions of graphics, ranging from static images to animated GIFs, are available for your free use. Some of these can be found on your own computer in the form of clip art, and others can be downloaded from the Web. Take advantage of this valuable creative resource.

TRAP

As I've said, all Web designers learn from studying the work of others. This is one of the great community aspects of the Web. However, if you are going to use a graphic (or any Web element, for that matter) designed or programmed by others, be sure that you have their permission to do so, and cite them as the creator of the work if they require it.

Now, why don't you experiment with adding some graphics to your Web page. FrontPage has several options for inserting available graphics, so you will explore a few of them here:

1. From the preceding exercise, you should have the name of your company nicely formatted at the center of your page. (If you don't, that's okay. All these early exercises are designed just to get your virtual feet wet with the FrontPage interface.) Now, place your cursor below the text of your company name, and click the center icon again on the formatting toolbar (if your cursor is not already centered).

2. From the Insert menu, click Picture (see Figure 10.10). When the option menu slides out to the right, hold your mouse button over the down arrow at the bottom of this menu so that you can see all the options available to you.

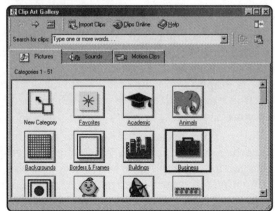

FIGURE 10.11

The Clip Art Gallery dialog box allows you to insert graphics, video, and sound easily into your Web pages.

3. Click the Clip Art option. This opens the Clip Art Gallery dialog box (see Figure 10.11).

Take a closer look at this dialog box:

- Note the three tabs: Pictures, Sounds, and Motion Clips.
- The Clip Art Gallery dialog box has a handy search feature, so if you're looking for a specific type of graphic, you can do a search for it.
- Note the two icons at the top: Import Clips and Clips Online. Import Clips allows you to insert different graphics you have collected on your own into the clip art collection. This is useful for organizational purposes; you can keep all your graphics in one place. Clips Online is a special service that Microsoft has established, where you can download new and interesting clip art directly into FrontPage.

4. With the Pictures tab selected, click the Business icon, which displays all the current clip art on your machine that has been placed into this category. Find a graphic that appeals to you, and click it once. This displays a special pop-up menu (see Figure 10.12).

5. If you click the first icon in the pop-up menu, the selected graphic is inserted directly into your Web page. If you click the second icon, you get a preview of the graphic. This is useful for seeing the entire graphic before you insert it into your page.

6. For now, click the Insert Clip icon. The graphic is then placed into your Web page (see Figure 10.13).

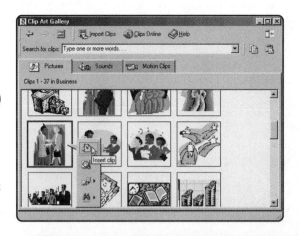

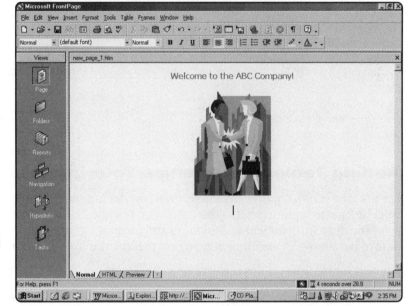

7. When the graphic is in your page, you can manipulate it in various ways. Click the graphic once. This causes the graphic to be outlined and also the Pictures toolbar to appear at the bottom of your screen (see Figure 10.14).

8. By clicking one of the squares outlining your graphic and then dragging your mouse, you can change the size and shape of your graphic. Also, take some time now to experiment with the Pictures toolbar. If you hover your cursor over the icons in the Pictures toolbar, a ToolTip appears, informing you of which action the specific icon executes. Go ahead and experiment with some of the icons in the Pictures toolbar, paying close attention to how they affect your picture.

TRICK

If the Pictures toolbar disappears, you've probably deselected your graphic. Simply click your graphic once to bring the Pictures toolbar back to your screen.

Pictures toolbar

Adding Tables to Organize Your Information

The greatest HTML tag ever invented? Well, maybe not quite that good, but you will quickly come to love—and hate—the <TABLE> tag. The good news is that FrontPage does a lot of the dirty work for you in designing and formatting tables, so you can have more time to be creative in deciding how to best present the content on your page.

The best way to learn tables is to experiment. So, let's do a little table experimenting.

1. Create a new page within FrontPage.

TRICK
You can quickly access recently opened files and Webs by selecting File, Recent Files, or File, Recent Webs.

2. From the Table menu, select Insert, Table. This produces the Insert Table dialog box. See Figure 10.15.

3. For now, go ahead and leave the default values in the Insert Table dialog box as they are. When you click OK, a table is drawn to the parameters you set within the Insert Table dialog box (that is, 2 rows by 2 columns). See Figure 10.16.

As you can see, using the Insert Table command isn't difficult. But FrontPage's table features don't stop with this simple (and, arguably, boring!) Insert feature. Rather, you can format and design your tables—not to mention insert graphics and text into the various table cells—to produce some really nice effects.

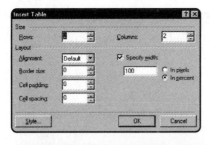

FIGURE 10.15

Accessing the table
features of
FrontPage.

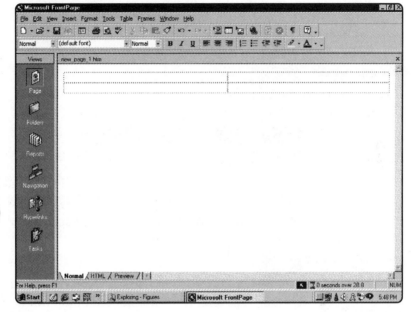

FIGURE 10.16

You can quickly
produce tables for
your Web pages
with the Insert
Table feature.

Formatting Tables

To access the table formatting features, click in any cell within your table. Then, from the Table menu, select Properties, Table. This displays the Table Properties dialog box, as shown in Figure 10.17.

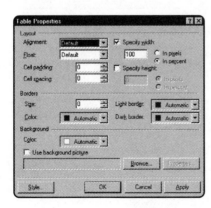

FIGURE 10.17

The Table Properties
dialog box.

Let's examine the different features of the Table Properties dialog box:

- **The Layout section** enables you to set the alignment of the table cells, as well as cell padding and cell spacing.
- **The Borders section** enables you to define both the size and color of your table borders.
- **The Background section** enables you to select images and graphics to use as background within your table. See Figure 10.18.

In addition to controlling the entire table properties, you can set specific cell properties of your tables. You can access the Cell Properties dialog box by selecting Properties, Cell from the Table menu, or right-clicking on the table and selecting Cell Properties from the pop-up menu. See Figure 10.19.

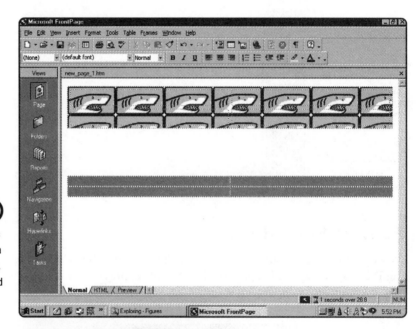

FIGURE 10.18

The first table uses ClipArt graphic as a background image, whereas the second table uses a simple design.

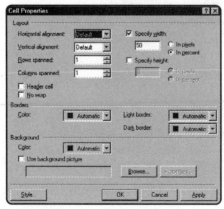

FIGURE 10.19

Use the Cell Properties dialog box to set specific cell characteristics within your table. Note the features are similar to the Table Properties dialog box.

Of course, once you initially insert your table, you can edit it by adding and deleting rows, columns, and cells.

- To insert an element into your table, click within your table, then select Insert from the Table menu and choose Rows, Columns, or Cells.

TRICK You can also add a caption to your table by selecting Insert, Caption from the Table menu. This will place your cursor directly above the table, from which you can add text.

- To delete an element, first select the element in the table. Then, from the Table menu, select the Delete Cells option that is highlighted, as shown in Figure 10.20.

Finally, you can also split and merge cells in a table to produce some interesting table structures.

1. In the table you created in the first exercise, select the first cell by clicking within the cell, then from the Table menu, click Select, Cell. The cell is highlighted.
2. Next, right-click in the selected cell and select Split Cells from the pop-up menu. See Figure 10.21.
3. The Split Cells dialog box will now appear. Go ahead and split the cell into four columns.
4. Next, select the upper-right cell, select Split Cells from the Table menu, and split this cell into two rows. See Figure 10.22.

FIGURE 10.20

In this example, the cell has been selected and can now be deleted from the Table menu.

FIGURE 10.21

Select Split Cells from the pop-up menu, when you right-click on a selected table cell.

The Split Cells dialog box. Here, we are splitting the cell into four columns.

TRICK

In addition to splitting cells, you can also merge cells. To merge cells, select all the split cell elements you want to merge. Then, from the Table menu, select Merge Cells.

Adding Text and Graphics to Your Tables

The table we've created is a little boring. Let's take some time to spice it up with text and graphics, in the process demonstrating what a powerful design element tables can be.

TRAP

As with nearly every element of Web design, tables are no exception to the "Test in different browsers" rule, to ensure that your tables (and entire Web site, for that matter) look neat and well-designed in both Internet Explorer and Netscape Navigator (and, other browsers, too, if you have access to them).

Netscape and IE can (and do) render tables differently. Sometimes, the differences are so small they are unnoticeable; other times, it seems as if you've created two entirely different versions of your table! Test, test, test!

1. Let's get rid of the boring table we have on the page right now. Select the entire table, then from the Table menu, select Delete Cells. This will erase your table.

2. Now that you have a clean slate, let's begin again. From the Table menu, select Insert, Table. Within the Insert Table dialog box, leave the number of rows set at 1, but change the number of columns to 2. Click OK.

3. The table is inserted. Now, select the right cell, right-click, and select Split Cells. From the Split Cells dialog box, divide the cell into two rows.

4. The basic structure of the table is now defined. Now, add a graphic to the left cell (that is, the cell that hasn't been split). Click in the cell, then from the Table menu, select Properties, Cell (or right-click in the selected cell and select Cell Properties from the pop-up menu).

5. In the Background section of the Cell Properties dialog box, click on Browse. The Select Background Picture dialog box appears. See Figure 10.23.

6. Browse through the image files (if you have any) on your machine, or click on the ClipArt button and find a graphic that appeals to you. Your graphic will be inserted in the left cell (in the sample table I've drawn above, the music pages are simple ClipArt).

7. Finally, format the two remaining (right) cells any way you want.

Take some time now to play around with formatting your table. Split and merge cells, add and delete elements, and format text and graphics.

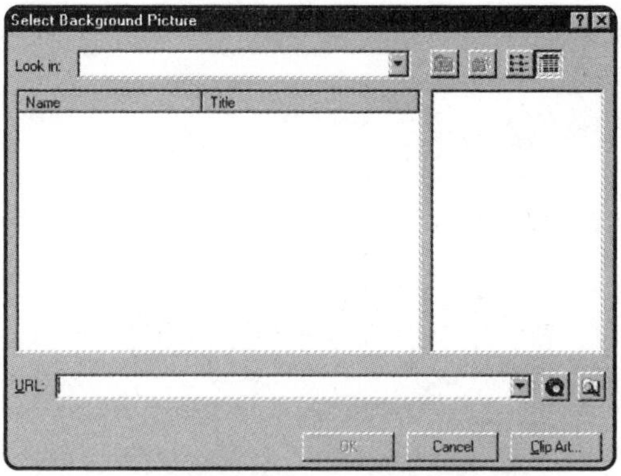

FIGURE 10.23

Either select a
graphic from your
computer or click on
the ClipArt button
and browse until
you find something
that appeals to you.

Chapter 10 ASP and HTML Scripting with FrontPage 2000

Working with FrontPage Components

At this point in your initial Web page creation, you have inserted and formatted some text, as well as placed a graphic or two on your page. Now, take a moment to investigate a unique feature of FrontPage as a Web development tool: the FrontPage components.

You can use the components to easily include some of the more common functionality you find on well-designed Web pages, such as

- **Hit counters**. Are used to visually track the number of visitors to your site. Well positioned, the hit counter can serve as a powerful PR tool, reflecting the (you hope) popularity of your site by highlighting the numbers of visitors who have loaded your site into their browser.

- **Hover buttons**. Allow special effects to occur when the user "hovers" his or her cursor over the button. For example, you could place within your Web page a hover button titled *Song Excerpt*. When the user hovers the cursor over this particular button, a short excerpt of a song (which you would also insert into the Web page) would begin to play.

- **Marquees**. Allow you to have text scrolling across the top of a page, much like an electronic marquee at a professional sports arena. Within FrontPage, you can customize not only the text that appears in the marquee but also the direction and speed at which the text scrolls.

- **Search forms**. Are essential tools for any well-designed site because they allow users to quickly enter a term (or terms) about which they are interested in learning more.

You can view the FrontPage components by selecting Component from the Insert menu (see Figure 10.24).

Now you insert the marquee component into the sample Web page:

1. Click underneath the picture you inserted during the preceding exercise.

2. Go to the Insert menu, select Component, and then choose Marquee from the list of options. This opens the Marquee Properties dialog box (see Figure 10.25).

3. Enter some text into the Text field. (Try to type a sentence or two, instead of just one word, so that you can see the full marquee effect in action.) Leave the other options as they are, and click OK.

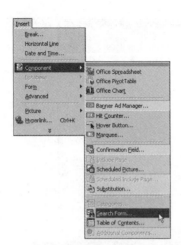

FIGURE 10.24

The FrontPage 2000
Component menu.

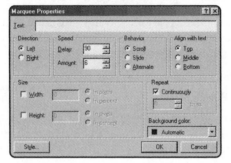

FIGURE 10.25

The Marquee
component
dialog box.

4. On your Web page (within FrontPage, that is—after your page is published, you will see the marquee in action), you will see the text you just typed into the Marquee Properties dialog box. Your Web page should now look something like Figure 10.26.

TRAP

Note that the marquee is only guaranteed to work 100% of the time when you use Internet Explorer. Again, use caution when relying too heavily on these Microsoft-centric capabilities that are built into FrontPage, lest visitors to your Web site using browsers other than IE may experience errors or a loss of your desired functionality.

5. Ready to see the marquee in action? Take a look at the bottom of the FrontPage window, and notice the three view tabs: Normal, HTML, and Preview. Up to this point, you have been working in Normal view. To get an immediate feel for how your page will look when it is live, you can click the Preview tab. Do that now. You should see the text you inserted in the Marquee dialog box scrolling across the screen (see Figure 10.27).

You should note that the Preview tab might not render a completely accurate representation of how your page will look in a Web browser. What do I mean? Not all elements you insert into your Web pages will be immediately visible using the Preview tab. Some elements (including some components, such as the hit counter component) have to be published first to be seen in action.

View tabs

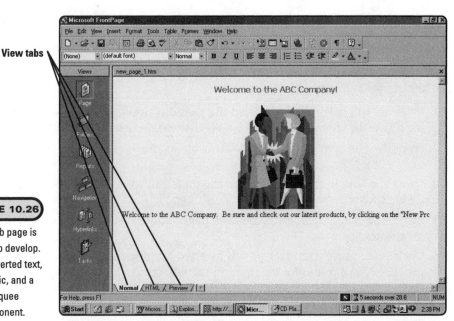

FIGURE 10.26

Your Web page is
starting to develop.
You've inserted text,
a graphic, and a
marquee
component.

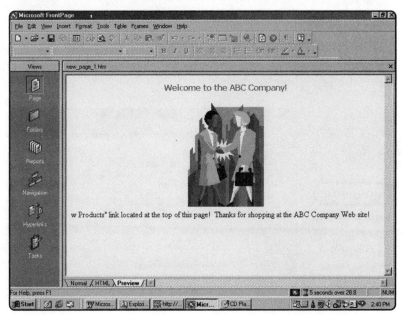

FIGURE 10.27

Your text scrolls
across the page.

This is why the installation of a Web server (again, either the PWS or IIS) is crucial. It allows you a complete development environment on your own computer so that you can get a true picture of how your site will function when it is live on the Web.

TRICK

The HTML view tab displays the HTML code used to build your Web pages. By utilizing HTML view, you can go in and tweak the HTML, as well as ASP code, to your specifications.

Saving Your Web Pages

You've done some significant Web page construction. Like all work on a computer, it is a good idea to save your work frequently, and FrontPage is no exception.

Go ahead now and save your Web page:

1. If you are still in Preview view from the preceding exercise (if your text is still scrolling across the screen, you are still in Preview view), click the Normal view tab.

2. From the File menu, click Save As. This opens the Save As dialog box (see Figure 10.28).

3. Using the Save In field, navigate to the folder on your hard drive where you'd like to save your Web page.

4. In the File Name field, give your Web page a name. Leave the Save as Type field set to Web pages.

5. Click Save to save your page. If you inserted graphics into your page (which you probably did if you followed along in the exercises), you are also presented with the Save Embedded Files dialog box (see Figure 10.29). Click OK to save these embedded pictures, along with your Web page.

Validating Forms

As with many things dealing with Web design, form validation used to be a difficult programming task. But, as with many Web-related tasks now, the use of FrontPage makes things a whole lot easier.

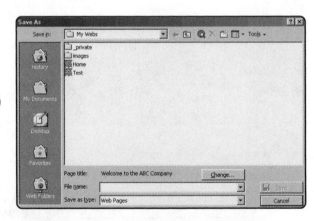

FIGURE 10.28

The FrontPage Save As dialog box. Note the similarities to Save As dialog boxes in the other Office applications.

FIGURE 10.29

The Save Embedded Files dialog box.

In this section, we'll take a look at how you can incorporate form validation into your own Web pages, to be sure you are capturing all required information from visitors to your site.

Determining Required Form Fields

To begin our discussion of form validation, the first thing to do is create a new page.

1. First, create a new page within FrontPage, and insert the form elements so that your page looks like Figure 10.30. Go ahead and save it as FormA.htm.

2. For this initial example, let's pretend that we've determined the textbox field (Enter Your Full Name Here:) to be a "required" field. Double-click on the actual form element to display the Text Box Properties dialog box. See Figure 10.31.

3. When the Validate button is clicked, the Text Box Validation dialog box is displayed. Note that different form elements will display different validation dialog boxes. For example, Radio Button Validation when a radio button is selected for validation. See Figure 10.32.

   This box appears complicated, but in actuality is quite simple to work with. Let's take a closer look at the different types of "validation" properties you can set:

   • The Data Type drop-down menu enables you to set the specific type of data that can be entered into the form element. Depending on which data type you

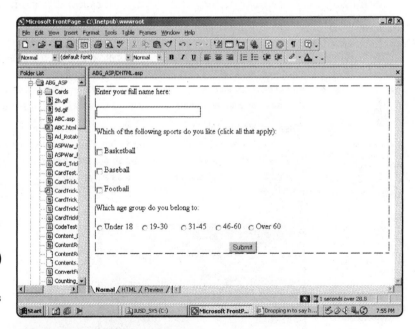

FIGURE 10.30

Preparing to set validation properties on a form.

FIGURE 10.31

Click on the Validate button to display the form elements validation properties.

FIGURE 10.32

The Validation dialog box for, in this case, a Text Box form element.

select (there are four types: No Constraints, Text, Integer, and Number), this can activate the Text Format options of the dialog box. For example, if you select the Text option, both the Text format options and the Display Name will become active. See Figure 10.33.

- In Figure 10.33, we have selected the Text option. This, in turn, enables us to select what type of text formats we'll allow to be entered into our textbox form element (for example, letters, digits, white space, other) as well as the message which will be displayed if the user does not enter information in the form field, or enters characters that are not acceptable.

TRAP

Use caution when setting the Text Format properties of a form element. In Figure 10.33, we have set the Text Format properties to allow for letters and white space. However, if the user were to enter any numbers in this field, or any special characters (such as a comma), the error message would be displayed upon submission.

When setting form validation, take time to think about the type of information your users will be entering into the form fields. For example, if you have a form field requiring a phone number, you'd want to set the Text Format property to allow for numbers and special characters (such as a hyphen).

FIGURE 10.33

By selecting different Data Types, you can access specific form validation properties.

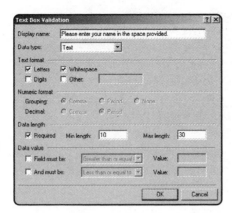

FIGURE 10.34

Setting validation properties for the textbox.

- The Data Length section enables you to determine the size of the information entered into the field. Note that there are both maximum and minimum value properties.
- Finally, note the Data Value section, which enables you to set specific parameters regarding not just the size of the information, but also within a range it must fall (this is especially useful for capturing numeric data).

4. Go ahead and set the validation properties for this form element so that your dialog box appears like Figure 10.34.

5. Save and close this page. Now, let's test our form validation properties in a browser.

Testing Form Validation in a Browser

We can test our form validation properties that have just been set, by loading the page within a Web browser and utilizing either IIS or the Personal Web Server.

1. Load the form page you created above into your Web browser. See Figure 10.35.

2. To see the effect of the validation on the textbox field, go ahead and click the Submit button, with no information entered into that field. See Figure 10.36.

3. When you click Submit without any information in the Name field, you are presented with a validation error, just as we specified in the Form Validation dialog box for this specific form element.

TRICK

Note that the Form Validation message box indicates it is using JavaScript. Through the magic (did someone say convenience?) of FrontPage, the underlying JavaScript code is inserted into your pages automatically—no programming involved!

4. When you created the FormA.htm page above, you set the Text Format properties to allow only for text and white space. Try entering some numbers in the Name field, but enter less than 10 numbers. Then, try entering more than 10 numbers and compare the differences in error message you receive. See Figures 10.37 and 10.38.

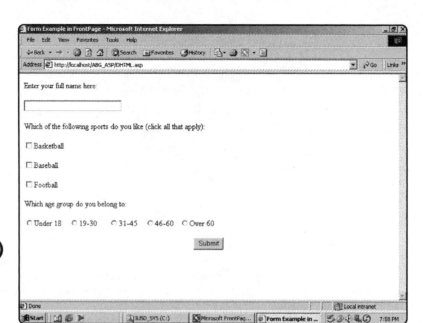

FIGURE 10.35

The form you created above, as viewed in a Web browser.

FIGURE 10.36

Form validation in action.

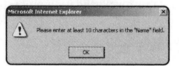

FIGURE 10.37

Because of our specified validation properties, when fewer than 10 numbers are entered, we are presented with the following error message.

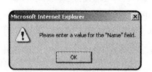

FIGURE 10.38

In this case, we've entered more than 10 characters so we've met that validation requirement. But, because we have entered numbers rather than text, we are presented with this error message.

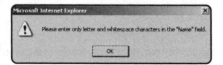

Validating Other Form Elements

You can use form validation with other form elements, too. In essence, they all follow the same principle as text boxes, in that you set specific requirements for the type of data that can be entered, selected, and checked.

Let's take a quick look at the other types of form elements you can apply form validation to, by again looking at our FormA.htm page.

- Double-click on one of the radio buttons, and then click on the Validate button in the Radio Button Properties dialog box. This will display the Radio Button Validation dialog box, as shown in Figure 10.39.

  If you don't select one of the radio button options when validation has been activated, you'll see the error message as presented in Figure 10.40.

- The other useful form validation feature is for drop-down menus. Although we don't have a drop-down menu on FormA.htm, Figure 10.41 illustrates the validation dialog box for this form element.

  The neat thing about the validation features of the drop-down menu is the Disallow First Item. By selecting this, you prevent the user from (surprise!) selecting the first item in the list. That way, you can use this item as an instructional option (for example, "Select from the following list...") without worrying about the user actually selecting this option.

TRAP

Remember, as with other practical and useful FrontPage functionality, form validation will require that the FrontPage components be installed on the server.

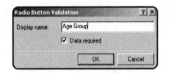

FIGURE 10.39

When you validate a group of radio buttons, you are in essence requiring that one of them be selected by the user.

FIGURE 10.40

Requiring the user to select one of the radio button choices.

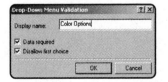

FIGURE 10.41

Setting validation for a drop-down menu form element.

Utilizing the FrontPage 2000 Database Results Wizard

As I said at the beginning of this chapter, before allowing FrontPage to automate any of your programming, you should do things by hand first. This includes general HTML code, as well as more advanced programming with ASP.

That said, however, I want to level you: After you gain a basic understanding of how everything fits together—for example, the relationship between ADO and ASP, discussed in Chapter 5—there is no reason not to use an application like FrontPage. If you've ever struggled with hand-coding an HTML table, you know how frustrating even the simplest of tables can be. With FrontPage (or another application development tool), you can automate this mundane or routine task, moving on to far more interesting aspects of programming, such as ASP scripting.

However (yes, another *however!*), you need to be aware of the downside of this, too. In the following sections, I'll show you how you can use FrontPage to generate automatically most of the code examples you worked through in Chapter 5, including the SQL examples utilizing the SELECT, UPDATE, and INSERT statements. As you work through the examples, you will see the advantages—and disadvantages—in using FrontPage to generate your ASP database connection scripts automatically.

Now you will work through a few examples to learn about the Database Results Wizard:

1. Create a new page within FrontPage, and save it under the name *FP_Test.asp* within your ABG_ASP folder.
2. From the Insert menu, select Database, Results (see Figure 10.42).
3. The first step in the Database Results Wizard is displayed (see Figure 10.43).
4. Select the Use a New Database Connection radio button, and then click the Create button. The Web Settings dialog box opens. Click the Database tab, and then click Add. The New Database Connection dialog box opens (see Figure 10.44).

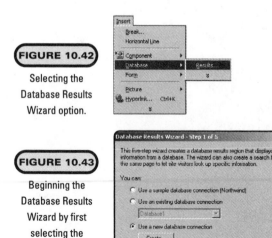

FIGURE 10.42

Selecting the Database Results Wizard option.

FIGURE 10.43

Beginning the Database Results Wizard by first selecting the appropriate database connection.

FIGURE 10.44

In using the Database Results Wizard, you work with a system DSN, which you learned how to create in Chapter 5.

5. In the Name field, enter **DBWizard**. Click the System Data Source on Web Server option, and then click Browse.

6. In the System Data Sources on Web Server dialog box, select the Music DSN (see Figure 10.45). You created this DSN during your work in Chapter 5.

7. Click OK, and you return to the New Database Connection dialog box. Click OK again to be returned to the Web Settings dialog box. Select the DBWizard name, and then click the Apply button (see Figure 10.46).

8. After a brief moment, the connection is made. Now, click the OK button to be returned to Step 1 of the Database Results Wizard. The Use an Existing Database Connection option should now be selected, with the DBWizard selection highlighted in the drop-down menu. Click Next, and you are presented with Step 2 of the Database Results Wizard (see Figure 10.47).

9. Leave the default Catalog Record Source option selected, and click Next. Step 3 of the Database Results Wizard is displayed (see Figure 10.48).

FIGURE 10.45

Selecting the system DSN to which you want to make a connection, with the Database Results Wizard.

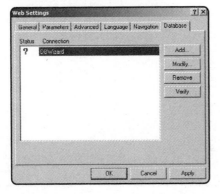

FIGURE 10.46

Completing the database connection process via the Database Results Wizard.

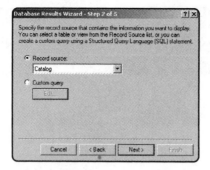

FIGURE 10.47

Specify the record source (in this case, an individual table of the Music database) to which you want to establish a connection and run a SQL query against.

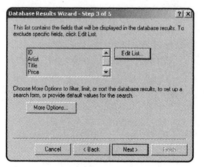

FIGURE 10.48

Note that in Step 3, you are asked to specify which fields from the Catalog table will be displayed when the Database Results Wizard performs its magic.

10. For this example, leave all the fields selected, and click Next. In the next dialog box (Step 4), leave the default selection, and click Next again. You are presented with the final dialog box (Step 5). Again, accept the default selection, and click Finish. Your screen should now look like Figure 10.49.

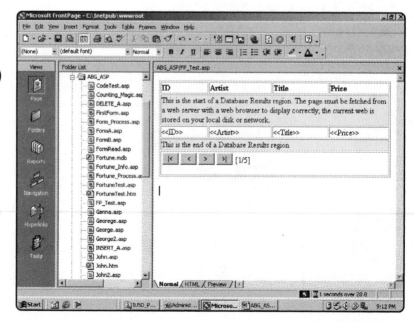

FIGURE 10.49

FrontPage, via the Database Results Wizard, automatically generates the ASP code, as well as a nicely formatted table (complete with navigation buttons) to view the results of the SQL query also generated as you worked through the wizard's steps.

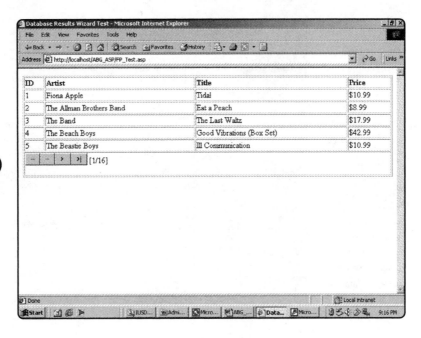

FIGURE 10.50

The Database Results Wizard automatically generates the ASP code that allows this type of interaction with your Music database.

11. Save this page now, and then open it in a Web browser. Your screen should look like Figure 10.50.

Viewing the Automatically Generated ASP Code

You probably have noticed, after working through the exercise, that by utilizing the Database Results Wizard you don't have to know anything about ASP. Also, after coming this far in the book, you probably have formed an opinion of ASP programming: Either you really like it or you are thinking—after looking at the preceding exercise— that the Database Results Wizard is a gift from heaven. That is, you can work with ASP without knowing anything about it.

I hope that your interest level, combined with the instructional nature of this book, is keeping you firmly in the "I like ASP and want to learn more" camp. Regardless, you should be aware of how FrontPage magically allows you fast and easy Web/database access with just a few clicks of the mouse instead of the programming you've been doing so far.

To illustrate this, here is the code generated by FrontPage to make the Database Results Wizard successful:

1. If it isn't still open, start FrontPage on your computer, and open the *FP_Test.asp* page, in which you created the Database Results Wizard.
2. Now, click the HTML tab, and view the code generated by FrontPage (see Figure 10.51).

If you're looking at this code and saying to yourself, "Well, hmm, I see some things in here that I'm familiar with—like SQL queries—but I see a lot of strange things I don't recognize," you are not alone. You are recognizing both the pros and cons of working

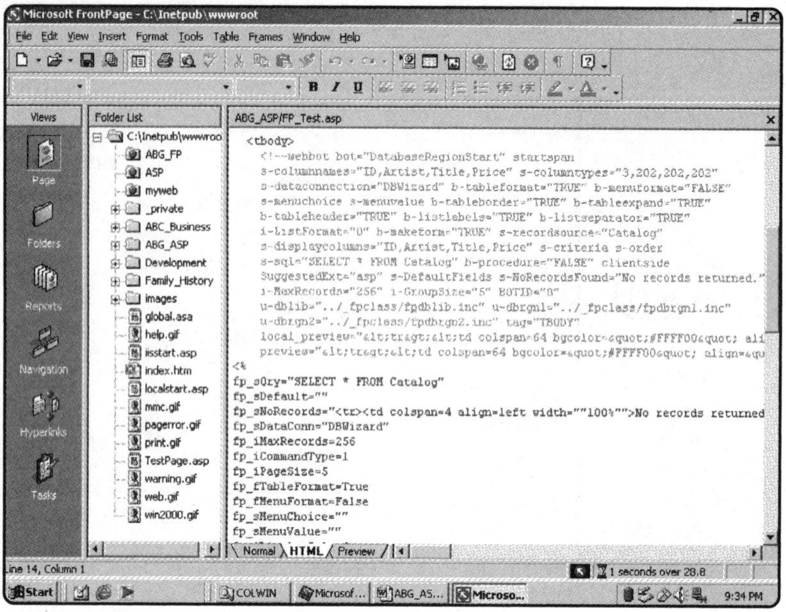

FIGURE 10.51

FrontPage automatically generates significant code to make the Database Results Wizard work its magic.

with this type of autogenerated ASP code. Yes, it's easy to use, and the Database Results Wizard gives you a powerful interface. The downside is that when you try to go into the code to understand and/or customize it, you can run into trouble.

It is for this exact reason that I waited until now to show you a tool like FrontPage and asked you to hand-code all your ASP programming. Admittedly, Notepad is not an ideal programming environment, and, yes, FrontPage handles the routine tasks of Web page development (creation of tables, general formatting, and so on) very, very well. As you've just seen, though, there are drawbacks in relying too heavily on all the automation that a tool like FrontPage provides.

Still, when you become familiar and experienced with the foundations of ASP programming (if you've made it this far into the book, you are well on your way to reaching that plateau), you should consider a tool like the Database Results Wizard. The following sections walk you through a few more examples of what you can do with it. I also show some of the form automation features of FrontPage and how you can use the two together.

Integrating Forms with the Database Results Wizard

In the example from the preceding section, I showed you a very simple illustration of the Database Results Wizard. Basically, you created a simple SELECT statement and then used the features of the wizard to put the results into a nicely formatted table. For the following example, I'll show you how to customize the wizard to bring it more in line with some of the other SQL statements you worked with in Chapter 5, "Database Access with ADO," and Chapter 6, "Using Forms."

For this example, I will first show you how to use some of the form automation features of FrontPage. Then, after you create your form, you can see how to integrate this with the Database Results Wizard. In essence, you will create two Web pages in this example:

- The first page is a typical HTML form, asking you to enter an artist's name. You will be using the Music database you worked with in Chapter 5.

- The second page, the form processing page, takes the information entered into the form on the first page and, utilizing the Database Results Wizard, displays to the user all records within the Catalog table of the Music database that match the search criteria (the artist's name you entered within the form).

1. Create a new page within FrontPage, and immediately save it as *SearchForm.asp* in your ABG_ASP folder.

2. Enter the text, **Please enter in the form field an artist for which you want to search in the Music database**.

3. Below this text, you insert the actual form field. From the Insert menu, select Form, One-Line Text Box (see Figure 10.52).

4. You can now use the automated form features of FrontPage to establish the specific properties of both the form field and the form itself. Double-click the form field to open the Text Box Properties dialog box. In the Name field, enter **Artist**. Your screen should look like Figure 10.53.

5. Click OK to apply your specifications. Now, right-click within the dotted line boundary of the form itself, and from the pop-up menu, select the Form Properties option.

FIGURE 10.52

Inserting a one-line textbox form field.

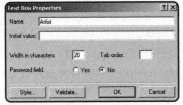

FIGURE 10.53

Rather than hand-code the specific properties of a form and its various elements, you use the FrontPage wizards and dialogs to automate these tasks quickly.

FIGURE 10.54

In the Custom Form Handler, you specify the location (the form processing page) to which you want to send your form data for processing.

6. The Form Properties dialog box opens. Click the Send to Other option, and then click the Options button. The Options for Custom Form Handler dialog box opens (see Figure 10.54).

7. Complete the form as illustrated in Figure 10.54 (you will be creating the *SearchForm_Process.asp* page in a few minutes), and then click OK. You are returned to the Form Properties dialog. Click OK to close this dialog.

8. Save this *SearchForm.asp* page. You are now ready to create the *SearchForm_Process.asp* page, which will utilize the Database Results Wizard.

Creating a Database Results Wizard Form Processing Page

As you remember from Chapters 5 and 6, you can easily create a form that integrates with a database. Undoubtedly, this type of ASP coding will become second nature to you, with a little experience, and your interest in programming will continue to increase. I hope that you will want to continue to hand-code and specially modify your own form and database ASP code.

Still, at times you might want to create a quick form that integrates with a database, without having to do any coding. In these cases, you can use FrontPage's Database Results Wizard.

In the preceding section, you created a simple form that asks users to enter a search criteria; remember, you named this form field *Artist*. Now you would like to have whatever information is entered in this form matched with all corresponding records in the Catalog table of the Music database. You saw some of the FrontPage tools for creating forms and form fields and setting their properties. You will now see how you can easily integrate these forms with a database:

1. Create a new page within FrontPage, and immediately save it as *SearchForm_Process.asp*. Remember that on the *SearchForm.asp* page, in the Options for Custom Form Handler dialog box (refer to Figure 10.54), you indicated that you wanted the form results to be processed on this page.

2. From the Insert menu, select Database, Results. The Step 1 dialog box of the Database Results Wizard opens.

3. Click the Use an Existing Database Connection option, and select Music from the drop-down list.

4. Click Next. In Step 2 of the wizard, select the Record Source option, and from the drop-down menu, select Catalog.

5. Click Next. It is here in Step 3 of the wizard that you will perform much of your custom form and database integration. First, you edit the Catalog table fields that will be returned for all records that match the form search criteria. Click the Edit List button to open the Displayed Fields dialog box (see Figure 10.55).

6. In the Available Fields column, select ID, and then click the Remove button. This prevents the ID field of the Catalog table from displaying in the Results table generated for all matching records. Note that you can also change the order of the displayed fields by selecting them and clicking the Move Down button.

7. Click OK to return to Step 3 of the wizard. Click the More Options button. In the dialog box that opens, click the Criteria button.

8. You are presented with a blank Criteria dialog box. Click the Add button to open the Add Criteria dialog box (see Figure 10.56).

9. Complete this dialog as shown in Figure 10.56. Again, remember that you gave the form field on the *SearchProcess.asp* page the name *Artist* and that you want

FIGURE 10.55

Use this dialog box to edit the database table fields that will be displayed for all matching records.

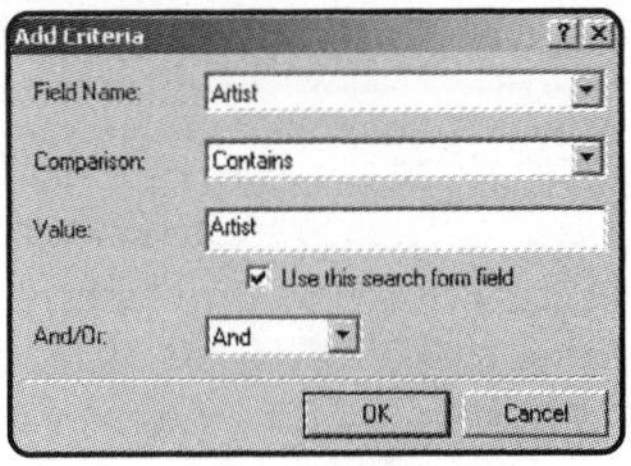

FIGURE 10.56

Use the Add Criteria dialog box to customize your search of the database, based on different factors. In this case, you want to search the Catalog table using the search criteria entered on the *SearchProcess.asp* page.

to use whatever information is entered into this field as a search criteria, looking for matches in the Artist column of the Catalog table of the Music database. The value field in the Add Criteria dialog box should equal the name—in this case—of your form field (*Artist*). Be sure to check the Use This Search Form Field so that the wizard knows that the value you are entering in the Value field corresponds to a form field.

10. Click OK to return to the Criteria dialog box. Note that your search criteria have been added to this list. Using the buttons at the bottom of this dialog, you can add, remove, or modify criteria.

11. Click OK, and then OK again to return to Step 3 of the wizard.

12. Click Next, and then Next again to reach the final step (Step 5) of the wizard. Click Finish, and all the ASP code for the Database Results Wizard is generated, including the formatted HTML table to display the results. Your screen should now look like Figure 10.57.

13. Save the page.

You are now ready to see the *SearchForm* and *SearchForm_Process* pages in action:

1. Open a Web browser, and load the *SearchForm.asp* page.

2. In the Search field, enter the name of a pop/rock band you like. For this example, enter **The Beatles** in the search field (see Figure 10.58).

3. When you click Submit Query, the information you entered is passed to the *SearchForm_Process.asp* page, where the code for the Database Results Wizard is executed. Your screen should look similar to Figure 10.59.

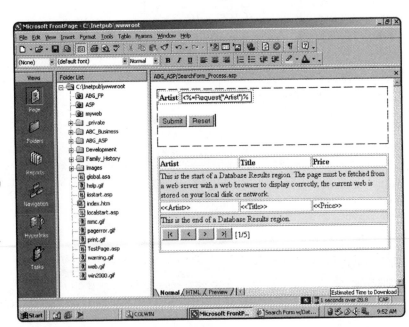

FIGURE 10.57

After providing the wizard with your query specifications, the ASP code and the HTML table to display the query results are generated.

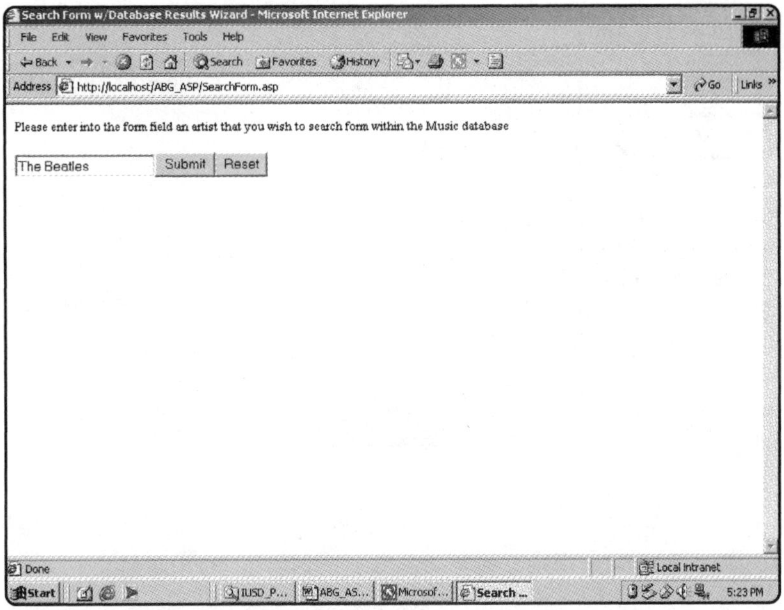

FIGURE 10.58

Using the
SearchForm.asp
page to look for
information in the
Catalog table of the
Music database.

FIGURE 10.58

Using the
SearchForm.asp
page to look for
information in the
Catalog table of the
Music database.

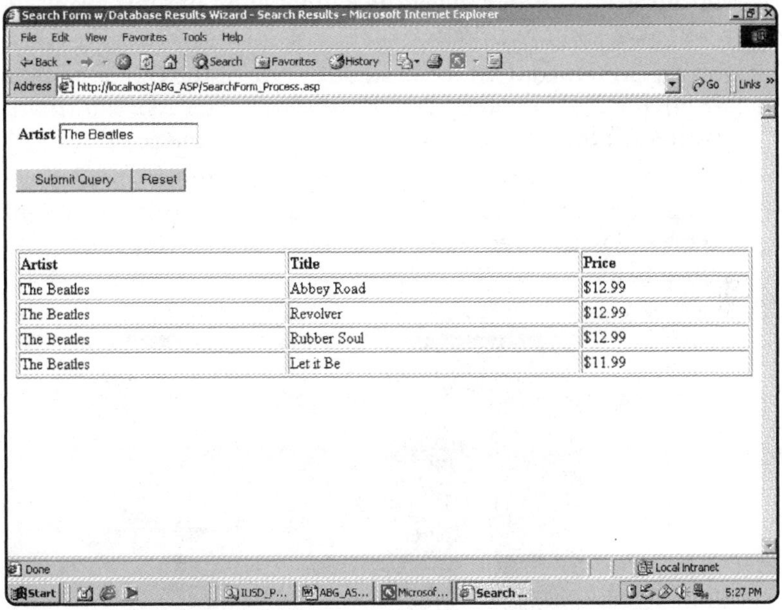

FIGURE 10.59

The Database
Results Wizard
returns all records
that match your
search criteria.

Working with Frames in FrontPage

Utilizing frames within your Web pages is a great way to add style and functionality to
your work. FrontPage offers a very powerful tool for creating and manipulating frame-
based Web pages.

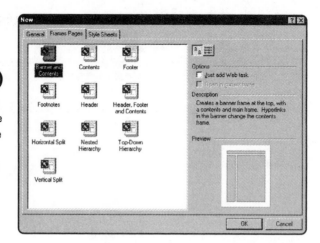

FIGURE 10.60

The Frames Pages tab of the New Page dialog box. Note the different types of frame layouts, and how you are provided a description and preview of each.

1. From within FrontPage, click on the File menu, and select New, Page. When the New Page dialog box appears, select the Frames Pages tab, as shown in Figure 10.60.

2. For this example, let's select the Banner and Contents layout. Be sure this choice is selected, and then click OK.

3. You are presented with the basic structure of the frame. Note that each frame is essentially three separate Web pages. FrontPage asks you whether you want to create each frame from scratch or use an existing page. See Figure 10.61.

4. For now, go ahead and click on the New Page button in each frame. After clicking on each of the three New Page buttons, you are presented (in FrontPage Page View) with three blank Web pages, each corresponding to a frame. See Figure 10.62.

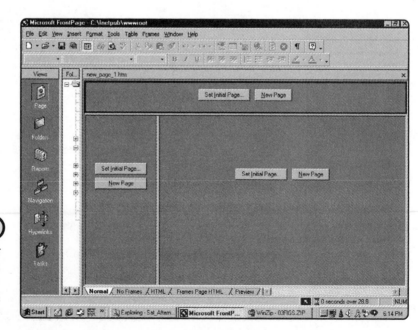

FIGURE 10.61

You can build your frames page from existing pages or create new pages from scratch.

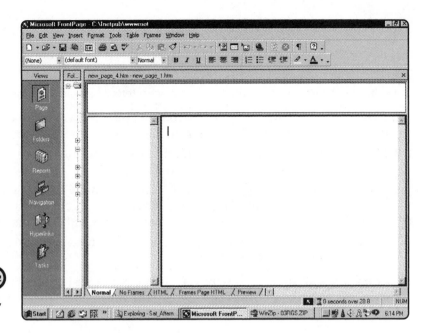

FIGURE 10.62

New frame pages,
ready to go.

5. Note the additional frame tabs at the bottom of your screen. For now, take special notice of the No Frames tab. Remember above when I mentioned that not all your customers might have browsers capable of displaying frames? Well, FrontPage has a built-in No Frames option, so you can construct a "no frames" page to display to these customers. See Figure 10.63.

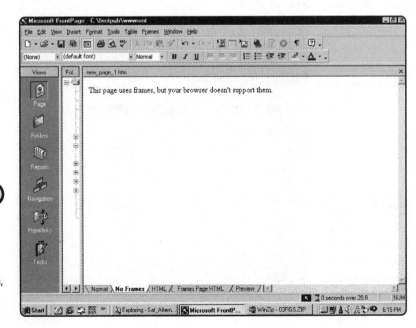

FIGURE 10.63

Use this page to
display special
messages to
customers with
(very) old browsers,
that can't display
frame pages.

Saving Frame Pages

As I mentioned above, building and saving frame pages is very similar to working with regular HTML pages in FrontPage, but with a few unique differences.

Now that we have a structure for our frame page, let's go ahead and immediately save it.

1. From the File menu, select Save As. You are presented with the Save As dialog box. Note how the structure of your frame page is presented. See Figure 10.64.

2. I have decided to name the entire frame page *FrameTest*. Enter a name for your frame page in the File Name field, and then click Save.

3. You are now asked to save the "table of contents" frame (remember, each frame is an individual Web page, so you have to save each page: This frame consists of three Web pages, so you'll need to save each one individually). See Figure 10.65.

   After you enter a name for each frame, you will be taken to the next frame, until all frames (Web pages) are saved.

Now that you have the structure of your frame page saved and displaying in a Web browser, let's go back into FrontPage and explore the unique properties that make up a frame page.

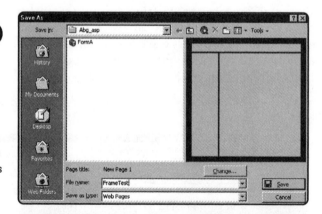

FIGURE 10.64

The first name you provide in the FileName field will be the name of the entire frame page, or the name of the page users will see in the URL when this frame page loads into the browser.

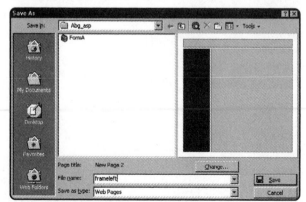

FIGURE 10.65

Saving the table of contents frame page. In this case, I've decided to just name it *frameleft.*

Understanding Frame Page Mechanics

Even though we haven't explored the actual HTML that builds your Web pages, let's examine how it works in relation to frames pages, because it will make your understanding of frames easier.

1. Return to FrontPage, and open *FrameTest.htm*.
2. Click on the Frames Page HTML tab at the bottom of the screen. This will display the HTML that comprises the *FrameTest.htm* page. See Figure 10.66.

HINT When you first began the save process of your frames page, the first filename FrontPage asked you to provide was the name of the "container" page: In this case, you gave it the name *FrameTest.htm*. The container page is, in essence, the structure of a frame page: it sets basic attributes of the page (the width of the scrollbars, the size of individual frames, and so on) and calls the actual Web pages that make up the frame (remember, each frame is a separate Web page).

3. Let's examine the following code:

Listing 10.1 Frame HTML

```html
<frameset rows="64,*">
  <frame name="banner" scrolling="no" noresize target="contents"
  src="frametop.htm">
  <frameset cols="150,*">
    <frame name="contents" target="main" src="frameleft.htm">
    <frame name="main" src="frameright.htm">
```

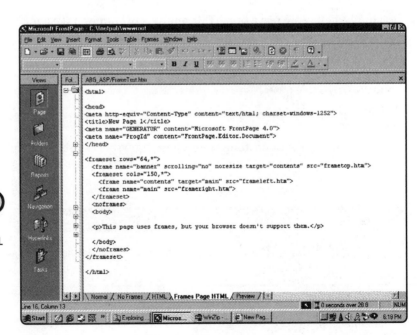

FIGURE 10.66

By utilizing the Frames Page HTML tab, you can see exactly how your frame page is constructed with HTML.

```
</frameset>
<noframes>
<body>

<p>This page uses frames, but your browser doesn't support them.</p>

</body>
</noframes>
</frameset>
```

4. Notice the three `<frame name>` tags: banner, contents, main. Also, notice the `src` of these three "frame names" (*frametop.htm*, *frameleft.htm*, and *frameright.htm*). Recall that when you were saving the frame, you were asked to provide a filename for each of the frames: these were the names (i.e., frametop, frameleft, and frameright) that you provided. FrontPage, in turn, correlated the names you provided with the "frame structure name" (banner, contents, main). So, the following is how the filenames you provided correlate to the "frame structure" names that FrontPage has inserted:

5. Next, notice in the HTML excerpt here the "target" component of each `<frame>` tag. For example, take a closer look at this piece of HTML:

```
<frame name="contents" target="main" src="frameleft.htm">
```

This tag refers to the "table of contents" frame (or, the left frame). The name of this frame is contents, and the Web page represented by this frame is *frameleft.htm*. The "target" attribute refers to which frame hyperlinks will point to. For example, if we place a hyperlink titled New Products in this frame, when the customer clicks on the link, the results of the hyperlink will be displayed in the "contents" frame (or, the *frameright.htm* page).

6. Finally, before we leave our HTML analysis of frames, take a look at the following code:

```
<noframes>
<body>
<p>This page uses frames, but your browser doesn't support them.</p>
</body>
</noframes>
```

Again, most of your customers will have browsers capable of displaying frames. However, for those who don't, the `<noframes>` tag displays a message to these users

TABLE 10.1 FILENAMES TRANSLATED TO FRAME NAMES

Filename You Provided During the Save Process	Correlating FrontPage Frame Name
frametop.htm	banner
frameleft.htm	contents
frameright.htm	main

(in this case, "This page uses frames, but your browser doesn't support them"). You can change this message to display anything you want: remember from our discussion earlier, you can click on the NoFrames tab within FrontPage to access and customize this no frame option.

Integrating E-mail with FrontPage Webs

By utilizing the FrontPage e-mail features, you can turn your Web site into your own personal secretary. But instead of having hundreds of those old "While You Were Out" message forms lying all over your desk, you can configure your small business Web site to automatically send you an e-mail when an order is placed.

How is this done? Quite simply. Let's take a look:

1. Since we've already added some nifty form validation to it, let's go ahead and continue to work with the *FormA.htm* page.
2. From within FrontPage, right-click anywhere within the form boundaries (not on a specific form element, but somewhere between the dotted lines), and select Form Properties from the pop-up menu. See Figure 10.67.
3. First, let's take a look at the "Where to Store Results" section of this dialog. In the preceding chapter, we were using the Send to Other option to specify a page to submit our form results (that is, so the information could be inserted into an Access database). For this example, though, click on the Send To option, and enter an e-mail address, such as your e-mail address. Then, click on OK. See Figure 10.68.
4. What is this rather detailed error message, and why are you receiving it? In order for FrontPage to automatically generate e-mail, the e-mail server needs to be properly configured. So, for this section, you'll have to take my word that this feature really does work(!), even though you might not be able to see a live demonstration on your own machine.

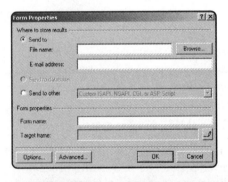

FIGURE 10.67

The Form Properties dialog box.

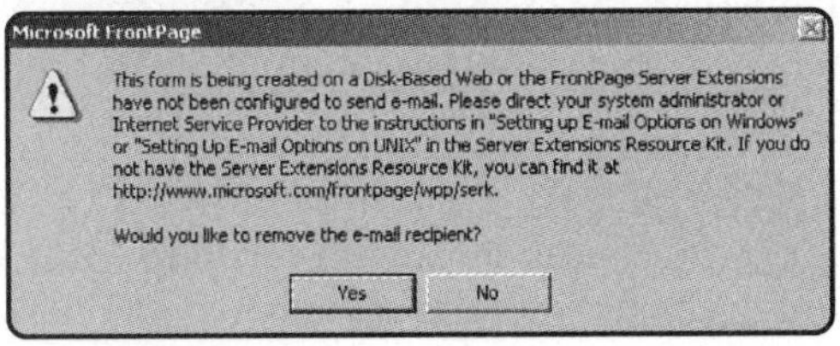

FIGURE 10.68

More than likely, you will receive this FrontPage error message, when you select Send To e-mail address.

FIGURE 10.69

Click on the E-mail Results tab to specify related e-mail features of FrontPage.

5. With the Send To...(e-mail address) option still selected, go ahead and click on the Options button in the Form Properties dialog box. This will display the Options for Saving Results of Form dialog box, as shown in Figure 10.69.

6. The E-mail Results tab of the Options for Saving Results of Form dialog box has a few specific properties you can set:

- **E-mail address to receive results**: the address for which you want to send the message (that is, your e-mail address).

- **E-mail format**: depending on the type of e-mail client being used (Microsoft Outlook, Netscape Messenger, and so on), the format of the e-mail text can have different styles (HTML formatting, formatted text, etc.). The default format is formatted text.

- **E-mail message header**: this allows you to specify the subject and reply-to line of the e-mail. Ideally, the subject line will be indicative of the message contents; the reply-to line can be an e-mail address (again, your e-mail address or your company's general e-mail address) that you want customers to respond to, if necessary.

7. After you specify the properties as described above, go ahead and click OK to return to the Form Properties dialog box. Click OK again to close this dialog, and be returned to the FrontPage editor.

Working with DHTML Effects

The Web is not a static medium. Given the ever-increasing bandwidth offered by such devices as cable modems, not to mention the increasing processor speeds and generally out-of-this-world cool applications that are being developed, we are truly in the digital revolution with the Web as our collective technological flagship.

That said, one of the recent advances has been in HTML itself. Originally designed to be a static method of displaying text (hence the "markup" in Hypertext Markup Language), not unlike preparing a book for a printer, HTML has received some much-needed "active" shots in the arm, through the use of such advances as DHTML, which we'll focus on in this section.

So what is DHTML? This stands for Dynamic Hypertext Markup Language, and in essence allows traditional HTML to come alive through the use of exact positioning of text on a screen, and all kinds of interesting special effects. A combination (usually) of something called cascading style sheets and JavaScript, skilled DHTML programmers can do some amazing things to bring a boring, static Web page to life.

However, you don't have to program to utilize the DHTML effects that are available through FrontPage. Let's see an example of how you can add DHTML to your Web pages, through the use of FrontPage.

TRAP

Despite the cool applications that Microsoft develops, they are not the only fish in the Web pond (they might be the biggest, but they are not the only one). That said, the technology used by Microsoft to implement DHTML in its browser (Internet Explorer) is not the same as how Netscape implements this technology in its browser.

So guess what? The DHTML effects you add to your Web pages with FrontPage may look fantastic in IE, but may not work at all in Navigator (or, they may work differently). Bottom line: don't be the farm on the use of DHTML effects in your Web pages, because they can very often be implemented quite differently, in different browsers.

1. Keeping the "Caution" on DHTML in mind, let's do a little experimenting. Create a new Web page and title it *Cool.asp*.
2. Type the following text: **Dropping in to say hello, this is an example of DHTML,** and format the text in some fashion (I've bolded, changed the font, and increased the size of my text).
3. With your cursor on the same line as the text, select Format, Dynamic HTML Effects. See Figure 10.70.
4. The DHTML toolbar is displayed, as shown in Figure 10.71. From the On drop-down menu, select Page Load, and from the Apply drop-down menu, select Drop in By Word. Note how the text you typed above is now outlined in blue.
5. Save your page.

FIGURE 10.70

Accessing the DHTML effects option through the Format menu.

FIGURE 10.71

Determining the type of DHTML effect you want to apply.

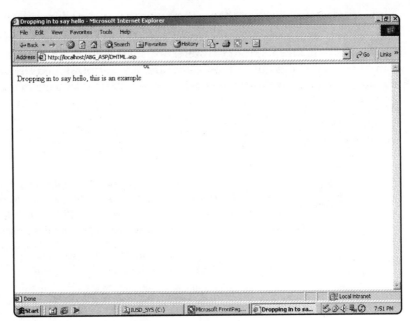

FIGURE 10.72

Your text "drops in" just as you specified in FrontPage.

6. Now, load this page into Internet Explorer. See Figure 10.72.

7. If you have Netscape Communicator, try loading the same page, and see the differences in effect. Instead of dropping in word by word, the entire sentence "drops in" at once. Still a cool effect, although admittedly not quite as snazzy as how it appears in Internet Explorer.

DHTML is fun, and with the use of FrontPage is easy to implement. However, as we've just seen, differences in how various browsers interpret it can result in mixed results, to say the least.

A much better alternative is to use an application that, through the use of a browser plug-in, can produce the same effect regardless of which browser your customers use. Probably the best such application available today is Macromedia Flash: while somewhat difficult to master, Flash can produce absolutely stunning audio and visual effects within your Web page (for a great example, check out the Chrysler Web site for its new PT Cruiser at: http://www.chryslercars.com/.

Summary

This chapter introduces you to FrontPage 2000, providing a quick overview of the application's interface, explaining how to create and save Webs and Web pages, and discussing some special features of the program, especially those that focus on ASP, including form processing and database integration. Although the product has a high degree of functionality and is easy to use, you learned the possible drawbacks of using an application like FrontPage. Specifically, it sometimes relies too much on proprietary technology, supporting only other Microsoft products, so you run the risk of alienating some visitors to your FrontPage-built Web sites.

To Use or Not to Use FrontPage? That Is a Good ASP Question!

This chapter gives you a cursory overview of all the FrontPage 2000 features. Used alone or as part of a group-based Web development project, FrontPage is a powerful, easy-to-use tool that takes the mundane tasks out of Web development and programming—it straight out makes designing and implementing Web pages more fun. Although FrontPage is not by any means the only HTML editing tool available (indeed, other products, such as Macromedia HomeSite, natively support ASP functionality), nothing comes close to FrontPage (and this should come as no surprise) in integrating with other Microsoft technologies, of which ASP is one, and making them easier and more productive to use.

Although this is good, there are some significant drawbacks to using FrontPage in the real world, especially if you are a seasoned programmer:

- Despite improvements in this area from previous editions, FrontPage 2000 still has a notorious habit of not necessarily changing your code but adding its own unique mark on the proceedings. If you recall from looking at the autogenerated Database Results Wizard code, the program adds several of its own FrontPage-isms to your code (ASP, HTML, or otherwise). Although most of this is easy to figure out, it can lead to some real frustrations, especially if you like to have exact control over every element of your programming.

- FrontPage is a Microsoft product and is designed to work best with other Microsoft products. Depending on which side of the fence you compute, this push towards homogenous computing amounts to either tremendous freedom for innovation or just one keystroke shy of totalitarianism. At any rate, you need to remember that some of the whiz-bang features of FrontPage (more specifically known as *FrontPage extensions*) function properly only in Internet Explorer. This is probably the most important thing you need to consider when deciding how much to rely on the automated features of FrontPage. You don't want to spend time developing a Web site based solely on the special features of FrontPage only to discover that it will function in only one browser. Long story short: Test, test, test your Web pages in various browsers (and different versions of browsers) to ensure maximum compatibility.

- Speaking of FrontPage extensions, if you want to publish your Web pages via a third-party ISP, you need to be sure that the ISP supports FrontPage extensions. Otherwise, many special features of FrontPage that make it so easy to use, for example, the FrontPage components, won't function. Unfortunately (or fortunately, depending on how you feel about Mr. Gates and his little company), some ISPs refuse to support the FrontPage extensions as a voice of protest against the Redmond machine. Again, the real story here is to test all your work, know your development environment, and be prepared to suffer the consequences of developing with a special tool. For example, some visitors might not be able to view special features of your site because they don't use a specific browser.

EXERCISES

To improve your understanding of FrontPage, work through the following exercises:

1. Within FrontPage, create a new Web site, assign it the proper access permissions, and name it *MyNewWeb*.

2. Create a page that has several form elements. Place and configure the elements using the FrontPage form tools.

3. Create a page that utilizes the Database Results Wizard. Query the Music database, but this time, create a search form that queries on the Title field (instead of Artist). Make sure that the resulting HTML table also displays the ID field from the Catalog table.

4. In the HTML table created in the preceding exercise, make the displayed ID field a hyperlink. Note that often you will want to hyperlink query results. For example, if you are running an e-commerce site, you might want all returned records from a customer search of your inventory to be directly hyperlinked to an order form.

5. Finally, after working through the preceding two exercises, try to duplicate all the ASP functionality presented in these exercises by just using Notepad, returning to coding by hand. What differences do you see in the code you wrote versus the autogenerated code of FrontPage? What elements or section of the code do you find easier or more difficult to create either by hand or by using FrontPage? Use your answers to these questions to help guide you in your decision as to whether to use a tool like FrontPage.

Looking Back and Looking Forward

I n this chapter, you will

- Get an overview of all the concepts and tools you learned to work with in this book. You can then use this chapter as a quick reference as you move forward with your ASP programming.

- Learn what's ahead for ASP, specifically the Microsoft .NET initiative, and about resources where you can discover more about this exciting, emerging technology.

As the Grateful Dead used to sing, "What a long, strange trip it's been." Perhaps this is the way you are feeling now after 10 chapters of intense immersion into the world of ASP and VBScript. Although strange as it undoubtedly was when you were introduced to new and exciting concepts, I sincerely hope that your trip has been an educational one. This trip should inspire you to continue working with this exciting Web development tool and to learn more about creating dynamic, powerful, functional, easy-to-use Web applications.

This final chapter reviews what you've learned and serves as a comprehensive quick reference tool to which you can return time and time again with your ASP questions. Also, I will describe what's ahead for ASP so that you can glimpse the future of Web development in this area.

Topics are presented in (roughly) the order in which they appear in this book. Note that I've provided specific page numbers for reference to the material discussed so that you can quickly find what you are looking for.

Configuring Your System for ASP

For ASP to function properly, you must work with a properly configured server, one that is capable of supporting ASP. In the Windows operating system discussed in this book, both the Personal Web Server (Windows NT and 98) and the Internet Information Server (Windows 2000) are capable of supporting ASP functionality.

Working with ASP on the Personal Web Server

The Personal Web Server (PWS) is designed to work with Windows 98 and NT (it is called *Peer Web Services* on Windows NT). Although not as functionally complete or powerful as the Internet Information Server (IIS), the PWS can be effectively used in conjunction with your personal computer as a development, testing, and staging platform for your work with ASP before you take it live on a production server. PWS also supports the FrontPage server extensions (discussed in more detail in Chapter 10, "ASP and HTML Scripting with FrontPage 2000"; also refer to Chapter 1, "Preparing to Work with ASP") and is easy to install and configure.

For more information on PWS, consult the following sections:

Working with ASP on the Internet Information Server

IIS is the full-featured Web server that comes packaged with Windows 2000 server, as well as the Windows 2000 Professional client. With IIS, you have a complete application tool that enables you to work with the Web via ASP (and other) applications in a variety of ways.

For more information on IIS, consult the following sections:

- "Configuring Your Web Server's ASP Functionality" in Chapter 1, page 13.
- "Installing Internet Information Server" in Chapter 1, page 5.
- "Confirming Your IIS Installation" in Chapter 1, page 7.

Working with Other ASP-Related Tools

Although a functional, properly configured Web server is an essential tool for your work with ASP, you will also find other resources useful. Specifically, some type of HTML and/or scripting editor comes in quite handy because you need an easy-to-use environment for entering and fine-tuning your code.

For more information on such tools, consult the following:

- "Choosing an ASP Application Development Tool" in Chapter 1, page 18.
- Chapter 10, "ASP and HTML Scripting with FrontPage 2000," for more information on Microsoft FrontPage, an excellent tool for working with ASP and general HTML coding.

FrontPage is by no means the only development tool that supports ASP functionality. However, given its ease of use and direct integration with ASP (because both are Microsoft products), FrontPage is the focus of this book.

Programming ASP Pages with VBScript

As you now know, VBScript is the default scripting language for use with ASP. Although not the only scripting language you can use, VBScript is relatively easy to learn without sacrificing any functionality for this ease of use. Because your ASP pages contain VBScript code, this code is processed on the server, and the results are sent to the Web browser for display.

Although nearly all the chapters in this book contain some element of or reference to VBScript, some chapters deal more specifically with the fundamental concepts of this powerful scripting language. For the essentials of VBScript, consult the following sections:

- "Understanding VBScript Variables" in Chapter 2, page 29.
- "The IF...THEN Statement" and "The FOR...NEXT Statement" in Chapter 2 for general information on essential programming statements, beginning on pages 33 and 37, respectively.
- "Commenting Your VBScript Code" in Chapter 2, page 39.
- "Working with Loops" in Chapter 7, page 151.
- "Introducing Arrays: Why Do You Need Them?" in Chapter 8, page 162.
- Chapter 8, "Essential Programming Logic, Part II," for general information on mathematical, time and date, and VBScript functions.
- Appendix A, "VBScript Variable Reference," for more general information on working with the variable subtypes available within the scripting language.

Integrating Your ASP Web Pages with a Database

As noted many times throughout this book, one of the most popular and useful features of ASP is how easy it is to have your Web pages interact with a database. This allows for an entirely new level of functionality because your pages become *dynamic*, able to respond to and display information based on specific user input.

For specific information on how to accomplish this integration, refer to the following chapters:

- Chapter 5, "Database Access with ADO," which describes the fundamental elements of this type of integration.

- Chapter 3, "Working with ASP Objects," which explains this essential component of working with ASP (a precursor to understanding the power of ADO and how it works).

- The Memory Game example from Chapter 6, "Using Forms" (beginning on page 110), which demonstrates how to integrate database access with other facets of your code, as well as how to accept user information and then query a database (and return results) based on that information.

- Appendix B, "SQL Reference," which provides an overview of the language in which you call and retrieve information from a database: SQL (Structured Query Language).

- Appendix C, "Access Essentials," which describes how to establish and configure basic Microsoft Access databases that you then integrate with your ASP Web pages (if you are not familiar with basic database concepts).

Looking Ahead—ASP+

The Web is in a state of constant change, fueled by thousands of ideas (some good, some not so good) that drive innovation, reinvention of existing ideas, market values, and, in general, how information is stored, distributed, and accessed.

ASP technology is but one tool in a sea of tools that shape the present—and future—of the Web. Like all other tools, to keep up with the ever-changing face of the Web, ASP must evolve or perish.

The Philosophy of Indispensability—Viewing the Web as an Automobile

Enter ASP.NET—or ASP+, or ASP 4.0 (it goes by many names)—the next iteration of ASP technology. As of this writing, the technology is still in *beta* (not yet officially released for public consumption) and is part of Microsoft's ambitious, sweeping vision of how the Web will evolve over the next several years, especially in the area of how information will be accessed on a multitude of devices, not just the traditional PC. As you probably know, *all* kinds of devices—from Web-enabled cell phones to handheld computing devices such as the Palm Pilot—are not essential tools in accessing information on a daily basis. With the ubiquitous nature of the Web in both our private and professional lives, it makes sense that these devices have the capability to link to information formerly accessible only via the desktop PC or laptop computer.

Besides multiple methods of access, there is also an ever-growing need to make the Web a more secure, personalized space. Think of the modern automobile. If you thought (frequently) that your car could break down at a moment's notice and, as you are sitting stranded on the side of the road, roaming bands of highway pirates would steal you blind while you watch hopelessly, you would not be inclined to drive often (or at the very least, any distance). Moreover, what if, instead of the literally hundreds of styles of cars available, you had only half-a-dozen models from which to choose and all in the same color? Again, you would probably feel stifled in how you use your automobile and—critical to how the Web will evolve—how you relate to your automobile. It is not only a necessary tool in your everyday life but also a metaphorical extension of your personality, desires, and goals.

If you think that what you've just read is heady and bordering on metaphysical gibberish, take a moment—seriously—to reflect on how you feel about your automobile. Why did you pick that particular model? Why that color? Also, why did you insist that the car have certain features (sunroof, multidisc CD player, and so on)? More than likely, you view your car not only as an invaluable machine in your everyday life but also as an important extension of your personality. It is this combination—practicality and intimacy—that many businesses (including Microsoft) want to see developed into the Web. For many of us, the Web and technology in general have already attained this sacred place in our lives—we can't live without them. However, for the vast majority of folks throughout the world, the Web is still very much in its infancy. An interesting gadget, one that has gained a tremendous amount of attention, but still alien and possessing nowhere near the status of being indispensable in our everyday lives.

The Promise of ASP+

ASP+ is about to enter the picture with the following goals:

- The availability of information on a variety of platforms and devices, not just the traditional PC.

- To quote a Microsoft press release, a shift of focus from "individual Web sites or devices connected to the Internet, to constellations of computers, devices, and services that work together to deliver broader, richer solutions" so that people can control "how, when, and what information is delivered to them."

- A universal vision of data access.

- Heavy use of XML (*eXtensible Markup Language*), allowing more exact control and placement of information.

- Intelligent data, which doesn't lose any of its integrity when transmitted across the Web and received (and manipulated) on a variety of platforms (handheld devices, desktop PCs, laptops, and the like).

- New levels of security so that data can be comfortably and securely shared.

- Personalization and customization of data (driven by customer information desires), including more control of your profile and how others access your personal information.

- A unified computing environment, enabling users to browse and author documents and information within a single interface.

- Cleaner, more powerful, and faster code, with advanced DHTML sent to browsers capable of displaying such content, as well as regular HTML.

- Extensive controls for both data binding and form control, which provide tremendous precision in how data is displayed within the client. This enhanced integration of the information and the process in which it is displayed or manipulated gives the information a life of its own. It doesn't just sit within your client; it communicates with the entire application structure.

Internet Information on ASP+

As of this writing, ASP+ and the entire Microsoft .NET are still very much in development. However, many developers (of which you are now one, having read this book!) are starting to look to ASP+ as their next tool for Web application development.

For more information, consult the following sources:

- `http://msdn.microsoft.com/msdnmag/issues/0900/ASPPlus/ASPPlus.asp`

- `http://www.devx.com/dotnet/resources/default.asp`

- `http://www-askasp-plus.com/articles.asp?View=ALL`

- `http://www.asp101.com/aspplus`

- `http://www.stardeveloper.com/asp_bk_aspplus_2.asp`

- `http://4guysfromrolla.com/webtech/amb/amb.ASPPlus.shtml`

Summary

Perhaps you are thinking that to stay on the cutting edge of ASP, you now need to run out and buy a book on ASP+. Perhaps you feel that all the material in this book is outdated and you would have been better off waiting for a book on ASP+. Think again. As with any new technology—especially one as sweeping in scope and vision as the .NET initiative—early implementers must spend much time not on the cutting edge but the bleeding edge. In short, there is something to be said for allowing the technology to evolve and work out its kinks and bugs before you invest time and resources in utilizing it as your primary solution. Moreover, you always benefit by having a solid understanding of the fundamentals, which are often found in earlier versions. Then you appreciate what the new enhancements mean and can best benefit from all the functionality they represent. You did a smart thing in purchasing and learning from this book because you now have a foundation from which to move forward into the world of .NET and ASP+. The technologies you now understand (VBScript, SQL, the integration of databases with Web pages, and so on) are cornerstones of ASP, both current and future. Build from what you've learned, and continue to experience the power and fun of working with this ever-evolving technology.

VBScript Variable Reference

Throughout this book, I've shown you how to tap the power of ASP using VBScript. This appendix serves as a quick reference, a convenient place for you to look up everyday questions in regard to VBScript variable behavior.

TRICK

You will discover, as you become more comfortable with ASP and VBScript, that you won't need to refer to a reference like this. Maybe you've already reached that level (if you're a quick learner!). For now, though, use this as a programming cheat sheet while you master the essentials of the language.

VBScript and ASP Essentials

To get your VBScript to perform correctly within your ASP pages, you need to keep the following in mind:

- Be sure that you save your VBScript-enabled Web pages with the *.asp* extension. This ensures that the VBScript included within your pages will execute on the server, sending only the results of that execution to the Web browser.

- Aside from giving your pages the *.asp* extension, you must also ensure that your ASP Web pages are presented (and processed) via a Web server capable of working with ASP. The Microsoft Personal Web Server and Internet Information Server you've been using throughout this book are good examples of Web servers capable of working with ASP.

- To integrate your VBScript into regular HTML, you must place the VBScript within `<%` and `%>` markings. For example, the following VBScript would properly execute in a Web page that has an *.asp* extension and is being processed by a Web server capable of working with ASP:

```
<html>
<body>
<%
TestVar="Active Server Pages"
%>
<b>Welcome to the exciting world of <%=TestVar%></b>
</body>
</html>
```

The following code would not work because the closing `%>` tag, after the definition of the `TestVar` variable, is not included. An error message would be displayed in the Web browser, attempting to access this page.

```
<html>
<body>
<%
TestVar="Active Server Pages"
<b>Welcome to the exciting world of <%=TestVar%></b>
</body>
</html>
```

I've shown you many coding examples utilizing these basic rules. Even though they are basic, they are essential. If you forget to follow these essentials of ASP programming with VBScript, your Web pages will, at best, not function and, at worst, present all kinds of nasty errors to the person visiting your site.

VBScript Variable Subtypes

Remember that a variable is a special programming component that can contain a variety of values, depending on how such values are set by the programming. For example, you could have a variable named *Age* to (temporarily) hold the age of each user as they are listed and read from a database.

Within VBScript are several variable subtypes, including the following:

- Byte
- Boolean
- Integer
- Long
- Single
- Double
- Currency
- Date
- Object
- String

Depending on the specific value you want to represent (for example, currency versus date), you can use these subtypes in different ways. I'll show you how to work with several subtypes in this appendix.

TRICK

Understanding and working with variables is about as essential as it gets in learning a programming language. Also, be sure to refer to Chapter 2, "Programming ASP Web Pages with VBScript," for more information on this subject and for more detailed examples of the information presented in this appendix.

Working with String Functions

The ability to manipulate and work with string functions is a major feature of VBScript. Within this section, I'll show you how to

- Concatenate strings.
- Search and replace strings.
- Compare one string to another.
- Extract strings.

Concatenating Strings

If you concatenate a string, you are literally building a larger string from two or more smaller strings. Consider the following example:

```
<html>
<body>
```

```
<%
ValueA="A good way to learn "
ValueB="to program in ASP is "
ValueC="to read ASP Programming for the Absolute Beginner"
ValueD=ValueA&ValueB&ValueC&ValueD
Response.Write(ValueD)
%>
</body>
</html>
```

When this ASP page executes, the text "A good way to learn to program in ASP is to read *ASP Programming for the Absolute Beginner*" is displayed. If you look closely at the code, you can see that three variables (ValueA, ValueB, and ValueC) have been assigned specific textual values. When combined together, using the & sign (and subsequently assigned to the ValueD variable), the entire concatenated value is displayed.

TRAP Note that the & sign is used only to concatenate strings. If you want to add numeric variables, you can use regular numeric operators (+, -, /, and so on). I'll talk more about numeric operators later in this appendix.

Searching and Replacing Strings

Often in your programming, you need to search for one string within another string. Fortunately, VBScript allows you to accomplish this task easily via the INSTR() function. By utilizing this function, you can determine the numeric position of one string within another string. Take a look at the following example:

```
<html>
<body>
<%=
INSTR("Now is the time for all good men to come to the aid of their
country", "good")%>
</body>
</html>
```

When this code executes, a numeric value of 25 is displayed on the screen. Why 25? Because in evaluating the string "Now is the time for all good men to come to the aid of their country", the INSTR function is looking for the position within the string that the word *good* begins. Starting at one and counting over the specific characters until the starting position of the word *good*, you will find that *good* starts at the twenty-fifth position. If you were searching for the starting position of the word *time*, the value returned would be 12 because time starts at the twelfth position in the string.

Note that you don't have to start at the first position of a string. Consider the following code:

```
<html>
<body>
```

```
<%=
INSTR(4, "My name is John", "name")
%>
</body>
</html>
```

In this example, a value of 4 is returned. You are asking the INSTR function to search for the word *name* and to begin the search at the fourth position of the string "My name is John". Because the word *name* starts at the fourth position of the string, a value of 4 is returned. However, look at the following code:

```
<html>
<body>
<%=
INSTR(5, "My first name is John", "first")
%>
</body>
</html>
```

In this case, a value of 0 is returned. Why? Because even though the word *first* is in the fifth position of the string included within it (that is, the letter *I*), a value of 0 is returned because the search starts at the fifth position. A full match on the word *first* is not found because the *f* in *first* is not accounted for, given that the search begins at the fifth character and the letter *f* is at the fourth position.

You should also be aware that the INSTR function is, by default, case-sensitive. The following code returns the value of 0 for this reason:

```
<html>
<body>
<%=
INSTR("My first name is John", "FIRST")
%>
</body>
</html>
```

If the search string were listed as "My FIRST name is John", a value of 4 would be returned.

 TRICK You can get around this case-sensitive default by placing a *1* at the end of the function, as shown here:

```
<html>
<body>
<%=
INSTR(4, "My first name is John", "FIRST", 1)
%>
</body>
</html>
```

TRICK In this example, a value of 4 is returned because you are telling the INSTR function to ignore its case-sensitive default. Be careful, though, when using this feature! You need to include the start position argument (4, . . .), or your code will produce an error.

Finally, even though the INSTR function searches by default from the left of a string, you can get it to search from the right. Examine the following code example:

```
<html>
<body>
<%=
INSTRREV("My first name is John", "J")
%>
</body>
</html>
```

In this example, a value of 4 is returned because the search begins from the right of the string and searches until, in this case, a capital *J* is found (because you've left the default case-sensitive feature turned on), which happens to be the fourth letter from the right of the string.

Replacing strings comes in handy in a variety of situations. Consider the following code:

```
<html>
<body>
<%
User="Robert Smith"
NewString="We should tell you that username is a great ASP programmer!"
NewString=REPLACE(newstring, "username", User)
%>
<b>A special message!</b>
<hr>
<%=NewString%>
</body>
</html>
```

When this code executes, the text "We should tell you that Robert Smith is a great ASP programmer!" appears on-screen under the boldface heading A special message!. As you can see in the code listing, the REPLACE function is used to tell your code what to look for (in this case, the word *username*) and replace it with the value assigned to the variable User.

Comparing One String to Another

At times, you want to compare two string values to see whether they are equal. Review the following code:

```
<html>
<body>
```

```
<%
VarA="My name is John"
VarB="My name is John"
IF VarA=VarB THEN %>
The two values are equal!
<% ELSE %>
The two values are not equal!
<% END IF%>
</body>
</html>
```

In this example, the text "The two values are equal!" is displayed because the two variables, VarA and VarB, are equal.

You should be aware, however, that the = operator is case-sensitive. To avoid returning false results when comparing strings (that is, returning a value indicating that the two strings being compared are not equal even though they are equal but have different capitalization), you can convert the strings to either uppercase or lowercase. Consider the following example:

```
<html>
<body>
<%
VarA="My name is John"
IF Ucase(VarA)="MY NAME IS JOHN" THEN %>
The two values are equal!
<% END IF %>
</body>
</html>
```

In this example, the variable VarA is converted to all uppercase, so the comparison is true.

TRICK **You can also convert to lowercase using the** LCASE **function in place of** UCASE**.**

Finally, use the STRCOMP() function to compare two strings quickly, as shown in the following example:

```
<html>
<body>
<%=
STRCOMP("My name is John", "My name is John")
STRCOMP("My NAME is John", "My name is John")
STRCOMP("My NAME is John", "My name is John", 1)
%>
</body>
</html>
```

What results are returned from this code listing? Take a look at each instance of the STRCOMP() function illustrated in the code:

- In the first example, a value of 1 (a true value) is returned because the two strings are identical.

- In the second example, a value of 0 (a false value) is returned because the two strings are not equal in regard to case.

- In the final example, a value of 1 (a true value) is returned. Even though the two strings are not identical in case, the inclusion of the ignore case argument (the 1 at the end of the third STRCOMP function) causes these two strings to compare as true because they are the same, with the exception of case.

Extracting Strings

Similar in scope to the search string function, the ability to extract string information is a powerful feature of VBScript and one you will use quite often.

In this section, you will take a look at the following functions:

- LEFT()

- RIGHT()

- MID()

Put simply, the LEFT function returns a specified number of characters starting from the left side of a string. The RIGHT function returns a specified number of characters starting from the right side of a string. Finally, the MID function returns a specified number of characters starting from the left side of the string and continuing for a specified number. Examine the following code example:

```
<html>
<body>
<%
ExampleText="My name is John, and I work with ASP"
%>
<%=LEFT(ExampleText, 7)%>
<%=RIGHT(ExampleText, 13)%>
<%=MID(ExampleText, 4, 4)%>
</body>
</html>
```

If this code were to execute, the following values would be returned:

- My name. This is representative of the LEFT function because it is returning the first seven characters (starting with one) and counting from the left.

- work with ASP. This is representative of the RIGHT function because it is returning the first 13 characters (starting with one) and counting from the right.

- name. This is representative of the MID function because it is returning a string of four characters, starting from the fourth position and counting from the left.

Replacing Strings

As you perform manipulations of your string functions, you will undoubtedly have a need to replace one value with another. This is where the REPLACE function comes in particularly handy:

```
<html>
<body>
<%=
TextValue="love"
NewTextValue="My name is John, and I like to program with ASP!"
NewTextValue=REPLACE(NewTextValue, "like", TextValue)
%>
<%=NewTextValue%>
</body>
</html>
```

Can you guess what happens when this executes? Take a look at each line of the code so that you can see how the REPLACE function works:

- First, the two variables TextValue and NewTextValue are assigned values ("love" and "My name is John, and I like to program with ASP!").

- Next, the REPLACE function is called into action. Because you want to replace some element of the NewTextValue string, you reassign this variable again (NextTextValue=REPLACE(NewTextValue…).

- The REPLACE function works like this: First, the variable you want to search through is listed (in this case, the initial value of the NewTextValue variable). Next, a value that you want to replace is listed (in this case, the word *like*). Finally, the variable or string (the variable TextValue, in this case) is listed. In essence, the REPLACE function works like this: You name the variable in which you want to replace something, you give a value you want to use to replace that something, and you list that something you want to replace.

TRICK

If you're starting to see some similarities between these various functions, at least in syntax, you are becoming a savvy ASP programmer. The syntax of many string manipulation functions is very similar. This is by design, to give VBScript a high degree of uniformity, usability, and functionality.

Working with Date and Time Functions

Knowing how to manipulate string variables is important—you will do lots of this in your work developing ASP. However, there are other common variable types you will find a need to work with just as often: date and time variables.

There are very simple (yet useful) time and date functions available for your use within VBScript:

- DATE(). This function returns the current date.
- TIME(). This function returns the current time.

- NOW(). This function returns the date and time as they are currently being kept on your Web server's clock.

- MONTH(), DAY(), WEEKDAY(), and YEAR(). These functions allow you to break the DATE() function into smaller parts, returning (not surprisingly) the specific month, day, and year of the current date.

- HOUR(), MINUTE(), and SECOND(). Like the preceding functions listed for deducing the current date into smaller components, these three functions allow you to perform similar tasks with the TIME() function by returning the exact hour, minute, and second (as recorded on your Web server).

The syntax of all these functions is very simple. Consider the following code example:

```
<html>
<body>
<b> Here is exact information about the current date and time!</b>
<hr>
The current month is: <%=MONTH(DATE)%><p>
The current day is: <%=DAY(DATE)%><p>
The current weekday is <%=WEEKDAY(DATE)%><p>
The current year is <%=YEAR(DATE)%><p>
<hr>
<b> And now, for some precise time measurements!<b>
<hr>
The current hour is <%=HOUR(TIME)%><p>
The current minute is <%=MINUTE(TIME)%><p>
The current second is <%=SECOND(TIME)%><p>
</body>
</html>
```

APPENDIX B

SQL Reference

Throughout this book, you have used Structured Query Language (SQL) to access and manipulate data in your Access databases via your ASP Web pages. You've come to the conclusion (I hope) that your Web pages are far more useful and interesting when you allow them to come alive and interact directly with a data source such as an Access database.

This appendix has been written to provide you with a general overview of the more common SQL commands, functions, and logical operators so that you can continue to utilize the power of SQL in your ASP programming.

TRICK

As I've said in other parts of this book, SQL is deceptively simple. Underneath those basic-looking commands lies a tremendous amount of power for data manipulation. This appendix touches only the surface of the fundamental SQL concepts. For more detailed information, be sure to check out *Microsoft SQL Server 7 Administrator's Guide* (Premier Press, Inc.) for more information.

TRICK

The examples in this appendix utilize the *Music.mdb* Access database, described in Chapter 5, "Database Access with ADO."

The SELECT Command

Use the SELECT command to return data from your database.

The following command returns all records from the Catalog table of the Music database:

```
SELECT * FROM CATALOG
```

The following command returns the record(s) from the Catalog table where the ID field has a value of 8:

```
SELECT * FROM CATALOG WHERE ID=8
```

The following command returns all records from the Catalog table where the ID field has a value between 25 and 30:

```
SELECT * FROM CATALOG WHERE ID >=25 AND WHERE ID <=30
```

The following command returns the record(s) from the Catalog table where the Artist name equals *The Beatles*:

```
SELECT * FROM CATALOG WHERE ARTIST='The Beatles'
```

TRAP

Be sure to include the single opening and closing quotation mark around any text field, as in the preceding SELECT example. Otherwise, you will receive an error message when the query is executed. Also, remember to use caution when including apostrophes in your queries. If you do use them, they must be doubled. For example:

```
SELECT * FROM CATALOG WHERE ARTIST = 'The Swanson's Beat'
```

would give an error, but the following code would function:

```
SELECT * FROM CATALOG WHERE ARTIST = 'The Swanson''s Beat'
```

As with many SQL commands illustrated in this appendix, you can generate queries with literally millions of permutations. That is the true power of SQL. By providing a simple syntax, you can access data in nearly any way imaginable. This holds true for not only the SELECT command but also any other SQL query you can dream up.

The INSERT Command

You use the INSERT command to place new information into your database.

The following example inserts a new record into the Catalog table. Note that all the individual fields in the Catalog table are assigned a value, with the exception of the ID field, which is an Autonumber field:

```
INSERT INTO CATALOG (Artist, Title, Price) VALUES ('Talking Heads',
'Remain in Light', '$8.99')
```

The next example inserts a new record into the Catalog table, but this time only the Artist field is assigned a value. When the new record is inserted, the other fields remain blank, with the exception of the ID field, which is an Autonumber field:

```
INSERT INTO CATALOG (Artist) VALUES ('Kid Rock')
```

Remember, the INSERT command is used to place new information into a database table. Use the UPDATE command to—you guessed it—update information that already exists.

The UPDATE Command

By using the UPDATE command, you change existing information in the database.

TRAP

As illustrated in this section, you must be very careful when using the UPDATE statement, making sure that you clearly specify which records you want to update. Using the UPDATE statement without providing any qualifying statement about what to update results in the updating of every record in your table. Although this is sometimes the desired result, usually you want to update only specific records.

The following example updates the record in the Catalog table where the ID record is equal to 15:

```
UPDATE CATALOG
SET Title='Sweetheart of the Rodeo'
WHERE ID=15
```

TRICK

In the preceding example, note how the SQL query is broken up into three lines. This type of formatting is useful in making the query syntax easier to read and easier to troubleshoot if you need to address problems at a later date. Note, however, that you can't break up statements like this in VBScript because it will result in errors.

You can use conjunctions (discussed later in this appendix) with the UPDATE statement, just as you can with other SQL commands. This is useful for gaining even more exact control over which data you want to update:

```
UPDATE CATALOG
Set Price='$15.99'
WHERE ID=25 AND WHERE ID=30
```

You can also use the UPDATE command without specifying what should be updated. Consider the following example:

```
UPDATE CATALOG
Set Artist='The Beatles'
```

Can you guess what the result of this query would be? If you said that all records in the Catalog table would have their Artist value set to *The Beatles*, you are absolutely right. Again, there might be situations where you want to make this type of global update. However, most of the time, you will be using the UPDATE command to make changes to a unique record. Be sure that you clearly specify which record you want to update!

The DELETE Command

The basic SQL command you use most often is the DELETE command. From a syntax perspective, it is similar to the UPDATE command:

```
DELETE FROM CATALOG
```

As with the UPDATE command, you must be very careful when using the DELETE command. If the preceding example was executed, all rows of data in the Catalog table would be deleted, wiping the table clean, in essence. Although you might have a need to perform this type of action, more than likely you will never want to delete all data from your tables! Therefore, as with the UPDATE command, you must clearly specify which data you want to delete. Consider the following example:

```
DELETE FROM CATALOG WHERE ID=15
```

In this example, only the record where the ID field is equal to 15 is deleted.

You can also use the DELETE statement to gain more exact control over which data is to be removed:

```
DELETE FROM CATALOG
WHERE ID >= 20 AND WHERE ID <=30
AND WHERE
Artist='Billy Joel'
```

In this example, all records with an ID value greater than or equal to 20 and less than or equal to 30 are deleted. Additionally, all records where the Artist field is equal to *Billy Joel* are deleted.

Logical Operators

Often, you want to determine whether specific relationships exist in your data, based on either information you have captured (from a Web form, for example) or the data itself. You use logical operators to perform this type of analysis.

This section describes the following commonly used logical operators:

- IS NULL
- BETWEEN
- IN
- LIKE

The IS NULL Operator

Depending on the type of information you capture in your database, you can have some records where not all fields are assigned a value. For example, imagine that you ask visitors to your Web site to enter not only their name and address but also specific contact information, such as telephone number, e-mail address, and fax. Although most visitors will undoubtedly have an e-mail account (and probably a telephone and fax, too), perhaps they won't want to provide you with all this information. In that case, when they complete the form your site uses to capture and insert their information into the database, specific fields for their unique records will be blank.

Now imagine that you have been asked by your supervisor to contact everyone who has a listing in your database. You'd rather not call everyone because this is too time-consuming, so you decide to use e-mail or fax. However, you are concerned that not all the individuals listed in the database have, or have provided, an e-mail or fax contact.

You can use the IS NULL operator to search through your database table for individuals whose records don't have a value assigned to the e-mail or fax field. Such a query might look like this:

```
SELECT * FROM CUSTOMERS WHERE EMAIL IS NULL AND WHERE FAX IS NULL
```

In this example, all the records in the Customers table where the Email and/or Fax fields are blank are returned as part of the SELECT command.

TRAP

Keep in mind that the following two queries are not the same:

```
SELECT * FROM CUSTOMERS WHERE EMAIL IS NULL
SELECT * FROM CUSTOMERS WHERE EMAIL=NULL
```

The first query returns all records where the Email field has a value of null. The second query returns all records where the Email field has a textual value of the word *null*. (Actually, this query would result in an error because it is missing the single quotes around NULL). Keep this important distinction in mind when working with the IS NULL operator.

The BETWEEN Operator

You use the very valuable BETWEEN operator to search for values that fall within a certain range. Take a look at the following example:

```
SELECT * FROM CATALOG WHERE ID BETWEEN 30 AND 40
```

In this example, all records that have an ID field value greater than or equal to 30 but less than or equal to 40 are returned.

The IN Operator

Imagine that you want to search through a specific table, looking for all records fields that have a specified value. Consider the following query:

```
SELECT * FROM CATALOG WHERE ARTIST IN ('The Beatles', 'The Byrds', 'Led Zeppelin')
```

When this query is executed, the records returned by the SELECT command have an Artist field where the value is equal to *The Beatles*, *The Byrds*, or *Led Zeppelin*. Use the IN operator to search quickly through your records as you look for a match (or matches) to a specified value.

The LIKE Operator

Imagine another scenario. You have a Web form that allows your customers to search through an inventory table to determine whether you carry the product in which they are interested. After you gather the desired product name from the customer, you use a simple SELECT query to return all matches, as follows:

```
SELECT * FROM CATALOG WHERE TITLE='" & Request.Form("Title") & " ' "
```

In this example, the only records returned are those where the Title field has an exact value specified by the customer. This is potentially useful, assuming that the customer knows the exact title of the CD he or she is interested in buying.

Often, customers do not know exact information, or they have only partial information. In this case, the preceding query would not work because it is looking for an exact match to return any data.

You need to use the LIKE operator, which allows your queries to generate results where the information provided is *like* what is found in the database table. Take a look at the following example:

```
SELECT * FROM CATALOG WHERE TITLE LIKE '%Live%'
```

In this example, the query returns the following records from the Catalog table of the *Music.mdb* database.

ID	Artist	Title
14	James Brown	Live at the Apollo
16	Johnny Cash	Live at Folsom Prison
54	Bob Seger	Live Bullet
75	The Who	Live at Leeds

By specifying the LIKE operator, using the syntax of %Live%, all records containing the word *Live* in the Title field are returned—it doesn't matter in what location the word *Live* appears. For example, if the title of a CD was *Absolutely Live*, this would be returned as well.

How you utilize the % or _ characters in the LIKE operator determines how this operator performs in a query. In the following query, all records where the Title field has the letters *RO* in the second and third position are returned:

```
SELECT * FROM CATALOG WHERE TITLE LIKE '_RO'
```

In the next example, all records that begin with the letter *P* are returned:

```
SELECT * FROM CATALOG WHERE TITLE LIKE 'P_%'
```

The next query returns all records in the Catalog table that have, in the Title field, a value that ends with the letter *P*:

```
SELECT * FROM CATALOG WHERE TITLE LIKE '%P'
```

The following query returns all records in the Catalog table with a value in the Title field that has the letter *O* in the second position and ends with the letter *R*:

```
SELECT * FROM CATALOG WHERE TITLE LIKE '%_O%R'
```

As you see from these examples, there is virtually no limit to the way you can use the LIKE operator to help locate data based on partial information. As you develop more advanced SQL queries in your ASP Web pages, you will return to the LIKE operator frequently. Be sure to use its power to your advantage.

TRICK

A useful spin on all these operators is the use of the word *NOT* before them. This allows you to search for the reverse of the condition you are specifying in the operator statement. Consider the following example:

```
SELECT * FROM CATALOG WHERE ID NOT BETWEEN 40 AND 50
```

In this example, all records that have an ID value *not* between 40 and 50 are returned.

Take advantage of the NOT operator when you want to exclude records from being returned that meet specific criteria.

Useful Data-Sorting Functions

In your ASP programming, you often want to return the minimum, maximum, sum, and average values from a table of values. The specific SQL functions you use to help with such tasks are discussed in this section.

The COUNT Function

Imagine that you want to return the number of records in a specific table. Using the COUNT function, you can do just that. Examine the following query:

```
SELECT COUNT(*) FROM CATALOG
```

When this query is executed, the number *80* is returned because there are 80 records in the Catalog table. (Note that if you run this query on your own Catalog table, the number of records returned can vary, depending on which actions you have performed on the table.)

Remember the IS NULL operator? You can use the COUNT function in a similar fashion:

```
SELECT COUNT (FAX) FROM CUSTOMERS
```

In this query, the number returned is all the records in the Customers table that have a value (other than null) for the Fax field.

The SUM Function

You use the SUM function if you have a particular numeric field in a database table that you want to sum for all records. Imagine that you have a Scores table to track how your class of third-grade students is progressing. Each individual record you enter into this table has a value entered into the Point field (in this case, the Point field is used to record the student's score on each quiz, test, and so on). In the following example, the executed query returns the sum of all points for all students:

```
SELECT SUM (POINT) FROM SCORES
```

Although this type of all-inclusive query is useful when you want to see the grand total points achieved by all your students, you use the SUM function to return the total number of points for each student in the table. That said, consider the following query:

```
SELECT SUM (POINT) FROM SCORES WHERE STUDENT_ID=15
```

In this example, only the records where the Student_ID field equals 15 are totaled—and again, only the Point field for each record is totaled.

TRAP

The SUM **function can be used only on fields that have a numeric value.**

The AVG Function

Similar to the SUM function, you use the AVG function to return the average value across rows in your database table. Using the same student database example, take a look at the following query:

```
SELECT AVG (TOTAL_POINTS) FROM SCORES
```

When this query is executed, the average for all records that contain a value for the Total_Points field is returned.

The MAX Function

Keeping with the student database example, take a look at an example of the MAX function:

```
SELECT MAX (TOTAL_POINTS) FROM SCORES
```

Can you guess what value is returned? That's right—the maximum value in the Total_Points field for all records that have a value in this field.

The MIN Function

The following query uses the MIN function:

```
SELECT MIN (TOTAL_POINTS) FROM SCORES
```

As I'm sure you guessed, when this query is executed, it returns the minimum value in the Total_Points field for all records that have a value in this field.

APPENDIX C

Access Essentials

Throughout this book, I've shown you how to integrate an Access 2000 database with your ASP pages to produce Web applications that sport far more functionality (and fun!) than simple static Web pages. This short appendix has been written to serve as an Access primer, a handy reference if you're familiar with the program and a comprehensive introduction if you're new to Access.

Access 2000 is a deceptively simple program. Don't let that perceived simplicity convince you that it is not a robust, powerful member of the Office 2000 suite. Check out *Microsoft Access 2002 Fast & Easy* by Faithe Wempen (Premier Press, Inc.) for a solid, more complete overview of Access.

You have learned how to program your Web pages to interact with an Access database—or, more specifically, you've learned how to work with ADO and ASP to empower your Web pages with a data source. In reality, you don't need to know much at all about Access to integrate your databases with your Web pages, but what if you need a refresher in the fundamentals, such as how to create a database from scratch, insert tables, and modify fields? Well, you've come to the right place! This short appendix introduces you to Access essentials. Along the way, you can take a peek at some of the query-generating tools that are also available in the application.

Creating an Access Database

To begin, take some time here to go through the process of creating a database from scratch:

1. Open Access. You are immediately presented with a dialog box, asking you to either create a new database or open an existing file (see Figure C.1).
2. Select the Blank Access Database option, and click OK. You are presented with the File New Database dialog box, asking you to which location you want to save your new database (see Figure C.2).

FIGURE C.1

Determining how to create your new Access database.

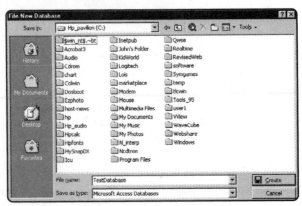

FIGURE C.2

In this example, I'm saving the database to my C: drive and giving it the name *TestDatabase*.

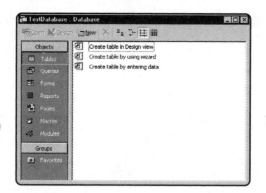

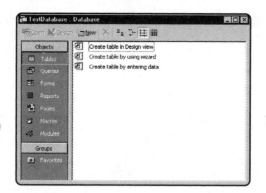

FIGURE C.3

Your newly created
Access database.
Congratulations!.

3. Give your database a name (I named my database *TestDatabase*), and select a location in which to save it.

4. Click the Create button (refer to Figure C.2). After a few seconds, your database is created (see Figure C.3).

You are ready to begin working in your new database. Now I'll show you some essential functionality of the application by explaining how to create and modify tables and specific fields in those tables.

Creating Tables in Design View

To work with information in your database, you need a place to store that information. This is where tables come into play.

Access tables are powerful repositories of data, allowing you to view your information in a variety of ways—through the use of simple sorting features, not unlike Excel, as well as SQL queries. Creating them is very easy, and I'll show you how it's done.

There are three ways to create a table with Access 2000: in Design view, through the use of a wizard, or by entering data. For this example, you will go through the traditional process of table creation in Design view:

1. Double-click the Create Table in Design View option (refer to Figure C.3). The Design view for a new table appears, as shown in Figure C.4.

2. Notice the three column names in Design view: *Field Name*, *Data Type*, and *Description*. As you create specific fields in a table, each of these columns will contain a value. Your cursor should be flashing in the first Field Name position; if it is not, click there now.

3. For this example, you are going to create a table to store information for a personal address book. You will name the first field *ID*. Type **ID** in the first field column, and tab across so that your cursor is in the Data Type field (see Figure C.5).

TRICK

It's a good idea to name the first field ID or Recnum (short for record number) so you have an easily identifiable field that can also be used as a primary key for the table.

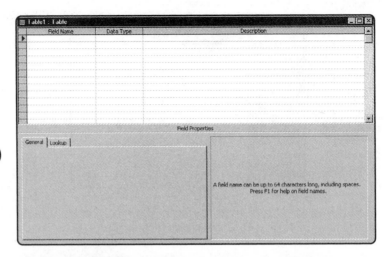

FIGURE C.4

Design view in a
new table. Note the
default naming
convention applied:
Table1.

FIGURE C.5

Naming your first
field *ID*. Notice that
when you tab
across to the Data
Type column, more
information
appears.

4. The Data Type column is where you specify the type of data you are going to be
   storing in this field. Click the down arrow in the Data Type heading to display
   the available data types (see Figure C.6).

5. You're going to make this ID field the primary key field for your database. You
   want it to increment automatically in values of 1 so that as new records are entered into the database, they are assigned a unique identifier. In other words,
   they are given a specific ID. From the Data Type menu, select AutoNumber as the
   data type for this field (refer to Figure C.6).

HINT

**A *primary key* field uniquely identifies each record stored in the table. By doing so,
this allows the full relational powers of Access to function because data can be
quickly located, sorted, and manipulated using this primary key. Every table should
have a primary key, usually named ID or Recnum (again, short for record number).**

6. To assign the ID field as your primary key, right-click in the ID field column, and
   select Primary Key from the menu that appears (see Figure C.7).

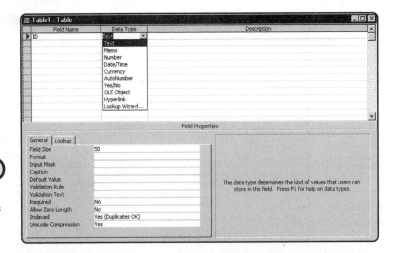

FIGURE C.6

Exploring the
various data types
available in
Access 2000.

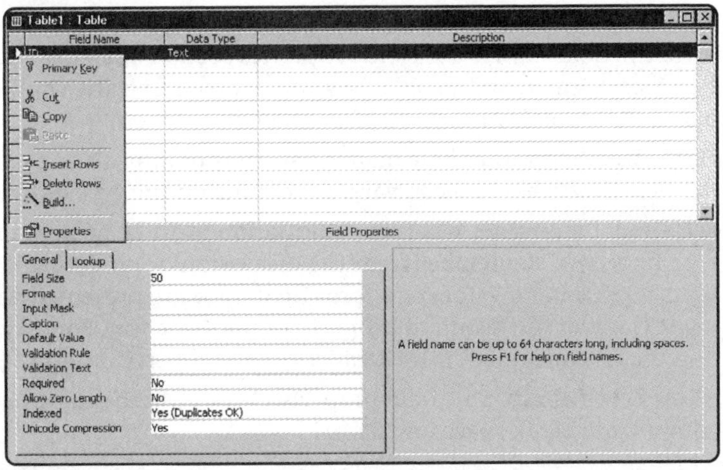

FIGURE C.7

Assigning the ID
field as the primary
key for this table.

7. Create a few other fields for your address book table. Say that you want to store the following information about each person in your address book:

- First name
- Last name
- Street address
- City
- State
- Zip code
- Phone number

There are seven fields of information you want to store about each person in your address book, so you need to create seven fields in your Access table. Place your cursor in the field column directly under the ID field, and type **Firstname** (no space between *First* and *Name*). Then, tab across to the Data Type field, and select Text from the menu, just as you selected AutoNumber for the ID field (refer to Figure C.6).

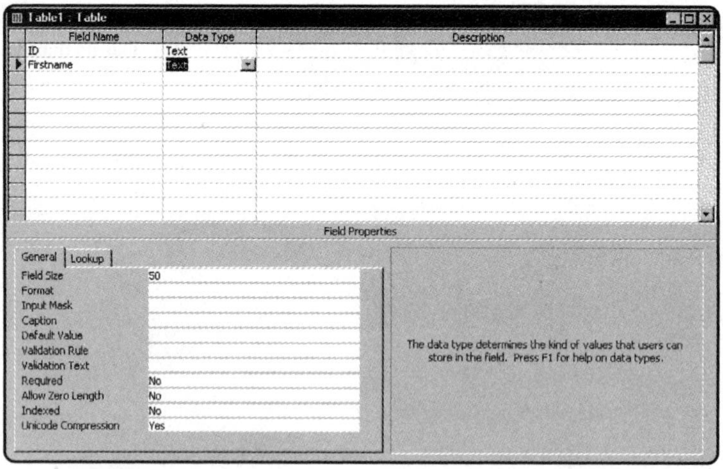

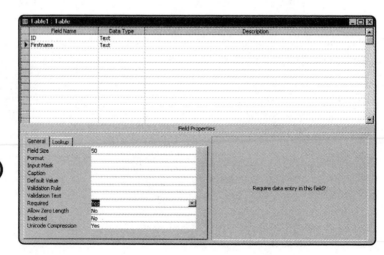

FIGURE C.8

Creating the Firstname field and assigning it as a text field.

8. Notice the fields under the Field Properties section of Figure C.8. These fields (Field Size, Format, and so on) allow you to assign specific characteristics to each field in the table. For now, note these field properties:

- **Field Size.** Determines how many characters of information can be stored in the field. Note that this can vary, depending on the type of field you select.

- **Required.** Determines whether information must be present in the field for the specific record. Remember from the discussion of validating Web forms that if users don't enter a value for a form field, they are presented with an error message? Think of the Required property in the same way. Some type of information must be included if the Required field property is set to Yes.

- **Allow Zero Length.** This field property checks whether a zero-length input is allowed or a blank space for the field is okay.

For the Firstname field, leave the Field Size property set to its default setting of 50. Then, set the Required property to Yes and the Allow Zero Length property to No (see Figure C.9).

FIGURE C.9

Setting all field attribute properties for the Firstname field.

HINT Generally speaking, if you have the Required field property set to Yes, you should set the Allow Zero Length property to No. This ensures that some type of information will be entered into this field in your table.

9. You are now ready to create the fields for the remaining pieces of information (last name, street address, and so on) for each record in your address book. Repeat steps 7 and 8 for each field you want to create for your address book, making sure that you set the following attributes for each field:

- Data Type should be set to Text for each field.
- The Field Size property can be left at the default of 50 except for the StreetAddress field, which you set to 255 (see Figure C.10).
- The Required property should be set to Yes.
- The Allow Zero Length property should be set to No.

When you finish creating all your fields, your table should like Figure C.10.

10. Now that you have created all the fields, it is time to save the table. Click the Save icon on the toolbar (the icon that looks like a computer disc). The Save As dialog box opens (see Figure C.11).

11. Your table is now saved (see Figure C.12). Close the Design view for this table by selecting File, Close.

That's it for table creation. Of course, this is a very quick introduction, to put it mildly! This process is easy, but planning which tables to create and which fields to store in them can be complex, depending on the amount of information you are storing and the relationships you want to establish between specific tables. A complete discussion of database creation is far beyond the scope of this book. For now, though, remember the following tips to table creation:

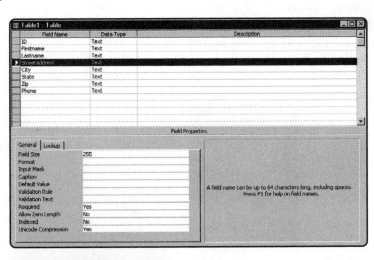

FIGURE C.10

All fields have been entered. Note that the field size for the StreetAddress field changed from 50 to the maximum of 255.

FIGURE C.11

Saving your new table by giving it a name.

ASP Programming for the Absolute Beginner

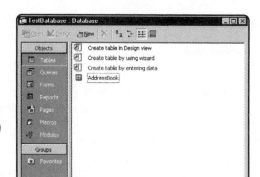

FIGURE C.12

Your AddressBook
table is now part of
the TestDatabase.

- Set a primary key in each table you create.
- Assign data types (text, autonumber, and the like) and field properties for each field you create.
- Plan ahead. Think about the kinds of information you want to store in tables and how that information can be divided into fields. For example, in the AddressBook table created here, you want to store the usual pieces of information for each person listed in your address book (first name, last name, address, and so on). By deciding which types of information you want to store, you make the table creation process much easier and save yourself time later because you don't have to go back and add fields you forgot to create in the beginning.

Entering Data into a Table via the Datasheet View

Now that you have created a table, it's easy to enter data into the table from directly within Access:

1. In your TestDatabase database, double-click the AddressBook table. The table appears in Datasheet view (see Figure C.13).

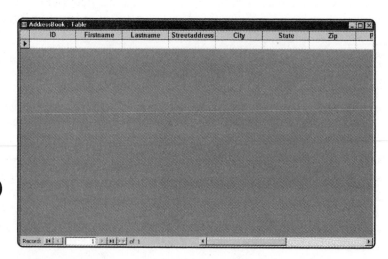

FIGURE C.13

Preparing to enter
data in the
Datasheet view.

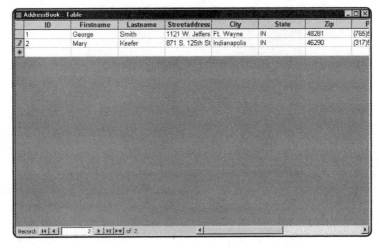

FIGURE C.14

Entering data into a
table via the
Datasheet view.

What's the difference between Design view and Datasheet view? Use Design view to create or modify your table (as you just did) so that you can easily designate your names, data types, and field properties. Use Datasheet view to enter data.

2. Begin entering data (in this case, you are transcribing information from your old-fashioned pen and paper address book into the high-tech world of an Access database. Note that as you enter records, the ID field automatically increments by 1 (see Figure C.14).

Modifying a Table That Contains Data

Imagine that you want to add a field to a table after you've begun entering data. Do you have to start from the beginning again and lose all the data you already entered?

Of course not! Access 2000 makes it easy to insert a new field or delete an existing field, for that matter, even if you've already started entering information into a table.

Inserting a New Field into an Existing Table

Follow these steps to insert a field quickly into an existing table:

1. Imagine that you want to add a Fax field to your existing AddressBook table. This is easily done in Design view, so open the table in Design view now. See Figure C.15.

2. You could simply tack on the field to the end of the field listing, after the Phone field, but say that you want to place it right after the StreetAddress field. To do so, click the City field to highlight it, as shown in Figure C.16, right-click to display the menu, and select Insert Rows.

3. There should now be a blank space between the StreetAddress and City fields. Type **Fax** into this blank space, tab over, and select Text as the data type for this new field, as illustrated in Figure C.17.

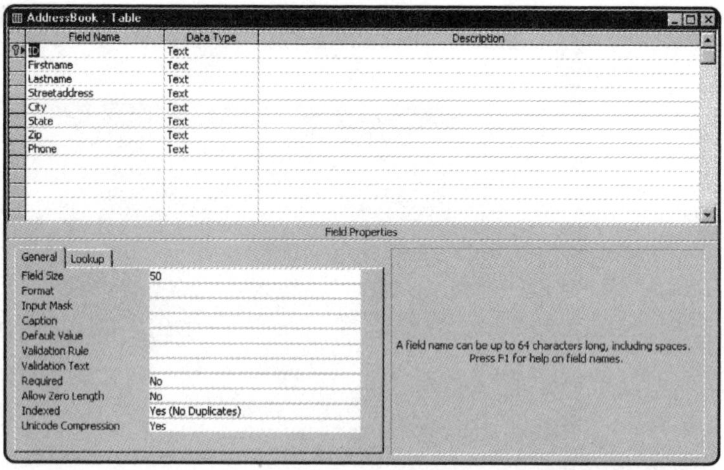

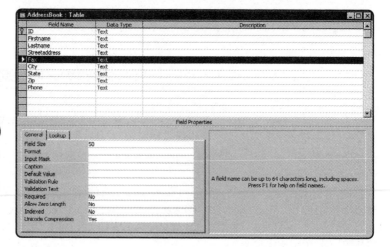

FIGURE C.15

Another look at the AddressBook table in Design view.

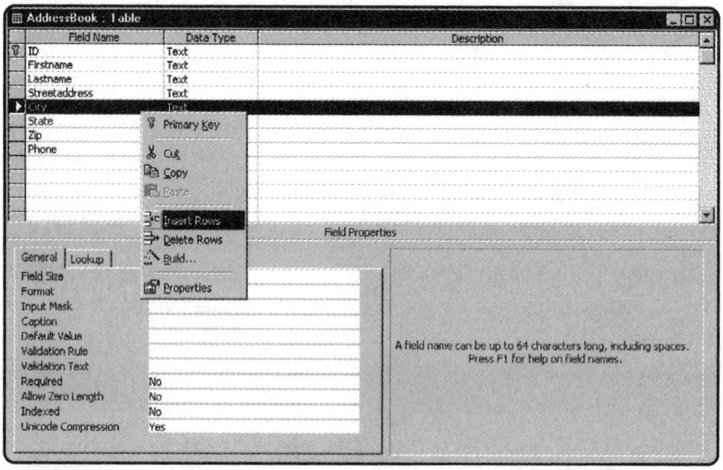

FIGURE C.16

Preparing to insert a new field into an existing table.

FIGURE C.17

You can easily add a new field to an existing table. Don't forget to set the field data type and properties.

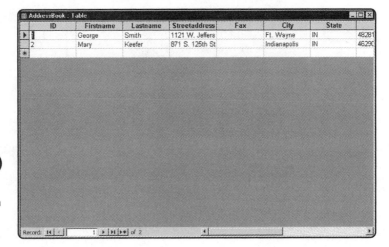

Now, when you view the table in Datasheet view, you see the new field in place. You need to go back and enter the specified information (in this case, a fax number) for each record that exists in the table (see Figure C.18).

Deleting a Field from an Existing Table

You can also delete fields easily from an existing table. To do so, follow these steps:

1. Open the AddressBook table in Design view.
2. Delete the newly created Fax field. Select it, right-click to display the menu, and select Delete Rows, as illustrated in Figure C.19.
3. Before the deletion process goes any further, Access cautions you about the action you are about to take, as shown in Figure C.20.
4. Click Yes. The field is deleted.

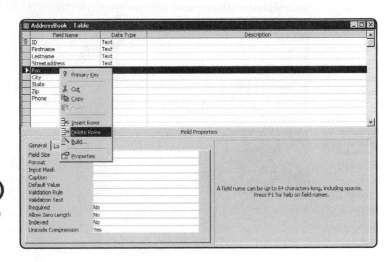

FIGURE C.20

Use the Delete
action with caution.

Modifying a Field Data Type

Another modification you might want to make on an existing table is to change a field's data type:

1. Open the AddressBook field in Design view.
2. Place your cursor in the Data Type column for the Phone field.
3. Click the down arrow, and change the data type from Text to Number, as shown in Figure C.21.
4. Save this table, but notice the dialog box that opens when you try to save (see Figure C.22).

What does this mean? When you entered data into your AddressBook table for the Phone field, you used the following format: (Area Code)XXX-XXXX. A typical phone number was listed as (317)555-1212. Because this field is a text field, the parentheses around the area code and the hyphen between the prefix and remaining four digits are okay, but now that you're changing the field data type from text to number, the parentheses and hyphen can no longer be part of the

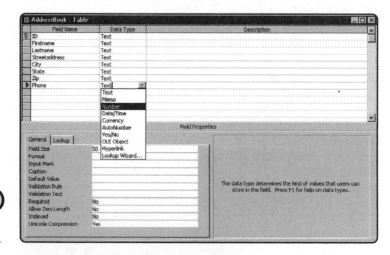

FIGURE C.21

Changing a field's
data type attribute.

FIGURE C.22

Again, Access
warns you about
potential data loss,
this time due to a
changing of data
type properties.

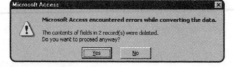

number—they are text elements, not numbers. Access is telling you that, for the data type change to occur, you have to delete the information previously entered into the Phone field.

5. For this example, click Yes. If this were a real application, you'd have to go back and re-enter the information into the Phone field (without any text elements such as parentheses or hyphens).

Again, this example illustrates the need to do some planning before you start constructing your database tables or, at the very least, before you get too deep into entering data. Plan ahead as much as possible.

Using the Access 2000 Simple Query Wizard

Remember from previous discussions that a query is a way of sorting and looking at your data in a specific way. The universal database language of SQL (*Structured Query Language*) offers a powerful method for querying your data.

As with most things, Access has a helpful wizard to guide you through the process of querying your data so that you don't have to worry about learning SQL to manipulate your data to see new informational relationships.

In this section, you will take a quick look at the Access Simple Query Wizard, which does most of the legwork for you in sorting your data. You will be using the *Music.mdb* sample database included on the enclosed CD-ROM and discussed in Chapter 5, "Database Access with ADO."

1. Open the *Music.mdb* file, and click the Queries tab. You will see two methods of creating queries display (see Figure C.23).
2. Double-click the Create Query by Using Wizard option. After a few moments, the first step of the Simple Query Wizard appears (see Figure C.24).
3. In the Tables/Queries field, select the Catalog table.
4. For this query, you will include the Artist and Price fields. One at a time, select each of these fields, and click the > button to add them to the Selected Fields (see Figure C.25).
5. Click Next. You are presented with the final dialog box for the Simple Query Wizard (see Figure C.26).

FIGURE C.23

Two methods of creating a query: in Design view or with a wizard.

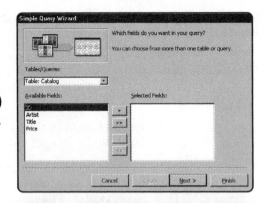

Beginning the query
creation process,
compliments of the
Simple Query
Wizard.

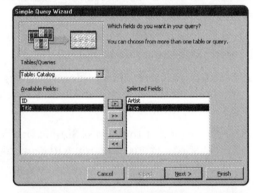

Determining which
fields you want to
include in the query.

The final steps in
the Simple Query
Wizard.

6. Leave the title of the query as the default, Catalog Query1. Also, leave the selected radio button, Open the Query to View Information.

7. Click Finish. After a few moments, the Catalog table is sorted by artist and price,
as specified in your query (see Figure C.27).

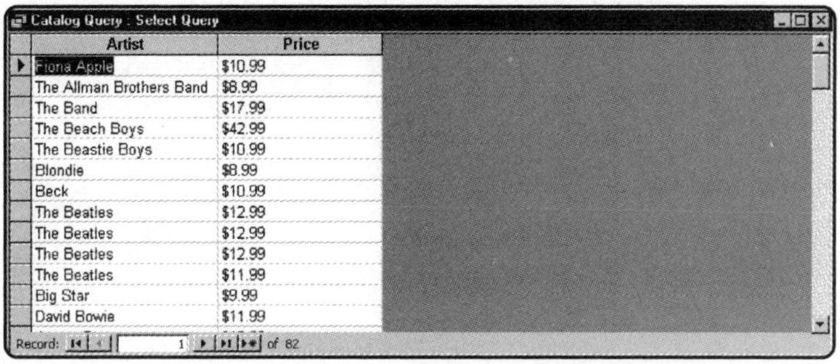

FIGURE C.27

The Simple Query Wizard can quickly return your information sorted in the way you specified.

Artist	Price
Fiona Apple	$10.99
The Allman Brothers Band	$8.99
The Band	$17.99
The Beach Boys	$42.99
The Beastie Boys	$10.99
Blondie	$8.99
Beck	$10.99
The Beatles	$12.99
The Beatles	$12.99
The Beatles	$12.99
The Beatles	$11.99
Big Star	$9.99
David Bowie	$11.99

Catalog Query : Select Query

Record: 14 ◄ 1 ► ►I ►* of 82

Index

License Agreement/Notice of Limited Warranty

By opening the sealed disc container in this book, you agree to the following terms and conditions. If, upon reading the following license agreement and notice of limited warranty, you cannot agree to the terms and conditions set forth, return the unused book with unopened disc to the place where you purchased it for a refund.

License:

The enclosed software is copyrighted by the copyright holder(s) indicated on the software disc. You are licensed to copy the software onto a single computer for use by a single user and to a backup disc. You may not reproduce, make copies, or distribute copies or rent or lease the software in whole or in part, except with written permission of the copyright holder(s). You may transfer the enclosed disc only together with this license, and only if you destroy all other copies of the software and the transferee agrees to the terms of the license. You may not decompile, reverse assemble, or reverse engineer the software.

Notice of Limited Warranty:

The enclosed disc is warranted by Premier Press, Inc. to be free of physical defects in materials and workmanship for a period of sixty (60) days from end user's purchase of the book/disc combination. During the sixty-day term of the limited warranty, Premier Press will provide a replacement disc upon the return of a defective disc.

Limited Liability:

THE SOLE REMEDY FOR BREACH OF THIS LIMITED WARRANTY SHALL CONSIST ENTIRELY OF REPLACEMENT OF THE DEFECTIVE DISC. IN NO EVENT SHALL PREMIER OR THE AUTHORS BE LIABLE FOR ANY OTHER DAMAGES, INCLUDING LOSS OR CORRUPTION OF DATA, CHANGES IN THE FUNCTIONAL CHARACTERISTICS OF THE HARDWARE OR OPERATING SYSTEM, DELETERIOUS INTERACTION WITH OTHER SOFTWARE, OR ANY OTHER SPECIAL, INCIDENTAL, OR CONSEQUENTIAL DAMAGES THAT MAY ARISE, EVEN IF PREMIER AND/OR THE AUTHORS HAVE PREVIOUSLY BEEN NOTIFIED THAT THE POSSIBILITY OF SUCH DAMAGES EXISTS.

Disclaimer of Warranties:

PREMIER AND THE AUTHORS SPECIFICALLY DISCLAIM ANY AND ALL OTHER WARRANTIES, EITHER EXPRESS OR IMPLIED, INCLUDING WARRANTIES OF MERCHANTABILITY, SUITABILITY TO A PARTICULAR TASK OR PURPOSE, OR FREEDOM FROM ERRORS. SOME STATES DO NOT ALLOW FOR EXCLUSION OF IMPLIED WARRANTIES OR LIMITATION OF INCIDENTAL OR CONSEQUENTIAL DAMAGES, SO THESE LIMITATIONS MIGHT NOT APPLY TO YOU.

Other:

This Agreement is governed by the laws of the State of Indiana without regard to choice of law principles. The United Convention of Contracts for the International Sale of Goods is specifically disclaimed. This Agreement constitutes the entire agreement between you and Premier Press regarding use of the software.